PRIMER ON ERISA

Fourth Edition

PRIMER ON ERISA

Fourth Edition

Barbara J. Coleman

The Bureau of National Affairs, Inc., Washington, D.C.

Copyright © 1989, 1993
The Bureau of National Affairs, Inc.

Library of Congress Cataloging-in-Publication Data

Coleman, Barbara J.
   Primer on ERISA / Barbara J. Coleman. —4th ed.
      p.   cm.

   Includes index.
   ISBN 0-87179-781-X
   1. Pension trusts—Law and legislation—United States.
I. Title.
KF3512.Z9C6   1993
344.73'01252—dc20
[347.3041252]   92-35173
                                                      CIP

Published by BNA Books, 1250 23rd St., N.W., Washington, D.C. 20037

Printed in the United States of America
International Standard Book Number: 0-87179-781-X

PREFACE

This *Primer* summarizes the major provisions of the Employee Retirement Income Security Act of 1974 (ERISA). Although the word "retirement" appears in the title of the law, ERISA goes beyond regulating pension plans to cover a wide range of other benefit plans as well—plans that provide employee health care, disability, and accident benefits. ERISA calls these programs "employee welfare plans."

But ERISA developed largely out of concern in Congress that abuses in the private pension system were denying pensions to many workers, and most of the provisions of the law are directed at safeguarding employee pensions. For that reason, the greater part of the *Primer* is devoted to ERISA regulation of pension plans. The *Primer* does include a section, however, that discusses ERISA provisions affecting employee benefit plans in general—welfare plans as well as pension plans.

This book has an introduction and five chapters. The introduction traces the history of pension plan regulation and the reasons for the enactment of ERISA. Chapter 1 explains which employee benefit plans are covered by ERISA and which are exempt. It summarizes the main provisions of the law as amended by subsequent legislation such as the Tax Reform Act of 1986 and the Omnibus Budget Reconciliation Act of 1987. It covers the additional changes made to these amendments by the Omnibus Budget Reconciliation Acts of 1989 and 1990, as well as by the 1989 repeal of Section 89 of the Tax Reform Act of 1986. In addition, Chapter 1 describes the effects of the Americans With Disabilities Act of 1991 and legislation attached to the extension of unemployment compensation in 1992.

Chapters 2 and 3 describe in greater detail how ERISA governs pension plans and include information on how pension benefits are protected if a pension plan folds. Chapter 4 looks at the ERISA provisions that cover both pension plans and welfare plans. Chapter 5 describes the federal agencies that administer ERISA and the criminal and civil sanctions in the law. Citations to legal decisions discussed in the text include references to BNA's *Employee Benefits Cases (EBC)*. A glossary of key terms is also provided.

The reader should be cautioned that ERISA is a complex law that employs a number of technical legal and actuarial terms and concepts. The *Primer* does not attempt a detailed explanation of these concepts. For such an explanation, the reader should consult *Employee Benefits Dictionary*, published by BNA Books. For more in-depth analysis of ERISA the reader should consult the following BNA publications: *ERISA: The Law and the Code*, a complete text of the law and amending legislation; *ERISA Regulations*, which covers the text of related regulations; *Employee Benefits Law*, a complete legal treatise in the subject area; and *Pension Reporter* or *Benefits Today* for current information on changes to ERISA.

Contents

INTRODUCTION

The major impetus for the enactment of the Employee Retirement Income Security Act of 1974 (ERISA) was abuse and mismanagement in the private pension system. Employers were taking tax deductions for their contributions to pension plans, but many employees were not receiving the pensions they had been promised. Workers were often denied pensions because they failed to meet rigorous requirements concerning length of service or because their employers went out of business, leaving behind bankrupt pension funds.

Until the enactment of ERISA, private pension plans were regulated largely under the Internal Revenue Code. Employers were permitted to deduct from gross income—for income tax purposes—their payments to employees for pensions or their direct contributions to a pension trust. If the payments were reasonable in amount and were intended to provide pensions for at least some employees, the Internal Revenue Service would grant the pension plan "tax-qualified" status. These contributions to a qualified pension plan were deductible as ordinary and necessary business expenses.

Under the Revenue Acts of 1921 and 1926, additional tax breaks were granted for tax-qualified plans, as the income earned by stock bonus and profit-sharing plans and pension trusts was exempted from current taxation.

1

Later, during and shortly after World War II, the number of pension plans began to increase rapidly for the following reasons:

- Wage and price controls prevented employers from increasing worker compensation, but not from providing fringe benefits such as pensions.
- Normal and excess-profit taxes were extremely high, leading employers to look for tax deductions, including those offered by pension plan contributions.
- Unions, aided by a 1948 decision of the National Labor Relations Board that held that pensions were a mandatory subject for collective bargaining, pressured employers to provide pension benefits.

Revenue Act of 1942

As more employers established pension plans, Congress began taking a closer look at the tax breaks those plans were receiving. Since a pension plan did not need to cover all employees of a company in order to become qualified for favorable tax treatment, many employers set up plans primarily for officers and other highly paid executives.

Congress decided that employers would have to include more employees in company pension plans if they wanted tax breaks for their payments to the plans. The new tax qualification requirements established in the Revenue Act of 1942 included the following:

- Pension plans had to cover a broad cross-section of employees, not just executives.
- Pension plans could not discriminate in the benefits paid to or contributions made for officers, stockholders, or other highly compensated employees.
- Pension plans had to be in writing, be permanent, and be communicated to employees.

Welfare and Pension Plans Disclosure Act of 1958

Although the Revenue Act of 1942 broadened coverage of employees under tax-qualified pension plans, the management and administration of the funds of employee benefit plans, including pension plans, were not regulated. Congressional studies and investigations began uncovering cases of corrupt and inept management of many plans, including examples of exorbitant fees and commissions, kickbacks, excessively high administrative costs, and other abuses.

The first major legislative attempt to curb these abuses was the Welfare and Pension Plans Disclosure Act of 1958 (WPPDA). The intent of the law was to provide employees with more information about the operation and financing of their benefit plans so they could police the plans and administrators themselves.

The law was weak, however, even when amended in 1962 to give the Department of Labor investigatory authority over employee benefit plans. The WPPDA did not address many other problems about pension plans that were beginning to come to public attention. These problems included inadequate funding for the plans, lack of standards for those who managed plan money, and restrictive requirements that prevented many workers from ever qualifying for pensions.

The lack of safeguards for worker pensions at many companies was most dramatically illustrated by the Studebaker case. When Studebaker stopped producing automobiles and closed its plants in 1963, over 4,000 workers with vested pension rights lost some or all of their pensions.

The stories of the Studebaker workers and of the employees of other companies who suffered similar hardships became the focus of a number of congressional hearings and drew increased media attention.

Still, it was not until 1967 that the first broad pension reform bill was introduced by Senator Jacob Javits. It took seven more years of congressional hearings and legislative action before ERISA became law on September 2, 1974.

1

OVERVIEW

The Employee Retirement Income Security act of 1974 (ERISA) is a voluminous document—a complex, technical piece of legislation that deals with the establishment, operation, and administration of two types of employee benefit plans: welfare plans and pension plans.

The term "welfare plan" refers to a wide variety of benefit programs, ranging from medical and hospital care to accident, death, disability, and unemployment benefits. A "pension plan" is a plan that provides retirement income to employees. (See Chapter 4, in which the two terms are described more fully.)

ERISA contains a number of provisions that apply only to pension plans. It also contains provisions that cover both pension plans and welfare plans. When ERISA provisions apply to both types of plans, the *Primer* will use the same term ERISA does when discussing both plans—"employee benefit plans."

Employee benefit plans that are regulated by ERISA include the following:

- Plans established or maintained by employers engaged in commerce or in any industry or activity affecting commerce or by an employee organization representing employees engaged in commerce
- Plans that qualify for tax-favored status

5

Employee benefit plans that are exempt from ERISA include the following:

- Government plans, including plans established under the Railroad Retirement Act and state and municipal plans
- Church plans for which no election has been made for coverage under the Internal Revenue Code (IRC) (Although exempt, a church association can make an irrevocable election to be covered by the participation, vesting, and funding requirements.)
- Plans of fraternal or similar organizations that receive no contributions from employers of the participants
- Plans maintained solely to comply with workers' compensation, unemployment compensation, or disability insurance laws
- Plans maintained outside the United States primarily for nonresident aliens

Except for the exclusions noted above, both welfare and pension plans are subject to the reporting and disclosure requirements and fiduciary standards of ERISA. The participation, vesting, and funding provisions, however, do not apply to the following plans:

- Employee welfare plans
- Unfunded excess benefit plans maintained solely to provide benefits or contributions in excess of the allowable limits established for tax-qualified plans
- Unfunded, nonqualified deferred compensation plans for a select group of top management or highly compensated executives

Insurance contract plans are excluded from the funding provisions. The termination insurance provisions of Title IV apply only to defined benefit pension plans.

ERISA PROVISIONS

ERISA retains the basic provisions for plan qualification established in the Revenue Act of 1942. But ERISA and subsequent legislation, particularly the Tax Reform Act of 1986, have developed new standards that must be met by all employee benefit plans to qualify for favorable tax treatment and to avoid tough civil and criminal penalities.

Failure to meet these standards can mean disqualification and, in some cases for pension plans, an excise tax. Penalties on employees who receive benefits above certain limits range from additional taxes to loss of tax exclusion for the benefits.

This use of tax exemptions and the threat of their withdrawal—the "carrot and stick" approach—combined with the growing use of civil and criminal sanctions have allowed the government to help shape the private benefit system in the United States.

ERISA has several major objectives:

- To ensure that workers and beneficiaries receive adequate information about their employee benefit plans
- To set standards of conduct for those managing employee benefit plans and plan funds
- To determine that adequate funds are being set aside to pay promised pension benefits
- To ensure that workers receive pension benefits after they have satisfied certain minimum requirements
- To safeguard pension benefits for workers whose pension plans are terminated

A summary of ERISA's major provisions follows. Where these provisions have been amended by more recent legislation, the current provisions are given.

TITLE I. PROTECTION OF EMPLOYEE BENEFITS

Title I contains the labor provisions of ERISA, which provide protections for employee benefit rights. In the declaration of policy that introduces Title I, Congress listed the following reasons why it believed the protections were needed:

- Workers were losing pensions after long years of employment when they had any break in service before retirement.
- Workers were losing retirement benefits because their pension plans terminated without adequate funds to continue to pay the benefits.
- Information was not available to workers about their benefit plans, and there were inadequate safeguards for the operation of those plans.
- Many pension plans were not required to meet any federal minimum standards to ensure solvency and were financially unstable.

Most of these concerns are addressed by provisions on reporting and disclosure of plan information, participation, vesting, funding, fiduciary responsibilities, and enforcement and administration. (Insuring pensions against plan termination is covered in Title IV.) These provisions are summarized below.

Reporting and Disclosure

Employees are protected by the following reporting and disclosure provisions:

- Employees must be furnished with understandable and reasonably comprehensive summaries of employee benefit plans, updates when major changes are made, summaries of annual reports on the financing and operation of the plans, and advance notification if the employer intends to terminate the pension plan.
- At their request, employees must be given a report on the status of their vesting and accrued pension benefits. If they leave their employer on a temporary or permanent basis, they must be given such a report automatically.

- Employee benefit plans must report certain detailed financial and actuarial data annually to the Department of the Treasury and submit audited financial statements to federal agencies.

Participation

With regard to participation in a pension plan, the following rules apply:

- Employees must be allowed to begin participation in a pension plan after they have reached age 21 and have completed one year of service (which includes at least 1,000 hours of work). The service requirement can be two years instead of one year if the employee is 100 percent vested after the two years.
- Employees cannot be excluded from a pension plan on the ground that they are too old even if they begin their employment with the plan sponsor within a few years of the plan's normal retirement age (defined benefit plans).

Vesting

Vesting requirements are as follows:

- Employees acquire nonforfeitable or vested rights to pension benefits under one of two schedules. Employees must be either 100 percent vested after no more than five years of service (ten years for multiemployer collectively bargained plans) or partially vested after no more than three years of service and 100 percent vested after no more than seven years of service.
- Once 100 percent vested, employees cannot lose their pension benefits even if they leave their jobs before retirement. If they leave and return, their years of service before and after the break must be added together in determining the amount of their pension.
- Pension plans must contain provisions for automatic survivor annuities and pre-retirement survivor benefits to married employees, with an option for employees to

waive survivor benefits if they wish, but only with a spouse's written consent.

Funding

The following funding requirements apply:

- Employers are required to fund annually all pension benefits earned that year by employees. They also must amortize over time the cost of benefit increases, investment losses or gains, and benefit credits for the past service of employees that were not previously funded.
- Employers who fail to meet the minimum funding standards must pay an excise tax penalty of 10 percent of the amount that should have been contributed. A 100-percent tax can be levied if an employer fails to correct a funding deficiency within a certain period of time.
- Plans that become underfunded because of benefit increases or other reasons must speed up the amortization schedule for covering certain liabilities.
- The Secretary of the Treasury can waive the funding requirement for companies that would suffer financial hardship by complying with the minimum standards, but may require security if the amount to be waived exceeds $1 million.
- A lien may be levied against an employer's assets if the employer fails to meet minimum funding standards. The employer must also notify plan participants and beneficiaries of any failure by the plan to meet the funding requirements.
- An employer who by increasing benefits causes the pension plan to be less than 60 percent funded in terms of what would be owed to the workers if the plan terminated must post a security bond to keep the plan qualified for tax breaks.
- Employer deductions for contributions to a fully funded pension plan may not exceed 150 percent of current liabilities—the value of all vested and nonvested benefits

that would be owed to plan participants if the plan terminated.

Fiduciary Standards

Fiduciary standards are covered by the following provisions:

- The persons who control and manage employee benefit plans and plan funds (fiduciaries) must exercise their duties in a prudent manner, solely for the benefit of participants and beneficiaries.
- Fiduciaries are prohibited from engaging in certain transactions with parties having interests adverse to those of the participants or the plan and from dealing with the income or assets of the employee benefit plan in their own interest.
- Fiduciaries are required to diversify pension fund investments to minimize the risk of large losses.

Enforcement and Administration

Title I includes the following punitive and administrative provisions:

- Civil actions may be brought by employees or beneficiaries to recover benefits, clarify rights to benefits, or seek relief from violations of the fiduciary standards.
- Criminal penalties are provided for individuals or corporations violating the reporting and disclosure regulations.

TITLE II. IRS RULES

Title II covers the tax provisions of ERISA, which consist of amendments to the Internal Revenue Code (IRC), including amendments that mirror the participation, vesting, and funding provisions of Title I. Other amendments to the IRC include the following.

IRAs and Keogh Plans

Individual Retirement Accounts (IRAs) and Keogh plans for self-employed persons are provided for, as follows:

- If an individual or his or her spouse is not covered by an employer-sponsored pension plan, that person may make an annual tax-deductible contribution of up to $2,000 (or 100 percent of earnings, whichever is less) to an IRA.
- Persons who are covered by employer-sponsored plans may also make the maximum $2,000 IRA contribution if they are single with an annual income under $25,000 or married (and filing jointly) with an annual income under $40,000. The $2,000 maximum is reduced for single persons with an annual income between $25,000 and $35,000 and for married couples with incomes between $40,000 and $50,000. No deductions are allowed if incomes exceed $35,000 and $50,000 for singles and married persons, respectively.
- Self-employed persons who establish pension plans for themselves (Keogh plans) can make annual tax deductible contributions of up to $30,000 or 25 percent of income, whichever is less.

Contribution and Benefit Limits

- The limit on an annual benefit payable from a defined benefit pension plan is the lesser of 100 percent of average salary or $90,000, indexed for inflation beginning in 1988. (The limit was $112,221 in 1992.)
- Annual additions under a defined contribution plan are limited to the lesser of 25 percent of compensation or $30,000, whichever is less. ("Annual additions" are the amounts contributed by the employer, plus employee after-tax contributions.)
- The $30,000 limit is frozen until the defined benefit dollar limit, indexed for inflation, reaches $120,000. Thereafter, a 4-to-1 ratio is maintained between the two limits.
- The ceiling on annual retirement benefits paid before the Social Security retirement age is reduced to the actuarial

equivalent of a $90,000 (inflation-adjusted) benefit beginning at the Social Security age. (The Social Security retirement age of 65 increases to age 66 in 2005 and to age 67 in 2022.)

Nondiscrimination Coverage Requirements

- Qualified employee benefit plans have to meet minimum nondiscrimination requirements designed to ensure that the plans are not providing disproportionate benefits to officers, shareholders, or highly paid employees.
- Pension plans have to meet one of three coverage tests: a percentage test, a ratio test, or an average benefits test. (For details of the three tests, see "Coverage Requirements" in Chapter 2.)
- Welfare benefit plans also must meet nondiscrimination coverage standards that differ by type of plan, either by covering a fair cross-section of workers or by satisfying various percentage tests.
- Employers of 20 or more workers must offer continued health care coverage to terminated employees and certain spouses and dependents for a specified period of time, but they are permitted to charge the beneficiary up to 102 percent of the cost to the employer.

TITLE III. JURISDICTION

Title III covers the responsibilities of the two federal agencies that administer and enforce ERISA and establishes the following arrangements:

- The Treasury Department has primary jurisdiction over participation, vesting, and funding issues and enforces compliance through tax exemption disqualification and through imposition of excise taxes.
- The Labor Department has primary jurisdiction over reporting and disclosure and fiduciary matters and can, in certain circumstances, enforce employee benefit rights and reporting and disclosure through civil or criminal actions.

TITLE IV. TERMINATION INSURANCE

The Pension Benefit Guaranty Corporation (PBGC), created by ERISA, is responsible for insuring against loss of pension benefits when plans collapse or are folded. Defined benefit plans are required to purchase termination insurance through the payment of annual premiums whose rates are based on the number of participants in the pension plan and whether the plan covers the employees of one employer (a "single-employer plan") or is a plan maintained under a collective bargaining agreement to which more than one employer contributes (a "multiemployer plan").

In the case of termination of a single-employer plan, PBGC insurance kicks in only if plan assets are insufficient to cover all benefits to which workers are entitled and the employer demonstrates financial distress.

In a "distress termination," an employer is liable for a percentage of the company's net worth, plus a percentage of employee benefits for which the plan has no funds.

Employers who pull out of a multiemployer pension plan must still pay their share of the unfunded pension obligations of the plan. (For details of plan termination, see Chapter 3, "Termination of Pension Plans.")

UPDATES TO ERISA

Legislative activity affecting pension plans has not abated since the passage of ERISA, with most of the substantive changes in the law coming through tax legislation. The preceding summary included provisions that were updated by the following measures.

Tax Legislation From 1975 to 1978

The Tax Reduction Act of 1975 increased the investment tax credit to 10 percent and permitted a corporation an additional 1 percent credit if it established an employee stock ownership plan (a "Tax Reduction Act Stock Ownership Plan," or

"TRASOP") and transferred to the plan an amount equal to the 1-percent credit.

An additional 0.5-percent annual investment tax credit if matched by employee contributions was provided for by the Tax Reform Act of 1976. The Reform Act also liberalized IRA contribution limits, which at that time were $1,500 for persons with earned income. Thereafter, a worker could set aside an additional $250 for a nonworking spouse.

The Revenue Act of 1978 extended the annual 1.5-percent employer credit for several more years. The law also introduced a new tax-favored retirement plan aimed largely at small employers—the "Simplified Employee Pension" (SEP). A SEP is an arrangement under which the employer establishes and finances an IRA for each of its employees.

The 1978 tax act also permitted employers to establish qualified profit-sharing and stock bonus plans with cash-or-deferred arrangements as long as the plans satisfied special nondiscrimination rules to prevent disproportionate participation and income deferral by highly paid employees.

These plans became known as 401(k) plans for the section of the IRC in which they are described.

Multiemployer Pension Plan Amendments Act

The provisions of ERISA covering multiemployer plans were believed to be unworkable almost as soon as they were drafted. Problems were anticipated because ERISA failed to provide any mechanism to help financially troubled plans stay solvent and because the law would have allowed many employers to bail out of plans without any liability for unfunded benefits.

After postponing implementation of ERISA provisions for multiemployer plans several times, Congress in 1980 enacted the Multiemployer Pension Plan Amendments Act (MPPAA), which provided relief for financially troubled plans and required employers withdrawing from plans to meet their obligations for unfunded benefits. (For an extensive discussion of this law, see "Termination in Multiemployer Plans" in Chapter 3.)

Economic Recovery Tax Act

The Economic Recovery Tax Act of 1981 (ERTA) doubled the amount that could be contributed to Keogh plans and SEPs and raised from $1,500 to $2,000 the maximum deductible limit for an IRA contribution.

Under ERISA, tax-deductible IRAs had been available only for persons not covered by pension plans at work. ERTA opened up IRAs to all persons with earned income, whether or not they were covered by an employer-provided pension plan.

The 1981 law also created a payroll-based employee stock ownership plan ("PAYSOP") intended to replace TRASOPs, which were scheduled to expire December 31, 1983. The tax credit became available to all employers as a percentage of payroll rather than as an investment tax credit on property. Under the plan, a company received tax credits for its contributions to the PAYSOP, which went into a trust fund to buy company stock for employee accounts. (The tax credit for PAYSOPs was eliminated as of December 31, 1986.)

Tax Equity and Fiscal Responsibility Act

The next major tax bill to affect employee benefits was the Tax Equity and Fiscal Responsibility Act of 1982 (TEFRA).

TEFRA cut back maximum contribution and benefit limits for pension plans, restricted the types of loans that could be made to individuals from their pension accounts without tax consequences, and permitted partial rollovers from one IRA to another.

TEFRA also radically revised Keogh plan rules, mainly by eliminating the distinctions between corporate plans and Keogh plans. Self-employed individuals using Keogh plans became subject to the same minimum age and service requirements that apply to other pension plans. Maximum benefit and contribution levels were set at the same amounts as for other pension plans.

New rules were also developed in TEFRA for so-called "top-heavy" pension plans in which benefits for "key" employees (officers, owners, and highly paid employees) exceed the benefits of all other employees by a certain percentage. If a plan is found to be top-heavy, special vesting schedules have to be used for rank-and-file employees and minimum benefits or contributions have to be provided for these employees. (For a more detailed discussion of these provisions, see "Faster Vesting Schedule for Top Heavy Plans" in Chapter 2.)

Deficit Reduction Act of 1984

The Deficit Reduction Act of 1984 was a massive tax measure intended to increase federal revenues largely by closing a number of tax loopholes. Many of its provisions relate to employee benefit plans, as follows:

- A limit was placed on flexible compensation plans (also known as "cafeteria plans"). Under these plans, employees can choose among taxable and nontaxable benefit options offered and paid for by the employer. The IRS had challenged certain types of cafeteria plans as providing tax-free reimbursement to employees for benefits that would have been subject to taxes if offered outside a cafeteria plan. Under the Deficit Reduction Act, only benefits specifically excluded from gross income under the IRC can be provided under a cafeteria plan without tax consequences. Examples include group term life insurance, health care benefits, and group legal services.
- The dollar limits that TEFRA imposed on pension plan benefits and contributions were extended until 1988.
- A 10-percent excise tax penalty will be assessed against the owners of a company who receive a premature distribution from their pension plan. A distribution is "premature" if it comes before an owner is 59½ years of age, is disabled, or has died.
- The maximum tax credit for employer contributions to a PAYSOP was frozen at 0.5 percent through 1987.
- Banks were allowed to exclude from taxable income half the interest they earned on loans to Employee Stock Ownership Plans (ESOPs).

- Employers were allowed to deduct dividends paid on employee stock in an ESOP if the dividends passed through to employees in cash.

Retirement Equity Act

As the 10th anniversary of ERISA neared, efforts accelerated to complete legislation aimed at improving pension opportunities for women. The Retirement Equity Act, signed into law on August 23, 1984, lowers the age at which workers must be allowed to join a pension plan and lengthens the time they can interrupt work without losing pension credits—provisions intended to ensure that women who leave the work force for a few years to raise children will, nevertheless, earn and retain some pension credits. (For additional details, see "Break in Service" and "Vesting" in Chapter 2.)

The Retirement Equity Act also makes survivor annuities possible for men and women whose spouses die before retirement if the spouses had vested rights to pension benefits. Automatic survivor benefits were previously available only for the spouses of retired workers or spouses of workers who were within a certain number of years of retirement. Written consent of a spouse must be obtained before workers can waive survivor benefits. (For additional details of the survivor provisions, see "Survivor Benefits" in Chapter 2.)

Single-Employer Pension Plan Amendments Act

Originally a separate bill, the final provisions of the Single-Employer Pension Plan Amendments Act (SEPPAA) were incorporated into the Consolidated Omnibus Budget Reconciliation Act of 1985 (COBRA). The legislation had two main objectives: (1) to shore up the financially troubled single-employer insurance fund of the Pension Benefit Guaranty Corporation and (2) to discourage solvent companies from dumping their pension liabilities on the PBGC.

By 1985, the PBGC deficit had reached $1.4 billion. The PBGC was paying more in benefits than it was collecting in premiums, using reserves to make up the difference. Every year from 1982 on, the PBGC had requested a premium hike from Congress, but it had been unsuccessful in convincing lawmakers of the need.

The poor financial situation of the PBGC resulted from the collapse of several major companies whose pension debts the PBGC had to assume, and from loopholes in ERISA that allowed companies that could afford to stay in business to terminate underfunded pension plans. The PBGC had to pick up those pension obligations as well.

The legislation raised the premium that employers pay to the PBGC insurance fund from $2.60 to $8.50 per employee, effective January 1, 1986. (This flat rate schedule was changed to a variable rate schedule for plan years on or after January 1, 1988. See the provisions of the Omnibus Budget Reconciliation Act of 1987.) The law also changed the conditions under which plans can be terminated, distinguishing between "standard terminations" for which there are sufficient assets to pay all guaranteed benefits and "distress terminations" of financially troubled companies with underfunded plans. (For additional details, see Chapter 3, "Termination of Pension Plans.")

COBRA also required a major change in employee benefit plans in regard to continuation of health insurance coverage for terminated employees and certain spouses and dependents. Employers with a work force of at least 20 persons who provide their workers with group health insurance coverage are required to offer continued coverage for up to 18 months for terminated employees and for up to 36 months for spouses and dependents of deceased or divorced workers.

Employers can require these beneficiaries to pay up to 102 percent of the premium charged to the employer for each worker. An employer who fails to comply with these provisions can lose the tax deduction for contributions to the plan.

Tax Reform Act of 1986

Despite the many changes Congress had made to ERISA and to the IRC in the years after the enactment of ERISA, lawmakers were not satisfied that employee benefit plans were benefiting as many lower- and middle-income workers as possible, relative to the tax breaks received by employers for their contributions to the plan and relative to benefits provided for higher-paid employees.

Legislators were also concerned that upper-income tax-payers were using IRAs and 401(k) plans more as tax shelters than as retirement savings plans, at a cost to the Treasury of tax revenues.

As a result, Congress used a major tax overhaul bill in 1986 to make sweeping changes to the IRC affecting both pension and welfare benefit plans.

To broaden coverage and benefits, the Tax Reform Act

- Shortened the number of years of service that can be required of employees before they acquire vested rights to their pension benefits (For additional details, see "Vesting" in Chapter 2.)
- Limited the amount that a pension benefit can be reduced by an employer who integrates the pension plan with Social Security (For additional details, see "Integrated Pension Plans" in Chapter 2.)
- Required employers beginning in 1989 to meet one of three new nondiscrimination tests to satisfy the requirement that a qualified pension plan benefit a broad segment of workers, not just highly paid employees (For additional details, see "Coverage Requirements" in Chapter 2.)
- Replaced separate nondiscrimination coverage tests for various welfare benefit plans with a new uniform test for health, accident, and life insurance plans, known as "Section 89" rules for their place in the IRC. (These provisions were subsequently repealed. For additional details, see "Nondiscrimination Rules for Welfare Plans" in Chapter 4.)

The Tax Reform Act also made substantial changes to IRAs, 401(k) plans, and SEPs, including the following:

- Persons covered by employer-provided pension plans, or whose spouses are covered by such plans, can no longer make the maximum $2,000 annual tax-deductible contribution to an IRA, unless they are single with an annual income under $25,000 or married with an income under $40,000.

- Employee deferrals to 401(k) plans were reduced from a maximum of $30,000 annually to $7,000, indexed for inflation. (The maximum was $8,728 in 1992.) Special nondiscrimination rules for 401(k)s were made stiffer. (For additional details, see "Plan Categories" in Chapter 2.)
- Employees in firms with 25 or fewer workers may elect to defer a portion of their salary to a SEP, subject to the same $7,000 inflation-adjusted limit set for 401(k)s. (For additional details, see "Plan Categories" in Chapter 2.)

The Tax Reform Act also provided the following additional tax benefits for ESOPs:

- An estate is permitted to exclude 50 percent of the proceeds from a sale of employer securities to an ESOP through December 31, 1991.
- A deduction is allowed of dividends used to repay ESOP loans that are used to acquire the stock on which the dividends are paid.
- Any portion of a reversion transferred to an ESOP for the purchase of employer securities is exempt from the 10-percent excise tax on reversions of surplus assets.
- Early distributions from ESOPs are exempt from the 10-percent additional income tax imposed on early distributions from other retirement plans.
- ESOP participants who have reached age 55 and who have completed at least ten years of service are allowed to invest up to 25 percent of their account balances in investments other than employer securities. (The percentage increases to 50 percent at age 60.)

The Tax Reform Act also made it tougher to withdraw retirement plan money before age 59½ or for other than a limited number of exceptions by imposing a 10-percent penalty tax on the amounts withdrawn.

Omnibus Budget Reconciliation Act of 1986

The Omnibus Budget Reconciliation Act of 1986 contained amendments to the Age Discrimination in Employment Act that affected pension benefit accruals for workers 65 and older. Under ERISA, companies had not been required to give pension credits to workers who continued on the job past age 65. A worker would accrue benefits until reaching age 65, after which the benefit would be frozen. Thus, a worker who retired at age 68 would receive the same pension benefit as if he or she had retired at age 65.

The 1986 amendments require employers to continue to provide for benefit accruals without regard to age, effective for plan years beginning on or after January 1, 1988.

Omnibus Budget Reconciliation Act of 1987

Despite the increase in premium payments that Congress approved in 1985 to shore up the PBGC, the agency was almost $4 billion in debt by the beginning of 1987. The agency had been facing growing claims because of the termination of a number of seriously underfunded pension plans and the practice by some companies of dumping pension liabilities on the PBGC while still remaining in business. Under ERISA, it was possible for a company to satisfy existing minimum funding requirements and yet terminate a pension plan with large liabilities and few assets.

These developments led to the drafting of the Pension Protection Act, which subsequently became part of the Omnibus Budget Reconciliation Act of 1987 signed into law by President Reagan on December 22, 1987.

The 1987 law requires employers with underfunded pension plans to make additional pension contributions and to pay increased premiums to the PBGC insurance program. The revised rules also seek to ensure adequate plan funding by

- Requiring quarterly contributions
- Shortening the number of years over which under-

funded plans can amortize past liabilities from 30 years
to 18 years and over which the plans can pay back any
waived amounts of funding from 15 years to 5 years
- Restricting the availability of funding waivers from five
  to three in a 15-year period
- Requiring plans that are less than 60 percent funded to
  post a bond or other security before increasing benefits

Other major provisions of the Pension Protection Act are
aimed at strengthening the PBGC through higher premiums
and tighter restrictions on plan terminations. These provisions
include the following:

- The flat-rate premium system in effect since the enactment of ERISA is replaced with a variable-rate premium.
  All plans pay a basic annual premium of $16 per partici-
  pant. However, underfunded plans must pay an additional $6 per $1,000 of unfunded vested benefits, capped
  at $34 per employee. Thus, the total maximum premium
  per employee would be $50.
- A company that wants to terminate its pension plan on
  the grounds of a Chapter 11 bankruptcy proceeding
  must show that liquidation will follow if the plan is not
  terminated.
- The PBGC's claim for unfunded guaranteed benefits of
  terminated plans increases from 75 percent to 100 percent.
- Plan participants in terminated plans are given greater
  protection. In a standard termination, participants must
  receive full benefits, including nonvested amounts.

The Technical and Miscellaneous Revenue Act of 1988

Among the many significant benefit changes provided by
the 1986 Tax Reform Act were the Section 89 nondiscrimination
rules for welfare plans. Effective in 1989, the law provided
complex new eligibility and benefits tests, which group health,
accident, and life insurance plans had to meet to be tax qualified. The aim was to prevent plans from discriminating in favor

of higher-paid employees by providing them better benefits than those given to lower-paid workers. If a plan is found to be discriminating in this fashion, the higher-paid employees must pay taxes on the value of the "discriminatory excess." Employers face a penalty tax if they fail to report that these employees received a discriminatory benefit.

As the deadline for complying with the new rules approached, companies complained that they had received little guidance from the Treasury Department in the form of regulations. Employers said they were facing an administrative nightmare in trying to conform to the rules, particularly in terms of data collection required to satisfy the new nondiscrimination tests.

In the Technical and Miscellaneous Revenue Act of 1988, Congress sought to clarify and modify some of the requirements, although there was no attempt at any broad overhaul of the Section 89 rules. The changes included allowing employers to test for compliance through random sampling of employees rather than collecting data on all employees and allowing employers with multiple plans to use a common testing date and year for all plans of the same type. Employers were also given additional time to comply with the requirement that they provide written documentation of their welfare plans that describe the benefits and the classes of workers eligible to participate.

The legislation also addressed another issue that had been causing controversy for several years—asset reversions. Under ERISA, companies with assets in their pension plans that exceeded benefit obligations could recapture those assets only by terminating their pension plans. If they did end the plan, they were obligated to pay workers and retirees the benefits promised them. But any amounts in excess of those obligations could revert to the employer. Opponents of the practice argued that all the assets of a pension plan belonged to the participants in the plan and that any "surplus" assets should be distributed to the participants in the form of increased benefits.

From 1980 to 1987, over 1,600 pension plans had been terminated with over $18 billion in assets that reverted to plan sponsors. A Senate proposal would have slapped a 60-percent excise tax on asset reversions, which critics said would have effectively halted the practice. Although that proposal was not enacted, Congress did raise the existing excise tax on reversions from 10 percent to 15 percent in the Technical and Miscellaneous Revenue Act. The higher excise tax was effective for reversions received after October 20, 1988. However, on October 24, 1988, the Treasury Department announced a moratorium on asset reversions until May 1989.

Retiree Benefits Bankruptcy Protection Act

In 1986, when the LTV Steel Company filed for bankruptcy under Chapter 11, the company contended it could no longer pay retiree health benefits under existing law. Congress enacted several temporary measures to prevent the company from stopping payments.

Finally, in 1988, Congress enacted a measure that allows a company filing for bankruptcy to propose a reduction in benefits to retirees if the company notifies the retirees and negotiates the reduction in good faith with a retiree representative. A bankruptcy court can then order a modification of benefit amounts while the bankruptcy case is pending. However, a company's reorganization plan must contain provisions for paying benefits to retirees.

Omnibus Budget Reconciliation Act of 1989

As in previous years, Congress included several pension and welfare benefit provisions in the Omnibus Budget Reconciliation Act enacted toward the close of the year. The 1989 Act included the following provisions:

- A requirement that the Secretary of Labor assess a civil penalty for certain violations of fiduciary responsibility under ERISA (The penalty is set at 20 percent of the amount recovered either through a settlement or a court proceeding. The penalty can be waived if the Secretary finds that the fiduciary has acted reasonably and in good faith or if the fiduciary faces a "severe financial hardship" in restoring losses unless he or she is granted a waiver or reduction of the penalty.)

- Repeal of the estate tax deduction for certain sales of employer securities to an ESOP and of the tax exemption on early distributions and a narrowing of the conditions under which deductions can be taken on dividends used to repay ESOP loans (The 1989 Act also limits the 50-percent interest exclusion on ESOP loans to transactions that result in the ESOP owning 50 percent of employer stock.)
- Extension of the tax exclusion for employer-provided educational assistance and group legal assistance from December 1988 to September 30, 1990
- Extension of health insurance continuation (COBRA) coverage for former employees from 18 months to 29 months for those employees who were disabled when they terminated employment and authorization for employers to increase the premium for such coverage to 150 percent of the employer's cost for the extra months
- Authorization for the Department of Labor to assess a penalty of $100 a day against an employer who fails to notify workers and retirees if a required quarterly pension plan contribution has not been made
- A requirement that pension plans determine experience gains and losses and the valuation of plan liabilities annually instead of on the previous schedule of once every three years
- A requirement that plans with a funded ratio of less than 70 percent report that information on Schedule B of the Form 5500

Debt Ceiling Increase (Repeal of Section 89)

Opposition to the Section 89 nondiscrimination rules for welfare plans continued from employers, particularly small businesses, throughout 1988 and 1989. Congress bowed to the pressure in November 1989 by repealing the provisions outright after several attempts to amend the rules failed. The repeal had been attached to that year's budget reconciliation bill, but it was stripped from that bill as nongermane. The repeal was then tacked on to a bill raising the statutory ceiling on the national debt. (For additional details, see "Nondiscrimination Rules for Welfare Plans" in Chapter 4.)

Americans With Disabilities Act

The Americans with Disabilities Act (ADA) prohibits employers of 25 or more persons from discriminating against disabled persons either in hiring or in benefit programs, effective July 1992. (The law covers employers of between 15 and 24 workers beginning in July 1994.)

The ADA prohibits an employer from treating any disabled person in a way that adversely affects that individual's right to health insurance or pension benefits. Thus, an employer cannot refuse to hire or try to fire an individual because that person's disability or illness (or that of a dependent) might cause health plan costs to increase.

However, employers are not prohibited from providing health insurance that could have the effect of restricting coverage for certain disabled employees if the health care plan complies with state and federal law and the insurance follows accepted risk classification principles. Employers can, for example, limit coverage for preexisting conditions, as most employer plans have done in the past, or limit reimbursement for certain treatments, so long as those limits apply to all employees.

(For further information on the ADA, see *The Employer's Guide to the Americans With Disabilities Act*, published by BNA Books.)

Omnibus Budget Reconciliation Act of 1990

Congress continued to debate the issue of reversions of surplus assets from terminated defined benefit pension plans. From 1980 through 1989, nearly 2,000 plans with reversions in excess of $1 million were terminated. Plan sponsors recovered a total of over $20 billion in assets from those plans.

However, the practice began to decline after the peak year of 1985 when 582 plan terminations with large reversions took place. The plans, with $6.1 billion in assets, had covered over 700,000 participants. Less than half as many terminations of this size occurred the following year. The PBGC projected that total reversions for 1991 (in the $1 million-and-over category) would amount to about $100 million, compared with the $6.1 billion in reversions in 1985—from a total of about 44 plans.

Despite the decline in reversions, Congress, in the Omnibus Budget Reconciliation Act of 1990, increased the federal excise tax on reversions from 15 percent to 20 percent and required that the employer provide a replacement plan and leave a cushion in the plan equal to 25 percent of the surplus or give workers and retirees an immediate benefit equal to 20 percent of the reversion. The excise tax increases to 50 percent if the employer offers no replacement plan.

The 1990 Act also allows employers to transfer excess pension plan assets to a 401(h) account to pay for current retiree health benefits. The employer may make up to five annual tax-free transfers for each of the years 1991 through 1995 provided that the following conditions are met:

- The employer must maintain the same level of spending on retiree health benefits for each of the four years after a transfer.
- Accrued pension plan benefits must be vested as if the plan had terminated at the time of the transfer.

The 1990 Act also raised the premiums paid to the PBGC by employers from $16 per participant to $19. Underfunded plans must pay an additional $9 per $1,000 of underfunded liability (up from $6), capped at a maximum of $53 per participant. The maximum combined total is thus $72 per participant ($19 + $53).

The law also extended through 1991 the tax exclusion on employer-provided group legal services and educational assistance.

Unemployment Compensation Extension (Lump-Sum Distributions)

During the 102nd Congress (1991–1992), the Bush administration and several lawmakers proposed and debated various steps that could be taken to increase pension coverage by simplifying the administration of certain types of plans, such as 401(k) plans and SEPs, with the aim of encouraging more employers to offer pension coverage to their workers. Another proposal sought to discourage workers eligible for lump-sum benefit payments from cashing out those benefits when they leave an employer. Under current law, such cash payments are subject to a 10-percent penalty for premature distribution unless they are rolled over into an IRA or annuity within 60 days.

A number of "simplification" proposals were included in a tax measure vetoed by President Bush in February 1992. However, changes to the lump-sum distribution rules were attached to a bill extending unemployment compensation, which was signed into law July 3, 1992.

The law provides that if a worker does not direct the plan administrator to transfer a lump-sum payment to an IRA or an annuity, 20 percent of the distributed amount is to be withheld. The remaining 80 percent is to be taxed as ordinary income and subject to the 10-percent excise tax on premature distributions. Plan sponsors must provide workers with information on the mandatory withholding and rollover rules.

2

OPERATION OF
PENSION PLANS

ERISA defines an "employee pension benefit plan" or "pension plan" as any plan, fund, or program that provides retirement income to employees or results in a deferral of income by employees for periods extending to the termination of employment. For the purpose of the definition, it does not matter what method is used to calculate the contributions to or the benefits under the pension plan or the method of distributing the benefits.

PLAN CATEGORIES

From 1975 to 1988, the total number of tax-qualified employer-sponsored private pension plans increased from 311,000 to 730,000. In 1988, more than 42 million full-time workers (approximately 48 percent of all full-time private wage and salary workers) were covered by private plans.

Private-sector pension plans are divided into two broad categories: defined benefit plans and defined contribution plans. In 1988, there were 146,000 defined benefit plans and 584,000 defined contribution plans. In 1987, 35 percent of work-

31

ers with pension plans were covered solely by defined benefit plans, 32 percent were covered only under defined contribution plans, and 33 percent were covered under both types of plans.

According to the U.S. Department of Labor, the trend since the early 1970s has been a shift from defined benefit plans to defined contribution plans. Defined contribution plans covered only one-third of all active participants in plans established prior to 1975, compared with four-fifths of active participants in plans created since 1975. Substantial growth took place particularly in ESOPs and thrift or savings, profit-sharing, and 401(k) plans.

Defined Benefit Plans

A defined benefit pension plan promises a fixed monthly benefit upon retirement. ERISA does not specify a formula to be used or what the benefit levels should be, but it does require employers to contribute enough money each year to cover the benefits that employees have accrued that year. Employer contributions are determined actuarially on the basis of benefits payable, mortality, work force turnover, and other factors.

Employers often use a combination of length of service (years worked) and amount of earnings to establish what the benefit will be. Alternatively, the benefit could be a flat amount per month regardless of the earnings or years of service of the employee. Or a formula might be used that sets the benefit at a certain percentage of compensation or a percentage of compensation times years of service. The earnings used might be a career average or a "final" pay formula that uses a stated number of years at the end of an employee's career.

Defined Contribution Plans

A defined contribution plan, also known as an "individual account plan," provides for a separate account for each participant to which contributions are made by the employer under a specified formula, for example, a percentage of the employee's earnings. These payments accumulate, along with investment earnings, in the employee's account. The retirement benefit depends on the contributions made to the individual's account and on investment gains and losses. All defined contribution plans except money purchase plans are exempt from ERISA's funding requirements; all such plans are excluded from the plan termination insurance program.

Although a collectively bargained multiemployer pension plan will, under the terms of a contract, call for a specified level of contributions from employers, such an agreement will also provide for an agreed-upon level of benefits and so is considered a defined benefit plan (see above).

Another type of defined contribution plan is a target benefit plan, in which the contribution is determined in accordance with a formula that sets up a "target" benefit for participants. The employer contributes an amount each year intended to achieve the target, but that amount is allocated to an individual account for the employee.

Also included under the term "defined contribution plan" are profit-sharing, thrift, stock bonus, and employee stock ownership plans.

Profit-Sharing Plans

Profit-sharing plans involve the sharing of a fixed percentage of profits with employees each year. There must be a predetermined formula for allocating the contributions made to the plan. Typically, amounts are allocated in proportion to salary. Distribution of the funds has to be made after a fixed number of years; when the employee reaches a certain age; or upon a layoff, illness, disability, retirement, or death.

Although profit-sharing plans are exempt from the ERISA minimum funding standards, "substantial and recurring" contributions must be made out of profits if the plan is to be considered qualified by the Internal Revenue Service (IRS) for tax deductions.

Savings or Thrift Plans

Savings or thrift plans are voluntary and contributory. Once an employee chooses to participate, he or she must contribute to the plan along with the employer. The employee usually can choose the level of his or her contribution, with the range generally between 1 percent and 6 percent of salary. The employer usually matches or provides some fraction of the employee contribution.

Savings plans also differ from other defined contribution pension plans in that the employee is generally permitted to make withdrawals from his or her account before retirement, although there may be limits to the withdrawals and possible penalties. One form of penalty is the suspension of the employee's participation in the plan for a period of time following the withdrawal.

Cash or Deferred Arrangements (CODAs)

Under a cash or deferred arrangement (also known as a 401(k) plan), employees are permitted to forgo a portion of their salary in favor of a tax-deferred contribution to the plan. Employers frequently match employee contributions. In 1988, about 12.3 million workers were covered by 401(k) plans.

The IRC limits the amount that may be deferred and requires plans to meet special nondiscrimination rules with regard to the amounts that highly paid employees may defer relative to the amounts deferred by lower-paid employees.

Stock Plans

Stock bonus plans and ESOPs provide benefits similar to those of profit-sharing plans, except that contributions made by the employer are not necessarily dependent on profits and the benefits are in the stock of the company. There were about 9,900 ESOPs in the United States at the end of 1990, covering over 11.3 million workers.

Under an ESOP, employees who reach age 55 with at least 10 years of service may invest up to a quarter of their account balances in investments other than employer securities. When employees reach age 60, the percentage available for diversification increases to half of their account balances.

Simplified Employee Pensions (SEPs)

SEPs are intended to encourage small employers to set up retirement plans for their employees by removing much of the expense and paperwork associated with pension plans. An employer may contribute up to $30,000 a year or 15 percent of compensation, whichever is less, to individual accounts for each employee. Employees may elect to defer up to $8,728 (in 1992) of their salary to the SEP if at least 50 percent of the employees participate. (The employee contribution, which was originally set at $7,000, is indexed for inflation.)

COVERAGE REQUIREMENTS

ERISA builds on the foundation laid by the Revenue Act of 1942, which first established "nondiscrimination" guidelines for pension plans that wanted to qualify for tax breaks. ERISA required pension plans to benefit at least 70 percent of all employees or 80 percent of all eligible employees if at least 70 percent of all employees were eligible to benefit (that is, a plan had to benefit at least 56 percent of all employees who had satisfied minimum age and service requirements).

Alternatively, a plan could meet the nondiscriminatory criteria by satisfying a "reasonable classification test," which required a plan to benefit a fair cross-section of employees and not discriminate in favor of officers, shareholders, or highly paid employees.

The reasonable classification test was criticized for being too subjective. In the Tax Reform Act of 1986, Congress changed the nondiscrimination coverage rules in an effort to bring greater objectivity to the tests and to ensure that qualified plans were benefiting most of an employer's work force.

Beginning with plan years after December 31, 1988, pension plans must meet one of three tests:

- Percentage Test—A plan must benefit at least 70 percent of all nonhighly paid workers.
- Ratio Test—The percentage of nonhighly paid workers covered by the plan must be at least 70 percent of the

percentage of highly paid workers who are covered. For example, if 90 percent of highly paid workers are covered, then 63 percent of other workers also have to be covered.

- Average Benefits Test—A plan must satisfy the current reasonable classification test *and* provide an average benefit percentage for nonhighly paid workers that is at least 70 percent of the average benefit percentage for highly paid workers. (The benefit percentage is the employer-provided contributions or benefits expressed as a percentage of the employee's compensation.)

For example, if the average benefit percentage for highly paid employees is 18 percent, then that percentage for all other employees has to be at least 12.6 percent (70 percent of 18 percent).

Qualified plans must also satisfy a minimum participation test, which requires that they benefit at least the lesser of 50 employees or 40 percent of all employees.

Special nondiscrimination tests also apply to 401(k) plans, which limit the amounts that may be deferred by highly paid workers relative to the amounts that are being deferred by other employees in the plan.

The key to the application of nondiscrimination tests for *all* qualified pension plans is the definition of "highly compensated employee" in the 1986 Tax Reform Act. (Compensation figures are adjusted annually for inflation.) An employee is considered highly compensated if he or she was in any of the following categories during the *preceding* year:

- A 5-percent owner
- An officer who earned more than 50 percent of the dollar limitation amount for defined benefit plans ($56,111 in 1992)
- An employee who earned an annual salary of more than $75,000 ($95,518 in 1992), or
- An employee who earned an annual salary of more than $50,000 ($62,345 in 1992) and was among the top-paid group of employees

Also defined as highly compensated are those employees who during the *current* year are 5-percent owners or among the top 100 employees by pay *and* in one of the last three categories above.

(These same definitions of highly compensated apply to welfare benefit plans.)

ELIGIBILITY AND PARTICIPATION

When Congress first wrote nondiscrimination coverage rules for pension plans in the 1942 Revenue Act, lawmakers were trying to make sure that pension benefits were actually going to rank-and-file employees. But the coverage tests had to be applied only against those employees who were *eligible* for participation in the plan.

The term "eligibility" refers to the conditions an employee must meet before becoming a participant in, i.e., being covered by, a pension plan. These conditions generally involve attaining a minimum age and completing a minimum period of service with the employer.

Before ERISA, employers could impose whatever minimum service and minimum/maximum age requirements they wished. Because the nondiscrimination provisions did not address these restrictions on participation, plans could still qualify for tax-favored status while excluding many workers.

ERISA prevents plans from imposing unreasonable age and service requirements. Eligibility cannot be delayed beyond the time an employee reaches age 21 and has completed one year of service, whichever occurs later. (Originally, ERISA set the minimum age at 25, but this was lowered to 21 by the Retirement Equity Act.)

Alternatively, a pension plan can require two years of service for eligibility if at the end of the two years the employee is 100 percent vested in his or her benefits.

There is one major exception to the one-year/age-21 minimum requirement or the two-year/100-percent-vested alternative. Tax-exempt pension plans of educational institutions that provide for full and immediate vesting on becoming a participant may require an employee to have completed one year of service or to have reached age 26, whichever is later.

Once an employee has met the age and service requirements, actual participation in the pension plan begins on the first day of the next plan year or six months after satisfying the requirements, whichever comes first. The employee then begins earning pension benefits or accumulating funds in an individual account.

It should be noted that ERISA requires that pension plans be established for the "exclusive benefit of employees." An appellate court ruled in 1988 that a plan sponsored by a corporation that claimed as employees professionals who were leased to other organizations had not been established exclusively for the benefit of the employer's employees. The court contended that the leasing corporation did not exercise such control over the professionals as to satisfy the definition of an employer/employee relationship (*Professional & Executive Leasing, Inc. v. Commissioner*, 862 F.2d 751 (9th Cir. 1988)).

Maximum Age

ERISA prohibits pension plans from discriminating against workers who join a company at an older age, even if those workers are within a few years of retirement age. Originally, ERISA did allow a defined benefit pension plan to exclude from participation any employee hired within five years of the plan's normal retirement age. If the plan used age 65 as its normal retirement age, for instance, it could exclude persons hired after age 60. However, the 1986 budget reconciliation act repealed the five-year rule.

Defined contribution pension plans must allow an older worker to become a participant, once the worker has met the eligibility requirements, even if he or she is within a couple of years of retirement.

Definition of "Service"

ERISA establishes minimum standards for defining "year of service" and "break in service." The law also authorized the

Labor Department to define "hour of service" through regulation.

In general, an employee is credited with a year of service for any 12-month period during which he or she has 1,000 hours of service. The 12-month period could be a plan year, calendar year, or employment year.

For seasonal employment, the Secretary of Labor has authority to define a year of service, and for maritime industries 125 days of service is treated as a year of service. Part-time and seasonal employees cannot be excluded from pension plans if they meet the "year of service" definitions.

Hours of Service

Labor Department regulations define "hour of service" as follows:

- Each hour for which an employee is paid or is entitled to be paid for the performance of duties for an employer
- Each hour for which an employee is paid or is entitled to be paid although no duties are performed, such as for vacation, holiday, illness, incapacity (including disability), layoff, jury duty, military duty, or leave of absence (No more than 501 hours of service must be credited to an employee, however, for any single continuous period during which the employee performed no duties, such as during a leave of absence.)
- Each hour for which back pay is either awarded or agreed to by an employer, except that no more than 501 hours of service must be credited for a period of time during which an employee did not perform any duties

If payment is made to an employee under workers' compensation or unemployment compensation, no hours need be counted for the periods covered by these payments.

The Labor Department permits three different methods of crediting employees with hours of service, as discussed below.

Under the "general" or "standard-hours" method, an employee is credited with all hours worked. This method involves recording the hours actually worked by every employee, which can be difficult when some employees are not paid by the hour.

An "equivalency" system credits employees with 1,000 hours of service when they have worked an equivalent amount of time. For instance, an equivalency system can use time periods such as days, weeks, shifts, or payroll periods. If an employee is credited with at least one hour of service during the time period used, the employee must be credited with all the hours imputed to the period, regardless of whether he or she actually worked the whole time period.

In addition, use of time period equivalencies requires an employer to credit more hours than are actually worked in the selected time period, to compensate for overtime or other additional hours that might have been worked. Thus, if days are the time period used, the employer would have to credit the employee with 10 hours for each day instead of 8 hours; if a week, 45 hours. A pension plan that uses time periods must treat 870 hours worked as equivalent to 1,000 hours of service and 435 hours worked as equivalent to 500 hours of service.

The third method of crediting hours of service is called "elapsed time" and is based on periods of service. Under elapsed time, an employee will have satisfied a one-year eligibility requirement, for instance, one year after the starting date of employment. Actual hours are not counted in this method.

Break in Service

Before the enactment of ERISA, a frequent cause of employees losing their pensions was that they failed to work the continuous period required by their employer. They might have broken up their employment with a leave of absence or might have quit only to return years later. Women taking prolonged leaves to raise children thus faced the loss of any benefits they might have earned.

ERISA protects vested pension rights of employees who have a break in the continuity of their employment. The law also allows employees who were not yet vested when they left an employer to maintain their place on a vesting schedule if their absence is not longer than the time they worked before the leave.

The Retirement Equity Act added even more flexibility for employees by requiring pension plans to allow employees to leave for up to five years without losing credit for pre-break service, even if it is less than the period of the break.

A "break in service" takes place under ERISA only when an employee works 500 hours or less in a plan or calendar year. Under equivalency methods a break in service occurs only when an employee works 435 hours or less. And under the elapsed method, a break in service does not take place until a year has elapsed after severance from service.

If an employee is credited with more than 500 hours but less than 1,000 hours of service, the employer need not count that time toward vesting or benefit accrual, but the employee has not incurred a break in service. The relevant time periods for the equivalency method are 435 hours and 870 hours, respectively.

A break in service can mean an employee has to start over accruing benefits or completing the number of years required to vest. But ERISA allows employers to wipe out previous service only under certain conditions. The effect of the break in service depends on the type of pension plan (defined benefit or defined contribution), the length of time the employee worked before the break and the length of the break, and whether or not the employee was vested at the time of the break.

Under ERISA, if an employee had incurred a one-year break in service, the pension plan could require a one-year waiting period before the employee could re-enter the plan. Then the employee's pre-break and post-break service had to be aggregated if the employee was vested or if the number of one-year breaks in service was less than the number of years of service before the break.

The Retirement Equity Act amended the break-in-service rules to provide than an employee could be gone from a job as long as five years without losing participation or vesting credit for the time worked before the break. For example, if a nonvested employee with three years of service left the job for a year, when that employee resumed work, the plan would have to count the three years of prior work. However, if the employee was gone for over five years and then returned, the plan could disregard the years worked before the break.

Maternity or Paternity Leave

ERISA did not require pension plans to give employees participation or vesting credit for unpaid maternity or paternity leave. Employees who had paid maternity or paternity leave could take about three months (501 hours in most cases) off without incurring a break in service.

The Retirement Equity Act allows an employee to count as hours of service up to 501 hours taken off from work because of pregnancy and birth or adoption of a child. The employee can be credited with the hours in the year in which the leave is taken in order to prevent a break in service that year, or the hours can be credited to the next year.

VESTING

The heart of ERISA is a guarantee to workers that once they become participants in pension plans, and then work some specified minimum period, they will have earned a right to a pension at retirement. This goal is reached through "vesting"— the earning by employees of nonforfeitable rights to pension benefits.

Pension benefits begin to accrue as soon as an employee satisfies eligibility requirements and becomes a participant in a pension plan. But no legal right to receive those benefits exists until an employee becomes vested. Once the employee has a vested right to a pension, he or she cannot lose the benefits earned.

An employer cannot deny a worker vesting credit for periods of employment during which the employee was not a participant in the pension plan and accruing benefits. The U.S. Court of Appeals for the D.C. Circuit said in a 1987 case (*Holt v. Winpisinger*, 8 EBC 1169) that the right to vesting credit is derived from ERISA and cannot be waived by an employment contract.

The case involved a woman hired on contract as a part-time consultant for one year, performing clerical work in a union's office. She was put on permanent full-time status one year later doing the same type of work. She worked nine more years, after which she was laid off. Her employer said she had not gained the 10 years of service required for vesting under the pension plan. But the court said the employee had not waived her right to vesting credit for the first year of her employment, even though she had accepted part-time employment without fringe benefits.

Her status as an employee, the court said, was determined by the employer's exercise of control over the details of her work, rather than the fact that she was characterized as an independent contractor.

Contributions made by employees themselves to their pension plans are always vested. They cannot be forfeited, regardless of whether the employee remains under the plan or dies before retirement, and regardless of vesting requirements for employer contributions. Further, accrued benefits attributable to employer contributions must vest when the employee reaches normal retirement age, even if the employee has not satisfied the plan's vesting schedule by that time. Accrued benefits also vest for all participants in any pension plan that terminates.

Vesting Schedules

Until passage of the Tax Reform Act of 1986, employers had a choice among three minimum vesting schedules. One provided for full vesting after 10 years of service, whereas the other two called for gradual vesting over a number of years. Whichever option employers chose, they had to ensure that employees were at least 50 percent vested after 10 years of service and 100 percent vested after 15 years.

The Tax Reform Act replaced those schedules with two options:

- "Cliff" or 5-year vesting, which is full vesting after 5 years of service (for multiemployer plans, 10 years of service), or
- Graded vesting, under which an employee is 20 percent vested after three years of service and gains 20 percent each year thereafter, with full vesting coming after 7 years

The schedules went into effect with plan years beginning after December 31, 1988.

Faster Vesting Schedules for Top-Heavy Plans

The Tax Equity and Fiscal Responsibility Act requires an even faster vesting schedule for any pension plan found to be "top-heavy"—that is, one that is providing more than 60 percent of its benefits to key employees. Key employees are officers; employees owning at least 1 percent of the firm and receiving more than $150,000 a year; the 10 employees owning the largest interest in the employer; and 5-percent owners, no matter how much they are paid.

The question of whether a plan is top-heavy has to be resolved each year. A plan could be intermittently top-heavy, resulting from high turnover among lower-paid employees who leave without vested benefits.

If a pension plan does become top-heavy, it must reduce the number of years an employee is required to work to be vested in a pension. The plan will then have the two following vesting schedule options:

- An employee with at least three years of service must be 100 percent vested, or
- An employee must be credited with at least partial vesting after two years of service and with complete vesting after six years. Called "six-year graded vesting," this option allows the employee to earn a vested right to 20 percent of his or her benefit after two years and 20 percent for each year thereafter, reaching 100 percent vesting after the sixth year.

Other Vesting Rules

An employee's years of service with the employer count toward the vesting schedule, including years worked before becoming a participant in the plan. However, the plan is allowed to disregard the following:

- Years of service before age 18
- Periods during which the employee declined to contribute to a plan requiring employee contributions as a condition for being covered
- Periods during which the employer did not maintain the plan
- Periods during which the employee had less than one year of service
- Service prior to a break in service if the length of the break is equal to or longer than the pre-break service or longer than five years, whichever is greater

The employer can also require that the employee complete at least one year of service on return to employment in order for the previous service to count.

If one company acquires or merges with another, service with the original employer must be counted for vesting if the successor company continues the plan.

If an employer decides to change from one vesting schedule to another, any employee with at least five years of service can continue under the former vesting schedule. But if the employee fails to make the election to remain under the old schedule, he or she will automatically come under the new one.

Permitted Forfeitures

Once vested, an employee cannot lose accrued benefits. However, if a person retires, begins receiving benefits, and then returns to work for the same employer, benefits may be suspended during the period of re-employment.

In contributory pension plans, withdrawal of an employee's own contributions could forfeit the employer contributions if the employee is not at least 50 percent vested when the withdrawal is made. Pension plans that contain this forfeiture provision must, however, permit the employee to "buy back" the forfeited benefits by repaying the withdrawn amounts plus, in some cases, interest.

ACCRUED BENEFITS

In a defined benefit pension plan, once becoming a participant, an employee begins accruing a specific amount of money each year toward a monthly retirement benefit. The amount accrued each year is based on a formula generally applied to salary and years of service, such as a percentage of final or average pay times the number of years of service. An employee has no legal right to the accruals, however, until vested.

The accrual schedule must follow minimum standards imposed by ERISA. A pension plan meets those minimum standards if it satisfies at least one of the following three methods:

- Under the "3-percent method," an employee's accrued benefit each year must be at least equal to 3 percent of what is projected to be his or her benefit at retirement. In this way, the employee will have accrued 100 percent of the retirement benefit after no more than 33⅓ years.
- Under the "133⅓-percent rule," an employee's accrued benefit each year is the actual benefit earned to date, but no future rate of benefit accrual can be greater than 133⅓ percent of the current benefit accrual rate. The intent of this rule is to limit "back loading," a practice in which a plan provides much higher rates of accruals in the later years of service than it does in the earlier years. Under the 133⅓-percent rule, the amount of the benefit accrual for a later year of service cannot be more than 1⅓ times the amount of benefits accumulated for the current year.
- Under the "fractional rule," an employee's accrued benefit at any one point in time is a prorated share of the employee's retirement benefit, based on years in the pension plan at that point relative to expected total years in the plan.

In a defined contribution pension plan, the participant's accrued benefit is the balance in his or her individual account. For plans funded exclusively through insurance contracts, the accrued benefit is the cash surrender value of the contract.

Pension plans are not required to accrue benefits for an employee for any year in which the employee has less than one year of service (except for plans using the elapsed method of crediting service since hours are not counted). If an employee works less than full time, but still works enough hours to be credited with a year of service, he or she must be given credit for a ratable portion of the benefit that would have been earned at full-time work.

Employers were allowed to freeze benefit accruals for employees who reached normal retirement age even if the employees continued working. However, in the 1986 budget reconciliation act, Congress included a provision requiring employers to continue benefit accruals for these workers.

Benefit Reductions

A pension plan cannot be amended to reduce retroactively the benefits an employee has already accrued. In certain circumstances, however, ERISA does allow a pension plan to reduce benefits being accrued for the current year if an amendment specifying such reductions is adopted within 2½ months from the close of the plan year. The Labor Department has to approve the amendment on the grounds that the reductions are necessary to prevent substantial hardship to the plan sponsor. (Since multiemployer pension plans are negotiated under collective bargaining agreements that generally run for two years or longer, amendments reducing benefits would have to be adopted within two years of the close of the plan year in which the collective bargaining agreement was signed.)

Benefit Payouts

A person with vested rights to a pension who leaves a job before retirement may be required to wait until the plan's normal retirement age before receiving a pension. Plans may require a terminated employee to take a lump-sum payment at termination if the entire amount of his or her vested benefit is not greater than $3,500. Otherwise, a pension plan may offer a lump-sum option, but is not required to pay benefits until the employee reaches the normal retirement age in the plan, completes 10 years of participation in the plan, or ends employment, whichever comes latest.

If a pension plan permits employees to choose early retirement after reaching a certain age and/or completing a certain number of years of service, an employee who retires early must be given the right to be paid his or her benefit at that time; however, the benefit can be reduced actuarially to take into account the longer period over which the pension annuity must be paid.

Minimum Benefits for Top-Heavy Plans

In the years a pension plan is found to be top-heavy, it must provide minimum benefits or contributions for rank-and-file employees, as follows:

- A defined benefit plan must provide a benefit of no less than 2 percent of an employee's average pay multiplied by years of service up to a maximum of 10 years or 20 percent of pay.
- A defined contribution plan must contribute 3 percent of pay for each employee in the plan. If, however, the maximum employer contribution for any employee has been less than 3 percent, the percentage contribution that must be made for other than key employees cannot be less than the highest percentage contribution for a key employee.

INTEGRATED PENSION PLANS

In determining pension benefit or contribution levels, employers have been permitted by the IRC to take into account an employee's Social Security benefit. The employer is given credit in effort for Social Security taxes paid for each worker. This practice is called integration.

Linked with integration is the "replacement ratio" theory. Employers who integrate their pension plans with Social Security are trying to ensure that total retirement income (pension benefit plus Social Security) will replace about the same percentage of pay for all employees, no matter how much they earn. Thus, since Social Security replaces a larger percentage of pay for lower-paid employees than it does for highly paid employees, the plan will provide lower pension benefits to the former and higher benefits to the latter.

One integration method, for example, calls for subtracting a certain percentage of the Social Security benefit from the pension benefit. The maximum permissible reduction is 83⅓ percent of the Social Security benefit, although a more common reduction has been 50 percent. For instance, if a worker was expected to receive $550 monthly in Social Security, the employer using a 50-percent reduction would subtract $225 from the total monthly benefit to be paid from the pension plan.

A pension plan that used what an appellate court termed unrealistically high calculations of estimated Social Security benefits to offset pension benefits was held to have violated the nondiscrimination requirements and antiforfeiture provisions of ERISA and the IRC. The employer's method of using estimated Social Security benefits for the offset rather than actual benefits was "unreasonable," the court said, as well as the employer's assumption that each employee always had been covered by Social Security (*Dameron v. Sinai Hospital of Baltimore, Inc.*, 815 F.2d 975 (4th Cir. 1987)).

Another method applies the pension formula only to salaries above a certain level, such as the Social Security taxable wage base, or applies one percentage to earnings below the salary level selected and a higher percentage to earnings above that level.

Although the use of integration methods often considerably reduced or sometimes totally wiped out the pension benefits of lower-income workers, the practice did not violate nondiscrimination rules for qualified plans. But integration was criticized for its effect on lower-paid workers. A freeze on the practice was included in the versions of ERISA passed by both the House and the Senate, but the language was struck in the conference on the final draft of the law. What remains in ERISA is a prohibition against reductions in the benefits of retired workers under integrated plans because of cost-of-living increases in Social Security benefits or increases in the Social Security taxable wage base. The Social Security benefit amount used to reduce pensions thus remain fixed for retirees.

This same prohibition against reductions in pension amounts because of changes in Social Security applies in the case of vested benefits of employees who leave their companies before retirement.

With the passage of TEFRA, Congress took another step toward limiting integration. TEFRA prohibits top-heavy pension plans from counting Social Security benefits against the minimum benefits received by lower-paid employees when they retire and against contributions that the companies make to lower-paid employees' accounts under pension plans.

In the 1986 Tax Reform Act, Congress sought to ensure that no worker lost an entire pension benefit through application of an integration formula. In offset plans, for instance, no employee's pension benefit can be reduced by more than 50 percent when taking Social Security into account or .75 percent of the worker's final average salary times years of service, whichever is less.

The changes in the integration rules took effect beginning in 1989.

LIMITS ON BENEFITS AND CONTRIBUTIONS

The limit on a benefit under a defined benefit plan originally was $75,000, and was to be adjusted annually to reflect increases in the consumer price index (CPI). Under this provision, the dollar limit had increased to $136,425 by 1981.

TEFRA reduced the maximum, however, to $90,000 beginning in 1983 and provided that $90,000 would remain the limit at least through 1986. This limit was extended to 1988 by the Deficit Reduction Act of 1984.

Prior to TEFRA, workers could retire as early as age 55 without any reduction in the maximum dollar limit on benefits. But TEFRA required plans to reduce benefits for persons retiring before age 62 to an actuarial equivalent of the full benefit that would have been received at age 62. However, TEFRA also set a floor of $75,000 below which benefits could not be reduced for early retirement after age 55.

The Tax Reform Act continued the $90,000 annual benefit limit, but provided for the $90,000 to be adjusted to reflect increases in the CPI beginning in 1988. The annual benefit limit was $112,221 in 1992. The annual compensation that can be used to determine benefit and contribution limits originally was $200,000, but indexing raised it to $228,860 in 1992.

Early retirement reductions in the maximum have to be made for benefits paid to persons retiring before the Social Security retirement age (65 through 2004 but increasing to 66 in 2005 and 67 in 2022). In addition, the Tax Reform Act eliminated the $75,000 floor under early retirement benefit reductions.

Tax-exempt employers and organizations are exempt from the actuarial reduction provision and change in the normal retirement age.

For a defined contribution pension plan, annual additions are limited to the lesser of 25 percent of annual pay or $30,000. The dollar limit originally was $25,000 and was to be adjusted annually for increases in the CPI. The $25,000 had risen to $45,475 before TEFRA put a $30,000 ceiling on the amount beginning in 1983, to remain in effect through 1986. Subsequently that ceiling was also extended through 1988 by the Deficit Reduction Act.

The Tax Reform Act provided that the $30,000 defined contribution limit not be adjusted for inflation until the $90,000 defined benefit limit reaches $120,000. Thereafter, the defined benefit–defined contribution ratio is to be maintained at 4 to 1.

The 1986 law also requires that all nondeductible employee contributions be counted in the total annual additions to which the limits on contributions apply.

For purposes of the limitations on benefits and contributions, all pension plans of an employer are treated as one plan so that the limits cannot be avoided through the creation of multiple plans. For combined defined benefit and defined contribution plans, there is a combined limit of 125 percent of the limits considered individually. For example, if an employee receives a contribution of 10 percent of annual pay under the company defined contribution plan and if the company has *only* a defined contribution plan, the contribution amount would be limited to a maximum of 25 percent of salary. Thus, the actual contribution in this case would be 40 percent of the maximum for a defined contribution plan (10% ÷ 25%). But if the company has a defined benefit plan as well, the allowable limit of 125 percent for the defined benefit plan for this employee would be reduced by the contribution from the other plan to 85 percent (125%–40%). The combined limit could be applied to restrict contributions to either of the two plans.

The Tax Reform Act applies a 15-percent excise tax on aggregate annual distributions from all tax-qualified plans, tax-sheltered annuities, and IRAs that exceed $140,276 (in 1992) or 1.25 times the indexed dollar limit for defined benefit plans.

The changes made by the Tax Reform Act to benefit and contribution limits and the excise tax on excess distributions went into effect in 1987.

DISTRIBUTION RULES

Pension benefits are paid to workers generally in the form of an annuity—that is, periodic payments (usually monthly) for the lifetime of the recipient. Although age 65 has been considered "normal retirement age," a worker can retire under many plans with pension benefits as early as age 55.

Moreover, if the pension plan allows, a worker may elect to receive a lump-sum distribution at retirement instead of an annuity. Changes made to the IRC as part of the enactment of ERISA permitted favorable tax treatment for such distributions so long as the worker had reached 59½ or in the event of death, disability, or separation from service. The tax liability on the amount could be reduced through 10-year forward averaging, by which the amount was treated as being received over a 10-year period.

The Tax Reform Act repealed 10-year forward averaging beginning in 1987, and substituted instead a one-time election of 5-year forward averaging with respect to a single distribution received after age 59½. (However, special grandfather rules allow 10-year forward averaging for pension plan participants who were age 50 before January 1, 1986.)

Other IRC rules apply to early withdrawals from retirement plans. To discourage early withdrawals (defined as before age 59½) of IRA contributions, the law imposes an additional 10-percent tax on the amount withdrawn, except in cases of death or disability. The 10-percent penalty tax has also been imposed on early withdrawals by 5-percent owners since the 1984 Deficit Reduction Act.

The rules have been somewhat less restrictive for 401(k) plans, however. In addition to the age 59½, death, or disability exceptions, withdrawals from 401(k)s have been permitted in cases of "hardship," which Treasury Department rulings allowed to include the purchase of a home or payment of college expenses for one's children.

In the Tax Reform Act, lawmakers decided to discourage all early withdrawals. Beginning in 1987, the 10-percent penalty tax is imposed on withdrawals of any tax-deferred amounts before age 59½ except in the form of an annuity or because of death, disability, separation from service after age 55, certain types of payments in divorce settlements, or medical expenses in excess of 7½ percent of adjusted gross income.

To further discourage workers from cashing out lump-sum distributions from pension plans when they leave an employer, Congress enacted legislation in 1992 requiring 20-percent mandatory withholding on such distributions. The worker can avoid the withholding only by directing his or her pension plan to transfer the pension funds to an IRA or an annuity. If no transfer is made, 20 percent will be withheld, and the remaining

80 percent will be taxed as ordinary income. In addition, the distribution could be subject to the 10-percent penalty tax on premature distributions.

SURVIVOR BENEFITS

ERISA provides that pension plans that pay retirement benefits in the form of annuities (periodic monthly or annual pension payments) must offer automatic joint and survivor annuities at retirement for married employees. The Retirement Equity Act expands the concept of survivor benefits by requiring plans to provide pre-retirement survivor annuities for the spouses of married employees with vested benefit rights.

Joint and Survivor Annuities

A joint and survivor annuity is an annuity for the life of the employee with half of the annuity going to a surviving spouse following the death of the employee. The price of providing for a spouse with this form of annuity is a reduction in the benefit for the employee. If the employee is to receive $200 monthly under a single life annuity, for instance, the benefit might be reduced to $150 monthly for a joint and survivor annuity. If the employee dies first, the spouse would receive $75 monthly.

As amended by the Retirement Equity Act, ERISA requires pension plans to provide joint and survivor benefits under the following conditions:

- The employee has been married at least one year before retirement or death.
- The employee has not waived the survivor option. (If he or she does reject the option, the waiver must be in writing and include the consent of the spouse.)
- The employee has retired and started receiving benefits or is eligible to retire but is still working after reaching the normal retirement age.
- The employee has retired under an early retirement option, postpones receiving benefits until normal retire-

ment age, but dies in the interim between early and normal retirement age.

Pre-Retirement Survivor Benefits

The Retirement Equity Act considerably altered the ERISA provisions on survivor annuities for the spouses of employees who die before retirement. Under ERISA, a pension plan allowing early retirement had to offer a survivor annuity to married employees but did not have to provide it automatically: the employee had to elect the option.

If the employee made the election, survivor benefits did not have to be paid to the spouse unless the employee reached the age specified in the early retirement provision in the plan or reached an age 10 years younger than normal retirement age, whichever was later. If a pension plan had an early retirement age of 50, for instance, with a normal retirement age of 65, the spouse of an employee who retired at 50 and died at 52 would not be paid a survivor annuity. This was true even if the employee was vested.

Under the Retirement Equity Act, a survivor annuity becomes automatic before retirement as well as after. If an employee with vested benefits dies before retirement, his or her spouse will be paid the annuity unless the employee and spouse have waived the survivor benefit. But the spouse cannot begin receiving the annuity until the time when the employee would have reached the earliest retirement age specified in the pension plan. A spouse can also receive an immediate lump-sum distribution if the pension plan so provides and the spouse consents in writing to such a distribution.

An employee has the right to waive the survivor option with the consent of the spouse any time after age 35. An employee also must be given the opportunity to change his or her mind about a waiver.

Notification Procedures

Notification to employees about joint and survivor annuities must begin nine months before normal retirement age. The notice must be in the form of a written explanation of the terms and conditions of the annuity, the effect of rejecting a joint and survivor annuity, and the rights of the spouse. The pension plan must also allow employees a 90-day period before the annuity starting date in which to decide whether to waive the option.

An explanation of the employee's right to waive a preretirement survivor annuity can be included in a summary plan description; a pension plan does not have to make a separate announcement to employees.

If an employee declines either the joint and survivor annuity or the pre-retirement survivor benefit, the consent of the spouse on the written waiver must be witnessed by a representative of the pension plan or a notary public.

A pension plan can subsidize the joint and survivor or preretirement survivor annuity or both. If the plan fully subsidizes the cost of the benefit (which means there is no decrease in employee benefits or increase in employee contributions), then the plan is not required to inform employees of their right to waive the benefit.

Effective Dates

The provisions in the Retirement Equity Act applying to pre-retirement survivor benefits became effective December 31, 1984. For collectively bargained plans, the changes had to be incorporated as soon as new agreements were negotiated or January 1, 1987, whichever was earlier.

PENSION PLAN FUNDING

The term "funding" used in regard to a pension plan refers to the practice of employers contributing money or other assets each year to cover the pension benefits that will become due at some future date—in other words, financing or funding the benefits in advance of payment of the benefits. A plan is fully funded if plan assets equal or exceed plan liabilities.

ERISA imposes minimum funding requirements that require employers to contribute enough each year to cover the normal cost of the plan—the pension benefits earned that year by participants in the plan. Employers also have to pay installments on the costs of pension plan benefits if the plan covers past service of employees earned before the pension plan was created. They also have to pay installments to cover "supplemental" costs for any benefit increase made retroactive. The yearly normal and supplemental costs together constitute the annual cost.

For defined benefit pension plans, the purpose of the minimum funding rules established under ERISA is to ensure that the plans accumulate enough assets within a reasonable time to pay retiring workers or their beneficiaries their promised benefits. For defined contribution pension plans, minimum funding means making the annual contributions required by the plan formula. The funding rules do not apply to welfare plans.

Pension plans are subject to ERISA funding requirements whether they are tax-qualified plans or not, although some kinds of plans are exempted. Plans that are exempted include the following:

- Governmental and church plans
- Deferred compensation and excess benefit plans
- Plans to which an employer does not contribute, such as union plans funded exclusively by member contributions
- Profit-sharing and stock bonus plans
- Plans funded exclusively through insurance contracts

The funding provisions of ERISA remained largely intact until Congress enacted major changes in the Pension Protection Act, which were incorporated into the Omnibus Budget Reconciliation Act of 1987. This legislation tightening the funding standards reflected congressional concern over certain funding practices that were leading to terminations of seriously underfunded plans.

It was possible under existing law for single-employer

defined benefit pension plans to be underfunded while satisfying existing minimum funding standards. Those requirements called for annual employer contributions to cover only the benefits accrued by employees that year and a portion of the costs for benefit increases and other changes to the plan that were increasing its liabilities.

Employers were allowed 30 years over which to amortize benefit increases, for example, and if they were running into financial trouble, they could secure as many as five waivers of funding requirements over a 15-year period. Under these circumstances, some companies continued to give benefit increases when they were in financial straits and their plans were underfunded. It was not uncommon for such companies to then be forced to terminate their pension plans with few assets to cover benefit obligations.

Congress decided in the Pension Protection Act that if employers want to liberalize benefits, they will have to speed up the pace of funding the pension plan—that is, they will have to put more money in the plan in a given year than under previous standards. Thus, the law makes it more expensive over the short term for an underfunded plan to grant benefit increases.

Key to the new funding requirements is the concept of "current liability," the value of all vested and nonvested benefits that would be owed workers if the plan were terminating. This is the standard to be used by plan sponsors to determine the health of their plans—that is to say, to measure whether a plan is at its full funding limit and to determine minimum contributions. Under the previous standard, an employer had only to consider the obligation for vested benefits.

The funding rules are to be applied on a "controlled-group" basis, rather than plan by plan. The controlled group consists of all plans held or controlled by one employer. The effect is that if one plan fails to meet the minimum funding standards, the PBGC may enforce a lien against the controlled group, not just the single plan.

Instead of annual contributions, employers are now required to make quarterly payments, and the penalties for failing to meet minimum funding standards are stiffer.

Congress was also concerned about employers who might be excessively overfunding their pension plans so that they could take advantage of tax breaks for their contributions. The Pension Protection Act places limits on the amount of tax-deductible contributions employers can make to pension plans. The new funding standards are described more fully in the following sections.

Tax Treatment

Prior to ERISA, the IRC set a maximum on the amount an employer could deduct for contributions to a pension plan, but it did not require that employers meet any minimum funding standards.

Some employers used "pay-as-you-go" systems, paying retired employees their benefits as they became due, but not accumulating funds in advance for the benefits. If an employer used such a method, it could deduct only the benefits that it paid out at any time. And even if the employer did set up a reserve or earmark specific assets for the retirement benefits, it could not deduct the reserve unless it was placed in a trust out of the employer's control.

Another method used prior to ERISA—"terminal funding"—called for lump sums to be set aside at the employee's retirement to purchase an annuity or to go into a trust fund to provide the monthly pension benefit the employee had earned.

It was not until 1946 that the IRS issued a ruling that had the effect of compelling pension plans that sought tax-qualified status to cover their pension liabilities by maintaining certain minimum funding levels each year. The IRS ruling said that if a plan was found at any time to have greater liabilities than when the plan started—that is, the employer was not making enough of a contribution each year to keep up with the benefits that were accruing for employees and the liabilities of the plan were growing—the IRS would treat the plan as if it had been discontinued. This meant that all accrued benefits of employees would become vested. The company was responsible for paying those benefits whether or not the employees stayed with the company long enough to meet whatever vesting schedule the company plan had. To avoid the higher cost this would entail, companies began covering normal costs each year and interest on unfunded past-service liabilities.

The IRS ruling did not have the effect of law, however; it merely provided an economic incentive for pension plans to maintain minimum funding. It was not until the passage of ERISA that minimum funding became mandatory. After ERISA took effect, even if a pension plan met the requirements of the IRS revenue ruling it had to go one step further—unfunded liabilities had to be paid up, or amortized, over a stated number of years.

"Pay-as-you-go" systems and terminal funding practices are not permitted under ERISA.

Minimum Funding Standards

To meet ERISA's minimum funding requirements for defined benefit pension plans, employers have been required to contribute an annual amount sufficient to fund a portion of the projected retirement benefits of plan participants. Those costs include "normal costs" (the costs of the benefits accrued that year by participants) and a portion of the plan's supplemental liabilities, such as benefit increases and the costs for the service of employees before the plan went into effect.

These funding standards were modified by the Pension Protection Act by the addition of special funding rules for plans that are less than 100 percent funded.

An important concept of the new rules is the term "current liability," which is defined as the present value of all accrued benefits, both vested and nonvested, calculated as if the pension plan were terminating. An employer must use "current liability" to determine whether the pension plan is underfunded and to determine minimum funding contributions. In determining current liability, the employer must use an interest rate range that is not more than 10 percent above or below the average rate for 30-year Treasury bonds over the previous 4 years.

If a plan is less than 100 percent funded, the plan sponsor must satisfy additional funding requirements by calculating and adding a "deficit reduction contribution" to the required annual minimum contribution. Part of this additional payment will be an amortized portion of "unfunded old liability"—the unfunded liability of the plan in effect at the beginning of the first plan year after December 31, 1987. This liability, which does not include any benefit increases approved after October 17, 1987, has to be amortized over 18 years instead of the previously permissible 30-year amortization schedule.

Also part of the deficit reduction contribution is "unfunded new liability," such as benefit increases or other plan amendments after October 17, 1987, that increase liabilities. The amortization period for this liability depends on the degree to which the plan is underfunded. The higher the rate of underfunding, the greater the required payment. Thus, the better funded a plan is, the longer the period of time over which it may fund new liabilities created by benefit improvements.

In calculating unfunded new liability, the plan sponsor need not include an amount to cover liabilities for "unpredictable contingent event" benefits, resulting from such events as a plant shutdown or reductions in the work force. But if the plan becomes underfunded because such an event does take place, then an additional contribution (over and above the plan's minimum funding contribution) is required for the year in which the event takes place.

"Unpredictable event" benefits do not include benefits such as early retirement subsidies, Social Security supplements, survivor subsidies, or similar benefits that are dependent on certain eligibility conditions such as age and/or years of service.

The changes in the minimum funding requirements became effective for plan years beginning after December 31, 1988. The special rules do not apply to plans with 100 or fewer participants. For plans with between 101 and 150 participants, the amount of the additional contribution is determined by multiplying the otherwise required contribution by 2 percent for each participant in excess of 100.

The 1987 law also changed the required dates by which contributions must be made. Under ERISA, the minimum required annual contribution had to be made within 8½ months after the end of the plan year. The new rules require quarterly installments during the plan year, with the total contribution due within 8½ months after the end of the plan year. The quarterly payment schedule was phased in between 1989 and 1992.

Waivers From Minimum Requirements

ERISA provided that an employer facing financial problems could apply to the IRS for a waiver from the minimum funding requirements. As many as five waivers could be approved in any 15 consecutive years. The amount waived would have to be amortized over 15 years. The Single-Employer Pension Plan Amendments Act had authorized the IRS to require security from the plan if the funding deficiency to be waived was $2 million or more.

The Pension Protection Act tightened up the waiver provisions. Beginning with waiver applications filed after December 17, 1987, the number of allowable waivers is reduced to three in a 15-year period. The waived contributions must be amortized over 5 years, rather than the previously allowed 15 years. The limit does not include waivers granted for plan years before January 1, 1988; that is, employers are provided a fresh start in regard to the limit on waivers.

Waivers will be granted only for temporary business hardship that affects the entire controlled group, not just the plan sponsor. The plan must post security if the amount to be waived is $1 million or more.

Maximum Funding Limits

Under ERISA, employers had been able to make deductible contributions to defined benefit pension plans up to a "full funding limitation." This amount is the excess, if any, of the benefits owed to the employees (or plan liabilities) divided by the plan assets.

To derive the full funding limit, an employer was allowed to use a projection of benefits to be earned by employees at retirement rather than the benefits actually accrued as of the close of the current year.

The Pension Protection Act provides for a new full funding limit that is 150 percent of a plan's current liability; that is, the liabilities owed to plan participants and beneficiaries if the plan were terminating.

The new funding limits became effective for plan years beginning on or after January 1, 1988.

Accounting Requirements

For normal costs, pension plans can use a funding method, the "unit benefit cost method," that actually computes the unit of benefit accrued each year by each employee. Another general accounting approach, the "projected benefit cost method," pro-rates the expected total cost of the employee's benefits over the number of years he or she is expected to work until retirement, assigning a level amount to each year.

There are a number of variations to these basic techniques, each resulting in varying yearly levels of contributions from the employer. Total cost over an employee's work life should be the same, however, no matter which method is used.

In addition to making contributions to cover normal costs, a plan sponsor must amortize other costs: past-service liabilities such as retroactive benefit increases, gains or losses resulting from changes in actuarial assumptions, or experience gains or losses. Actuarial assumptions are made about the rate of turnovers, deaths, early retirements, terminations, and so forth. Experience gains and losses refer to the difference between the actual experience of the plan in payments or investment returns, for example, compared with what had been expected.

Under ERISA, plans started after 1974 had 30 years over which to amortize these liabilities (40 years for multiemployer plans), except for 15 years for experience gains or losses. The Pension Protection Act reduced the amortization periods.

Special rules apply for underfunded plans, as was described above under "Minimum Funding Standards." For these plans, unfunded old liabilities must be paid up over 18 years (except for multiemployer plans, which still have 30 years).

Unfunded new liability must be funded even more rapidly. The period over which the new liability has to be funded depends on the degree to which the plan becomes underfunded as a result of plan amendments that increase the plan's liabilities. The greater the underfunding, the more rapidly the unfunded new liabilities must be amortized.

Other amortization changes include the following:

- Increased liabilities resulting from changes in actuarial assumptions must be amortized over 10 years (previously 30 years).
- Increased liabilities resulting from experience losses must be amortized over 5 years (previously 15 years).
- Required contributions for which waivers are obtained must be amortized over 5 years (previously 15 years).
- Benefit increases under collective bargaining agreements ratified before October 17, 1987, must be amortized in equal annual installments over 18 years.

Multiemployer plans may continue to amortize gains or losses from changes in actuarial assumptions over 30 years and experience gains and losses over 15 years.

Funding Standard Account

Every pension plan covered by the funding rules in ERISA must set up a "funding standard account." This account is the vehicle by which both the government and the employer can ascertain each year whether the plan is on target in meeting its financial obligations. Maintaining the account also enables an employer to determine if there are gains in the pension plan, perhaps from a better-than-expected return on investments, that will allow the employer to reduce its contribution the following year.

Liabilities charged to the account each year include the following:

- Normal costs
- The minimum amount required to continue amortizing past-service liabilities

- Losses resulting from changes in actuarial assumptions
- Losses resulting from plan amendments that increase liabilities
- Experience losses

Credits to the account each year include the following:

- Employer contributions for normal costs
- Installment payments to continue amortizing past-service liabilities
- Gains resulting from changes in actuarial assumptions
- Gains resulting from amendments that reduce liabilities
- Experience gains

Penalties for Underfunding

The account may not show a negative balance by the end of the year or the pension plan will have incurred what ERISA terms an "accumulated funding deficiency." The following severe penalties will be assessed if the plan comes up short:

- The account will be charged with interest at the rate used to determine pension plan costs.
- An excise tax of 10 percent will be levied on the amount of the deficit. This excise tax will be increased to 100 percent of the deficit if the deficit is not erased within 90 days of notification by the Secretary of the Treasury.
- The employer may be subject to civil action for failure to meet the minimum funding standards.
- All members of the controlled group are made jointly and severally liable for any penalty tax imposed.

The excise tax had been 5 percent until passage of the Pension Protection Act as part of the Omnibus Budget Reconciliation Act of 1987. This law increased the tax to 10 percent and made the controlled group, not just the plan sponsor, liable for the penalty. The increase does not apply, however, to multiemployer plans.

The PBGC may impose a lien on all controlled group property if an unfunded plan fails to make a required contribution within 60 days of the due date and the amount of the missed contribution exceeds $1 million. A lien may arise if an employer fails to make an installment payment on time or if the total annual contribution is not paid in full.

If a pension plan is amended to provide for a benefit increase that reduces the funded ratio of the plan to less than 60 percent, the plan sponsor and all members of the controlled group must post a security bond for an amount that will bring the funded ratio up to at least 60 percent. The requirement does not apply to benefit increases totaling $10 million or less.

If a plan is less than 70 percent funded, the employer must report that information on the plan's annual report to the Treasury Department. Employers who fail to meet funding standards, including failure to make required installment payments, must notify plan participants and beneficiaries.

If the account has a positive balance, the fund managers will credit the balance with interest at the same rate used to determine plan costs. The balance and interest can be used to reduce the required minimum contribution in future years.

ERISA requires pension plans when valuing plan assets to use reasonable actuarial methods that take into account fair market value. The asset value must be within 20 percent of fair market value to satisfy the requirement. The actuarial assumptions used for costs and liabilities must be reasonable.

ERISA also requires that experience gains and losses be determined at least every three years, although the IRS can require a more frequent valuation for pension plans that have sustained such gains or losses for several years in a row.

Alternative Funding Standard

Under certain circumstances, ERISA allows pension plans to use an alternative minimum funding standard that results in lower annual contributions. The objective of the alternative minimum funding standard is to allow plans that normally fund at a fairly rapid rate to switch to a slower rate if the plans find it difficult to maintain their former levels, as might happen in a business downturn.

Pension plans that can use the alternative standard are those that normally use the projected benefit cost method, which requires employers to lay out money for benefits that have not yet accrued. ERISA allows the employer to change to a unit benefit method, under which costs build up more slowly because benefit accruals increase only as salaries and years of service increase.

Employers using the alternative funding standard must maintain two accounts—this account and the regular standard account—since the minimum requirement each year will be the lower contribution from the two accounts. No excise tax will be levied on the regular account if there is no deficiency in the alternative account.

3

TERMINATION OF PENSION PLANS

Before the passage of ERISA, companies were not legally liable for vested pension benefits if they merged with another company, went out of business with the pension plan underfunded (or totally unfunded), or simply decided to terminate the plan. In order to ensure that employees are paid at least part of their benefits, whether there is enough money in the pension fund or not, Congress created plan termination insurance.

THE PBGC PROGRAM

ERISA established an independent corporation, the Pension Benefit Guaranty Corporation, and created a termination insurance program for defined benefit pension plans. The PBGC is a tax-exempt, self-financed corporation. The income of the PBGC comes primarily from mandatory premiums paid by the private pension plans that are subject to the termination insurance program.

When a single-employer defined benefit plan terminates without enough assets to cover its pension obligations, the

PBGC is liable for the payment of all guaranteed or insured benefits in the plans. The PBGC also provides assistance in the form of loans to financially troubled multiemployer pension plans.

The termination insurance program covers about 85,000 private single-employer and multiemployer defined benefit plans that are tax-qualified or plans that in practice have met the IRS standards for qualification for the preceding five years.

Exempt Plans

Pension plans that are not covered by the termination insurance program include the following:

- Government and church plans
- Plans maintained by certain fraternal societies
- Plans established and maintained outside the United States for non–U.S. citizens
- Unfunded, non–tax-qualified deferred compensation plans for top executives
- Plans that do not provide for employer contributions
- Plans maintained solely to comply with workers' compensation, unemployment compensation, or disability insurance laws

Defined contribution plans are not covered because they do not guarantee a specific benefit at retirement.

Premiums

The yearly premium amount that an employer must pay is based on the number of participants in the pension plan on the last day of the preceding plan year. A regulation issued by the PBGC March 29, 1985, changed the date by which premiums have to paid from seven months to two months after the end of the plan year. Only plans with under 500 participants can continue to pay their premiums after the seven-month period. The effective date of the change for plans with more than 10,000 participants was May 31, 1985. The effective date for plans with over 500 but under 10,000 participants was January 1, 1986. (See Appendix 1 for a sample of Form PBGC-1.)

Initially, the annual premium rate for single-employer plans was $1.00 per participant, and the rate for multiemployer plans was $0.50 per participant. The PBGC has authority to revise rates when necessary, but only after obtaining congressional approval through a concurrent resolution.

In 1977, the PBGC recommended and Congress approved a premium increase to $2.60 per participant for single-employer plans. In 1980, a new schedule was approved for multiemployer plans, which called for a premium of $1.40 per participant after September 26, 1980, rising in stages over nine years to $2.60 in 1989. The Single-Employer Pension Plan Amendments Act raised the premium for single-employer plans to $8.50 per participant, effective January 1, 1986.

But even the increase to $8.50 was not enough to stem the red ink that was spilling at the PBGC because of the termination of several major steel industry companies in the 1980s. With a 1986 fiscal year deficit of $3.8 billion, the PBGC returned to Congress seeking higher premiums for single-employer plans.

As part of the Pension Protection Act, which was incorporated into the Omnibus Budget Reconcilation Act of 1987, Congress made a major change in the premium structure by introducing the concept of a variable premium. Fully funded plans were to pay a flat annual $16 premium per employee. Underfunded plans were to pay an additional $6 per $1,000 of underfunding, up to a maximum of $34 per employee. Thus, the total maximum premium could be as high as $50 per employee ($16 flat fee plus maximum of $34 variable fee).

These amounts were raised again in the Omnibus Budget Reconciliation Act of 1990. The flat premium was increased to $19 per participant. Underfunded plans must pay an additional variable premium of $9 per $1,000 of unfunded vested benefits, up to a maximum of $53 per participant.

All members of a controlled group are jointly and severally liable for premiums.

BENEFITS INSURED

The PBGC guarantees the payment of "basic benefits"—normal retirement benefits that have become vested under the terms of a pension plan. The PBGC also has the option of insuring "non-basic" benefits such as medical insurance and death and disability benefits not part of a basic retirement plan, but has not done so.

Vested employees are insured only for the benefits they have accrued up to the time the pension plan terminates. Retired employees are insured in full. But for both groups, the law sets limits on the monthly amounts the insurance will cover. The maximum benefit for employees of single-employer plans was $750 per month when ERISA was enacted, but the maximum has been adjusted over the years to reflect increases in the Social Security taxable wage base. Different limits were set for employees of multiemployer plans by the Multiemployer Pension Plan Amendments Act (MPPAA).

Insurance coverage of single-employer pension plans became effective with the passage of ERISA, but the law delayed coverage of multiemployer plans until January 1, 1978. That deadline was extended five times until the passage in 1980 of the MPPAA, under which the termination insurance program began covering insolvent multiemployer plans.

Benefit Maximums

The formula for determining the limits on benefit payments was originally the same for both single-employer and multiemployer plans, but it has since been changed for multiemployer plans. The maximum monthly payment for single-employer plans still is the lesser of (a) the employee's average monthly income during his or her five consecutive years of highest earnings or (b) $750, increased each year in proportion to the increase in the Social Security taxable wage base from the year ERISA took effect to the year concerned.

Shown below is the formula used to increase the original $750 maximum for single-employer plans; Y stands for the Social Security taxable wage base for the year in which benefits are calculated and $13,200 is the wage base for 1974, the year ERISA was enacted:

$$\frac{Y}{\$13,200} \times \$750 = \text{adjusted monthly maximum for single-employer plan beneficiary}$$

The formula for multiemployer plans is based on an accrual rate (in dollars) determined by dividing the monthly benefit to which the employee is entitled by the employee's years of service, as shown below:

$$\frac{\text{monthly benefit to which employee is entitled}}{\text{employee's years of service}} = \frac{\text{multiemployer plan}}{\text{accrual rate}}$$

Based on this accrual rate, the monthly benefit is 100 percent of the first $5 of the employee's accrual rate plus 75 percent of the lesser of (a) $15 or (b) the accrual rate in excess of $5; the resulting figure is then multiplied by the years of credited service.

There is, however, under either a single-employer or a multiemployer plan, the same aggregate monthly limit on the basic benefit that can be paid to any one person. The maximum in 1992 was $2,352. The rate is adjusted each year.

None of these limitations applies to the vested benefits accrued as of July 29, 1980, by retirees or by vested employees who were within 36 months of retirement on that date.

Insuring Benefit Increases

To be insured by the PBGC, the basic benefits must have been in effect under the provisions of the pension plan for 60 months or longer at the time of plan termination. If the plan is amended within 60 months of termination to increase benefits or if new benefits are adopted within that time frame, the increased benefits can be guaranteed in stages of either 20 percent of the increase per year or an amount equal to $20 per month multiplied by the number of years the increase had been in effect, whichever is greater.

The PBGC must find substantial evidence that a pension plan has been terminated for a reasonable business purpose before it will insure recent benefit increases; this is to discourage plans from raising benefits before termination with the expectation that the PBGC will cover the resulting costs to the plan.

TERMINATION ISSUES

Whether a sponsor of a pension plan has actually terminated the plan and, if so, on what exact date are often difficult questions to answer. However, the determination that a termination has occurred can be critical to the people whose pensions are at stake, to the plan sponsor, and to the PBGC. Once it is clear that termination has occurred, the employer's liability can be assessed and the assumption of liability by the PBGC for the plan begins.

ERISA tries to point to distinct, clearly identifiable events that define a termination. The law also gives the PBGC power to initiate action to end plans under certain circumstances.

In the late 1980s, the PBGC mounted a major challenge to a termination action that the agency characterized as an abuse of the pension termination insurance system. In 1986, the LTV Corporation filed for Chapter 11 bankruptcy and stopped payments to three of its pension plans. The PBGC took over the plans, which had a total liability of about $2 billion. Under the terms of the pension benefit guaranty program, many of the workers would receive reduced benefits.

While in bankruptcy, LTV and the United Steelworkers of America negotiated a new pension plan under which LTV agreed to pay benefits that would have come close to bridging the gap between the benefits of the terminated plans and the PBGC payments. This action led the PBGC in September 1987 to insist that LTV should take back the responsibility for the liabilities of the terminated plans.

The PBGC contended that LTV had violated the pension guaranty system by establishing a "follow-on" plan. PBGC officials said they were concerned that financially troubled companies would try to shift their pension liabilities to the termination insurance fund, leaving it with mounting deficits that could be alleviated only by continually raising premiums charged other companies in the system.

LTV was successful with its arguments in lower courts, but the U.S. Supreme Court ruled in the PBGC's favor in June 1990 (*Pension Benefit Guaranty Corp. v. LTV*, 496 U.S. 633). In its decision, the Supreme Court said: "The plain language of ERISA Section 4047 empowers the agency to restore when restoration would further the interests that Title IV of ERISA was designed to protect."

The "Insured Event"

ERISA defines the event that triggers insurance coverage for single-employer plans as the termination of a pension plan, either voluntarily by the plan sponsor or involuntarily if the PBGC initiates the action. Under ERISA, plan termination originally was the "insured event" for both single-employer and multiemployer plans.

For multiemployer plans, however, the insured event became plan insolvency under the terms of the MPPAA. The PBGC does not make payments to multiemployer plan participants until a plan's assets have been completely depleted. At that point, the PBGC will make a loan to the financially strapped plan. Only if the employers in the plan are financially unable after the loan to meet the plan's obligations (including repaying the PBGC loan) will the PBGC step in to take over the responsibility for the liabilities of the plan.

Voluntary and Involuntary Terminations

Pension plans can be terminated either voluntarily by the plan administrator or involuntarily by the PBGC. However, since a multiemployer plan usually involves a sizeable number of employers, termination of such a plan with all employers withdrawing is not very likely. A more likely event is the withdrawal (a so-called "mass withdrawal") of one or more employers who relocate, go out of business, become bankrupt, or cease to operate under a collective bargaining agreement.

Even if an employer is forced to terminate a plan because it is financially unable to meet its obligations under the plan, this is considered a voluntary termination.

The PBGC may initiate termination proceedings when a pension plan

- Fails to comply with the minimum funding standards
- Fails to pay benefits when due
- Has a "reportable event" (certain events that may indicate a termination could occur)
- Is in such severe financial circumstances that failure to terminate would result in greatly increased liability to the PBGC

The Single-Employer Pension Plan Amendments Act (SEPPAA) authorized the PBGC to terminate single-employer pension plans if the PBGC determines that the plan will be unable to pay benefits.

Allocating the Assets

If the pension plan can pay out the required benefits in the form of annuities or lump-sum payments, the PBGC will authorize the administrator to proceed with the termination and distribution of assets. If not, the plan will be placed in trusteeship, generally under the PBGC. The PBGC then takes over plan assets and assumes the liability for guaranteed benefits.

ERISA stipulates that the assets of a pension plan be allocated according to a specific set of priorities, in the following order:

1. The portion of an employee's accrued benefit that is attributable to the employee's own voluntary contributions
2. Benefits attributable to mandatory employee contributions
3. Benefits going to retirees or beneficiaries who have been receiving the payments for at least three years at the

time of termination (or who have been eligible to receive benefits during that time period)

4. The insured benefits of all other participants up to the maximum limits for monthly payments
5. The remaining vested benefits, beginning with benefits in effect for at least five years and followed by benefit increases that resulted from amendments to the plan within five years of termination
6. All other noninsured nonforfeitable benefits under the plan

At issue in the case of *Mead Corp. v. Tilley* (490 U.S. 714 (1989)) was whether Section 4044(a) of ERISA, which spells out this allocation scheme, requires a plan administrator to pay participants unreduced early retirement benefits provided under the plan before excess assets can revert to the employer. The U.S. Supreme Court held that Section 4044(a) provides a mechanism for distributing benefits but does not confer a right of a participant to unaccrued benefits.

Asset Reversions

Until passage of the Tax Reform Act of 1986, employers were allowed to recover without penalty assets remaining in a terminated plan after liabilities to participants and beneficiaries had been satisfied. However, some lawmakers were concerned about the pace at which many well-funded pension plans were being terminated in the 1980s so that employers could recover the excess or surplus assets. From 1980 to 1989, there were more than 2,000 plan terminations that involved asset reversions of $1 million or more. The question lawmakers asked was whether an employer had a right to those assets in a pension plan that exceeded benefits promised to workers or should be allocating those assets to the workers in the form of increased benefits.

To discourage the practice that some critics called "raiding" pension plans, Congress in the 1986 tax act imposed a 10-percent excise tax on the amount involved in an asset reversion. In the quarter that ended December 1987, the IRS collected $20 million from the 10-percent excise tax on asset reversions.

Although the number of reversions had slowed by 1987, congressional scrutiny of the practice continued. In the Pension Protection Act (part of the Omnibus Budget Reconciliation Act of 1987), lawmakers included a provision that prevents an employer from taking a reversion within five years of a plan amendment permitting a reversion or increasing the amount of a reversion. Also, if a reversion takes place, excess plan assets must be allocated between employer contributions and mandatory employee contributions on a pro rata basis. This provision could result in an increase in the portion of the surplus that must be distributed to employees.

In 1988, the Senate considered a bill that would have imposed a temporary 60-percent excise tax on reversions until May 1989. That bill did not become law, but in October 1988, Congress did raise the 10-percent excise tax to 15 percent in a bill making technical corrections to the Tax Reform Act.

The higher excise tax was made effective for reversions received by the Treasury Department after October 20, 1988, if notice of an intent to terminate the plan was not provided before October 21, 1988.

On October 24, 1988, the Treasury Department announced a moratorium until May 1989 on approvals of plan terminations that would involve reversions of plan assets to the employer.

In 1990, Congress took another step toward discouraging asset reversions. Lawmakers raised the federal excise tax on reversions from 15 percent to 20 percent and added the requirement that the employer establish a replacement plan with a cushion in the plan equal to 25 percent of the surplus. As an alternative, the employer can provide workers and retirees an immediate benefit equal to 20 percent of the reversion amount. If no replacement plan is established, the excise tax increases to 50 percent.

TERMINATIONS OF SINGLE-EMPLOYER PLANS

The merger, consolidation, or reorganization of a company does not result in termination of its pension plan in ERISA'S terms if the successor company assumes responsibility for the plan. In such a case, the benefit rights of the participants in the old plan must be maintained in the new one.

Several likely stages a financially troubled plan might go through without actually producing a termination include the following:

- Curtailment of ancillary benefits
- Reduction of the rate at which benefits accrue
- A plan freeze created by not allowing any future benefit accruals to take place but continuing contributions for those benefits that have already accrued or have vested and allowing the vesting schedule to continue as well
- Discontinuance not only of future benefit accruals, but also the crediting of future service for vesting purposes

SEPPAA requires plans to give participants and beneficiaries 15 days notice if the plan decides to freeze benefits.

Liability of a Single-Employer Plan

It was possible and legal under ERISA for a completely solvent employer to terminate an underfunded pension plan and force the PBGC to assume responsibility for the plan's pension liabilities. Since an employer could be held liable for a maximum of 30 percent of net worth for the unfunded liability of the plan, some employers had an incentive to end their plans if the amount they owed the plan was more than 30 percent of their assets and if the employer was having trouble keeping up with its funding obligation.

Congress took steps to discourage terminations when companies remain in business. In the Single-Employer Pension Plan Amendments Act, lawmakers created two types of terminations for single-employer pension plans: "standard" and "distress" terminations. Only in the latter case may the PBGC be compelled to assume the plan's unfunded liabilities.

To initiate a standard termination, the SEPPAA required that a plan have sufficient assets to pay all "benefit commitments" under the plan. Benefit commitments are greater than the benefits insured by the PBGC but less than "termination liability." The latter covers all benefits that have been promised under the plan up to the date that the plan is terminated. What this means is that participants must receive full benefits under the plan, including nonvested amounts.

The Pension Protection Act increased the employer's liability in a standard termination to the full amount of termination liability, but it uses the term "benefit liabilities" to refer to these obligations of the employer.

In a standard termination, the plan has to send a Notice of Intent to Terminate to participants and beneficiaries at least 60 days in advance of the termination. As soon as practicable after the notice to participants, the plan must notify the PBGC, including certification by an enrolled actuary of the plan's projected assets and value of benefit liabilities. That notice must also certify that the plan's assets are sufficient to fund all benefit liabilities.

The plan is required to provide each participant with information on the amount of his or her benefit and the factors (such as age and length of service) that have been used to calculate the benefit.

Distress terminations take place under the following circumstances:

- Chapter 7 bankruptcy liquidation
- Chapter 11 bankruptcy reorganization, if the employer can demonstrate to the court that liquidation would necessarily follow if the pension plan were not terminated
- PBGC determination that the employer is unable to pay debts when due and unable to remain in business
- PBGC determination that a decline in the employer's work force is making the pension plan "unreasonably burdensome" for the employer to maintain
- Each member, rather than just "substantial" members, of the plan sponsor's controlled group must prove financial hardship

In a distress termination, the plan must give the PBGC the same 60-day notice that it gives to participants and beneficiaries of the plan.

The employer is liable to the PBGC for 30 percent of net worth plus 100 percent of unfunded guaranteed benefits minus the 30 percent of net worth. At least 50 percent of the amount due in any year can be deferred for one year, however, if the plan sponsor makes no profits in that year.

The SEPPAA also created a new "termination trust" to distribute benefit amounts to participants who had unfunded nonguaranteed benefits and to collect liability amounts from employers. The Pension Protection Act eliminates the termination trust. As the PBGC collects the total amount of the plan's unfunded benefit liabilities, it must distribute a portion to plan participants. The amount of the distribution to each participant is based on a ratio of the amount of employer liability recovered by the PBGC from distress terminations after December 17, 1987, to the amount of unfunded benefit liabilities of those plans.

If the amount owed is less than $100,000, payment can be made in equal annual installments over 10 years.

Congress also sought to discourage companies from trying to evade liability for an unfunded plan through a merger, transfer, or sale. If such a transaction takes place and the plan terminates within five years of the transaction, the PBGC can hold the original company responsible for the plan's liabilities.

In 1991, the PBGC agreed to 7,500 standard terminations and to the distress or involuntary termination of 86 underfunded plans. Two of the largest underfunded plan terminations in the agency's history took place in 1990 and 1991—seven Eastern Air Lines pension plans ($700 million underfunded) and three Pan American Airways plans ($900 million underfunded).

TERMINATION IN MULTIEMPLOYER PLANS

Inadequate funding and a shrinking work force were contributing to the financial troubles of many multiemployer pension plans when ERISA was enacted. Mandatory termination insurance for multiemployer plans was delayed several times by Congress because many lawmakers were afraid the potential drain on PBGC funds because of the shaky state of many plans could put the new insurance program in considerable jeopardy. In a 1978 report, for instance, the PBGC found that about 10 percent of all multiemployer plans covering about 1.3 million workers were experiencing financial difficulties that could result in plan terminations within 10 years. Even a few terminations in any one year, the PBGC said, would be dangerous to the insurance program because premium rates were set too low to provide enough money to cover many terminations.

This situation, plus the language in ERISA that allowed employers in certain circumstances to bail out of multiemployer plans without any liability, led to the drafting of the Multiemployer Pension Plan Amendments Act, which was signed into law September 26, 1980.

The MPPAA defined a multiemployer plan as a pension plan maintained under a collective bargaining agreement to which two or more employers contribute. Generally, this involves a situation where more than one employer is dealing with locals of the same national or international union.

Multiemployer plans are generally found in the trucking, apparel, coal mining, construction, entertainment, food and baked goods, communication, and public utilities industries. Examples include plans that involve various employers having collective bargaining agreements with locals of the United Mine Workers or Amalgamated Clothing and Textile Workers or the International Typographical Union. In 1991, there were approximately 8.5 million participants in 2,100 multiemployer plans.

Since a number of employers participate together in a multiemployer plan, the possibility of one employer leaving a plan is greater than the possibility that the plan itself will fold. Under ERISA, an employer who withdrew from a plan had no further financial responsibility for any unfunded benefits as long as the plan itself did not terminate within five years of the time the employer withdrew. If the employer was a "substantial owner" (one whose contributions accounted for more than 10 percent of the total contributions to the plan), it had to escrow assets or post a bond. But if the plan did not fold during the five years after withdrawal the assets were released or the bond cancelled. The other employers in the plan had to assume the unfunded obligations, forcing up costs and encouraging other employers to think about pulling out lest they get saddled with ever-increasing costs.

The passage of the MPPAA in 1980 made it impossible for so-called "runaway employers" to withdraw without continuing contributions until the withdrawal liability was satisfied or payments had been made for 20 years, whichever came first.

Complete Withdrawal

A complete withdrawal takes place when an employer "permanently ceases to have an obligation to contribute under the plan" or "permanently ceases all covered operations under the plan." The term "obligation to contribute" means an obligation under one or more collective bargaining agreements or under labor–management law. (An employer may no longer be obligated to contribute to a plan because the union with which it had an agreement was decertified or because the employer has replaced union workers with non-union workers.)

Withdrawal does not take place because of changes in corporate structure as long as contributions continue to be made to the plan. A withdrawal also does not occur if the employer suspends contributions during a labor dispute.

Special definitions of complete withdrawal apply to the building and construction, entertainment, and long- and short-haul trucking industries. These definitions reflect the unique work patterns of each industry. In the entertainment and construction industries, for example, work is often performed on a temporary or project-by-project basis, with extreme fluctuations in hiring and limited duration of an employer's participation in a multiemployer plan.

Frequently, as legislators pointed out in their debate on the MPPAA, these employers would join a plan only long enough to complete the construction of one building or for the run of one Broadway play.

Therefore, for employers contributing to an entertainment plan or construction industry plan for a temporary project, complete withdrawal occurs only if, after the project has ended, the employer continues the same type of work or resumes such work within five years but does not continue or resume contributing to the plan. In other words, if an employer completed one project but initiated another within five years and resumed contributing to the pension plan, no withdrawal would have taken place.

Special rules are also provided for trucking industry plans if substantially all of the contributions are made by employers primarily engaged in the long- and short-haul trucking, household goods moving, or public warehousing industries. The "substantially all" requirement is satisfied if at least 85 percent of the contributions to the plan are made by employers in the specified industries.

For these industries, before assessing liability the PBGC has to determine that the cessation of contributions or operations would cause "substantial damage" to the plan. Even if the PBGC makes such a determination, the employer can avoid withdrawal liability by furnishing a bond or placing in escrow an amount equal to 50 percent of its withdrawal liability. If after 60 months the PBGC finds that no substantial damage will be done to the plan, the bond will be cancelled or the escrow refunded.

Partial Withdrawal

A partial withdrawal can take place if any of the three following conditions exist:

- There is a decline in the employer's "contribution base units"—the units that are used to determine employer contributions to the plan, such as hours worked or tons of coal produced. The decline in such units has to be 70 percent or more in each of the previous three years compared to a previous two-year period of higher contributions. In the retail food industry, a partial withdrawal can occur when the decline in contribution base units is only 35 percent.
- An employer stops contributions under one or more but not all of the collective bargaining agreements under which it performs work.

- An employer ceases work at one facility while continuing work at other locations.

In the construction industry, a partial withdrawal can occur when an employer's contribution obligation exists for only an insubstantial portion of its work with the craft and area jurisdiction of a collective bargaining agreement.

Employers have one chance to withdraw from a multiemployer pension plan without incurring any liability if they withdraw within six years of joining the plan. This is called the "free look" provision, and it is intended to encourage employers to join multiemployer plans without fear of having to face high withdrawal costs if they change their minds and decide to leave the plan in a few years. The provision can be used only by multiemployer plans whose assets are at least eight times their annual benefit payments and by employers whose contributions will be no more than 2 percent of the total contribution base. The provision does not apply to plans in the building and construction industry.

Withdrawal Liability

Pension plan trustees are responsible for determining the liability of employers who withdraw from the plan. A specific formula for calculating liability is included in the Multiemployer Pension Plan Amendments Act. Several alternative formulas are also provided. Unless a pension plan is specifically amended to provide for one of the alternatives, the first method described in the law applies automatically.

The key to all the methods is the concept of "unfunded vested benefits," the benefit obligations of the pension plan not covered by assets of the plan. Withdrawing employers are responsible for a prorated share of the plan's total unfunded liabilities based on either the number of years they were in the plan relative to the other employers or the length of service of their employees relative to the employees of the other employers.

ERISA provides that challenges by employers to the assessment of withdrawal liability made by plan trustees will be taken to arbitration. Then the decision of the arbitrator may be reviewed by a court. But the U.S. Supreme Court in 1987 affirmed a lower court ruling that pension plan trustees may sue for collection of withdrawal liability payments pending arbitration (*Teamsters Local 115 Pension Plan v. Yahn & McDonnell, Inc.*, 479 U.S. 1027).

Determining Annual Payments

After the amount of the withdrawal liability has been determined for the employer, payment is to be made through annual level installments until the total liability has been satisfied or 20 years have elapsed, whichever comes first. The amount of the annual payment is determined by multiplying the employer's contribution rate times the contribution base. The contribution rate is the highest rate required by the collective bargaining agreement in the previous 10 years. The contribution base is the average annual number of contribution base units for the 3 consecutive years for which employer contributions were the highest during the previous 10 years before withdrawal.

Limits on Liability

To help small employers, the MPPAA provides a mandatory de minimis rule under which an employer's liability is reduced by the lesser of $50,000 or .75 percent of the plan's unfunded liability. If the unfunded liability exceeds $100,000, the employer loses one dollar of the waiver for every dollar of liability between $100,000 and $150,000. If the liability is more than $150,000, there is no waiver.

Other limits on an employer's liability include the following:

- An insolvent employer undergoing liquidation or dissolution does not have to pay more than a total of 50 percent of its liability plus that portion of the remaining liability that does not exceed the liquidation or dissolution value.
- The liability of an individual employer— a sole proprietor or partner—does not reach personal assets exempt under bankruptcy laws.

- The liability of an employer whose assets are transferred in a bona fide sale in an arm's-length transaction to an unrelated party is limited to either 30 percent of the liquidation value or the unfunded benefits attributable to the employees of the employer, whichever is less. If the liquidation value exceeds $2 million, the 30-percent limitation is incrementally increased to reach 80 percent for a liquidation value exceeding $10 million.

Reorganization

The procedure known as "reorganization" in the MPPAA is designed to help plans that are experiencing financial problems to avoid insolvency, if possible. The absence of such assistance in ERISA was viewed as a major shortcoming by many legislators and by the PBGC, which feared that it would end up having to assume the pension obligations of a number of financially troubled multiemployer pension plans.

A plan must go into reorganization if the level of contributions made under normal funding requirements is insufficient to meet the "minimum contribution requirement." This standard is the level of funding that would be needed if the plan were to cover the benefits of all currently retired employees over a 10-year period and the vested benefits of all current employees over a 25-year period.

A plan in reorganization must either increase minimum contributions, reduce benefits that are not insured, or both. If the contributions are not increased to satisfy funding requirements in any year, the plan will have an "accumulated funding deficiency" that is subject to the excise tax for funding violations. (See "Penalties for Underfunding" in Chapter 2.)

Contribution Increase

As noted above, when a plan is in reorganization, contributions to the plan must be increased to meet the minimum contribution requirement. The increase cannot be any greater, however, than 7 percent of the funding requirement for the previous year plus an amount for benefit increases if the plan was not in reorganization during the preceding year.

However, pension plans that cover a large number of retirees can reduce the minimum contribution requirement through an "overburden credit"— a dollar amount that can be subtracted from the minimum contribution requirement. The credit is based on a formula using average monthly payments to retirees and the number of retirees compared to employees covered by the plan.

The minimum contribution requirement can also be reduced if there is a decline in contribution base units, such as, for example, hours worked.

Benefit Reduction

If an employer increases contributions but still has a problem covering all benefits in the pension plan, the employer can reduce uninsured benefits such as accrued benefits that have not vested. There are certain restrictions on these benefit reductions, however, as follows:

- Benefits cannot be proportionally reduced more for former employees and retirees than for current employees.
- If the plan reduces benefits by changing the form of the benefits or the requirements for benefit eligibility, those reductions cannot be applied to retirees, beneficiaries, or employees who are within five years of retirement.
- Six months' notice of the reductions must be given to participants, beneficiaries, contributing employers, and employee organizations.
- A plan cannot increase or restore benefits to current employees unless previously reduced benefits are raised to the same extent for retirees, beneficiaries, and employees within five years of retirement.
- Except for a death benefit distribution, no lump-sum payment of vested benefits may be made unless the PBGC approves the payment.

Insolvency

A multiemployer pension plan becomes insolvent when the plan's available resources are not sufficient to pay the benefits that are due that year. "Available resources" include cash, marketable assets, contributions, withdrawal liability payments, and earnings, less reasonable administrative expenses and any amounts already owed to the PBGC.

Insolvency also occurs if a plan in reorganiztion anticipates on the basis of recent financial experience that it will not have enough resources to cover benefit obligations in the next year.

A plan in reorganization must review every three years the value of its assets compared with the total amount of benefit payments that year. Unless plan assets exceed three times the total amount of benefit payments, the plan must determine whether the plan will become insolvent during any of the next three years.

Once insolvent, the plan sponsor must

- Determine and certify the "resource benefit level" of the plan—the highest level of monthly benefits that the plan can pay out of available resources.
- Suspend payment of benefits, other than basic benefits, that exceed the resource benefit level.
- Notify the PBGC that financial assistance is needed if the resource benefit level drops below the level needed to pay monthly basic benefits.
- Notify the Secretary of the Treasury.
- Inform plan participants and beneficiaries, employers contributing to the plan, and affected employee organizations.

When the PBGC verifies that a pension plan is unable to pay basic benefits, it must provide enough assistance in the form of a loan to meet the plan's obligations. Loans can be made more than once, but if the plan recovers, it must start repaying the loans.

Mergers and Transfers

Multiemployer pension plans cannot merge with one or more other multiemployer plans or transfer assets and liabilities unless the following requirements are met:

- Notice must be given to the PBGC within 120 days of the effective date of the merger or transfer.
- The accrued benefits of participants and beneficiaries cannot be lower immediately after the merger or transfer than they were immediately before that date.
- The merger or transfer cannot reasonably be expected to result in a suspension of benefits.
- Each multiemployer plan must have an actuary value the assets and liabilities for the plan year before the merger or transfer.

4

OPERATION OF EMPLOYEE BENEFIT PLANS

As discussed in Chapter 1, ERISA covers two types of employee benefit plans—pension plans and welfare plans. Certain provisions of ERISA apply only to pension plans; these provisions were covered in Chapters 2 and 3. Other provisions, which will be outlined below, apply to welfare plans as well as to pension plans.

Employee welfare plans provide any of the following to participants and beneficiaries:

- Medical, surgical, and hospital care
- Benefits in the event of sickness, accident, disability, death, or unemployment
- Vacation benefits, apprenticeship and other training programs, day care, dependent care, educational assistance, and prepaid legal services

The term "employee welfare plan" also includes any benefit described in Section 302(c) of the Labor Management Relations Act of 1947 (the Taft-Hartley Act). Under Taft-Hartley, employers are prohibited from making payments to union officials or union funds. However, employer contributions to union welfare funds are permitted, provided there is joint employer–union administration of the fund. The funds must be in trust and limited to certain purposes such as pensions, health benefits, workers' compensation, unemployment benefits, or accident and sickness benefits.

STRUCTURE OF EMPLOYEE BENEFIT PLANS

ERISA describes what an employee benefit plan should include and in what form it should be established and maintained. Under ERISA, an employee benefit plan must be in writing and provide procedures for the following:

- Establishing and carrying out a funding policy consistent with the objectives of the plan
- Allocating responsibility for the operation and administration of the plan
- Amending the plan
- Making payments to and from the plan

In most cases, the assets of an employee benefit plan must be held in trust with the trustee named in the trust instrument or in the benefit plan. The trustee manages and controls the assets of an employee benefit plan, although actual investment decisions might be turned over to an investment committee or an investment manager.

The trustee is not liable for the acts or omissions of an investment manager as long as care is taken in the selection of that person, nor is a trustee who properly follows the instructions of an investment committee legally responsible for any losses that are sustained as a result of the instructions.

If the trustee had actual knowledge, however, that the investment committee instructions would result in a loss, the trustee could be held liable if he or she followed the instructions. For instance, in February 1983, the Labor Department filed a complaint against a bank trustee that followed investment committee directions to invest in company stock when the bank knew of the company's financial difficulties (*Donovan v. Ashplant*, No. 83-CIV-1455 (S.D.N.Y. filed Feb. 24, 1983)).

Trusts do not have to be created if the assets of the employee benefit plan consist solely of insurance or annuity contracts issued by a life insurance company, nor do trusts have to be established for Keogh plans and Individual Retirement Accounts that are maintained in custodial accounts.

Recovery of Contributions to a Trust

An employer's contribution to a trust is considered irrevocable. The following three conditions, however, can lead to recovery by an employer of its contributions:

- If an employer makes its contributions to a newly created or amended employee benefit plan contingent on IRS approval of tax-qualified status that the plan does not receive, recovery can be made if the plan so provides and if the claim is made within one year.
- If an employer makes a contribution to the plan contingent on the tax deductibility of the entire contribution and a portion of that contribution is disallowed as a deduction, it can recover the portion that is disallowed if the plan so provides and if the claim is made within one year.
- If a mistake of fact is made in the calculation of the amount that the plan requires and the employer overpays, the amount attributable to the mathematical error can be recovered by the employer if the claim is made within one year of the time of the contribution.

Nondiscrimination Rules for Welfare Plans

Employer-provided contributions to group health insurance, group life insurance (up to a maximum of $50,000), child care, and other smaller benefits are not considered income to the employee (these contributions are tax-exempt). Tax exclusions also have existed for employer-provided educational assistance and prepaid legal services, but Congress has repeatedly debated the continuance of these exclusions. The Tax Reform Act of 1986 scheduled the exclusions to expire December 31, 1987, but lawmakers have since extended the exclusions in various legislation for one- and two-year periods.

To ensure that welfare benefit plans are not created for the exclusive benefit of highly paid employees or officers, Internal Revenue Code provisions have subjected each type of welfare benefit plan to separate broad nondiscrimination rules. For example, nondiscrimination standards for health plans have applied only to self-insured plans and are similar to the pre-Tax Reform Act requirements for qualified pension plans; that is, the plan must benefit 70 percent or more of all employees or 80 percent of all eligible employees if 70 percent of all employees are eligible to benefit. An alternative has been the fair cross-section test.

Group term life insurance plans have had the following tests:

- At least 70 percent of all employees benefit.
- At least 85 percent of all participants are not key employees, *or*
- The plan covers a fair cross-section of all employees.

The Tax Reform Act provided uniform and consistent nondiscrimination eligibility and benefits tests for group health (both self-insured and insured plans), accident, and life insurance plans. Employers could apply these tests also to dependent care, group legal, and educational assistance plans.

These tests included the following:

- At least 50 percent of those eligible to participate in the plan must include rank-and-file workers.
- At least 90 percent of the rank-and-file workers must be eligible for a benefit that is at least 50 percent of the most valuable benefit available to highly paid employees.
- The average benefit received by lower- and middle-income workers must be at least 75 percent of the average benefit received by highly paid employees.

As an alternative to these tests, a plan could satisfy the eligibility and benefits tests by benefiting at least 80 percent of nonhighly paid employees.

The Act provided a special test for dependent care assistance. The average benefits received by lower- and middle-income workers need to be at least 55 percent, rather than 75 percent, of the average benefit provided to highly paid workers.

There were also special rules for cafeteria plans. Each benefit under such a plan was subject to its own applicable nondiscrimination test.

In addition, the definition of "highly compensated employee" applied to qualified pension plans also became applicable to welfare benefit plans.

In recognition of the complexity of the new nondiscrimination rules, the Act provided that they not go into effect until after December 31, 1987, or three months after the Treasury Department issued regulations, whichever date was later. Collectively bargained plans had to meet the new rules no later than the first taxable year beginning on or after January 1, 1991.

The Tax Reform Act also requires all welfare benefit plans to be in writing, to be legally enforceable, and to be of indefinite duration. If a welfare benefit plan is found to be discriminating in favor of highly compensated employees, the latter are taxable on the value of the so-called "discriminatory excess." An employer who does not report the discriminatory excess (that is, include that amount in the highly compensated employee's income for tax purposes) is subject to a penalty tax calculated at the highest individual tax rate.

Technical and Miscellaneous Revenue Act of 1988

After passage of the Tax Reform Act, the Treasury Department was slow in issuing regulations covering the major provisions of the new nondiscrimination rules. The absence of regulations coupled with the extreme complexity of the new standards and a deadline of January 1989 for many provisions caused Congress to take another look at the rules as part of a 1988 review of other Tax Reform Act provisions. As a result, a comprehensive bill making technical corrections to the Tax Reform Act was passed in October 1988, which included provisions intended to clarify some of the welfare plan nondiscrimination rules.

Despite efforts to ease the Section 89 rules, employers continued to complain about the complexity of compliance. The Treasury Department delayed compliance first to July 1, 1989, and then to October 1, 1989, while Congress continued to search for acceptable alternatives, including the possibility of simpler testing methods. Finally, after various proposals to ease or simplify the rules failed, Congress in late 1989 repealed the Section 89 nondiscrimination tests as part of legislation raising the federal debt ceiling. The pre-1986 rules were reinstated.

FIDUCIARIES

The written plan document for an employee benefit plan must provide for one or more named fiduciaries who have authority to control and manage the operation and administration of the plan. A "named fiduciary" is a person either named in the plan itself or named by the employer or employee organization, or by both acting jointly, under a procedure set out in the plan.

Not the least of the sensitive and difficult questions that arise in the enforcement of ERISA is the definition of a fiduciary. The ERISA definition is very broad, and whether a given individual is found to be a fiduciary often turns upon the facts and circumstances of a specific situation. The resultant finding is important because of the legal responsibilities of a fiduciary.

The term "fiduciary" includes people who

- Exercise discretionary authority or control over the management or administration of an employee benefit plan or over the management or disposition of its assets
- Render investment advice for a fee or other direct or indirect compensation

The following are generally regarded as subject to the definition of a fiduciary:

- Directors, officers, and consultants with discretionary authority over the plan

- Plan administrators
- Bank trustees

In *Anoka Orthopaedic Association v. Lechner* (12 EBC 2241 (8th Cir. 1990)), the court held that attorneys, accountants, actuaries, and consultants who perform professional services for employee benefit plans would not be considered fiduciaries solely because they provided such services if their responsibilities did not also include giving investment advice on a regular basis. The case involved an accountant and attorney who provided administrative services to a pension plan. Although the attorney made two investment recommendations to the plan, his main function was to provide legal advice and help prepare financial statements.

Employee benefit plans can allow individuals to serve in more than one fiduciary capacity (e.g., as both trustee and administrator). A plan can also have co-fiduciaries, with each person responsible only for those duties to which he or she has been assigned. However, one fiduciary can be liable for the breaches of another if the former

- Participates in the breach
- Knowingly conceals the breach
- Imprudently allows the breach to occur

Any person designated by a fiduciary to carry out the fiduciary's responsibility becomes a fiduciary by reason of that delegation. Persons responsible for the selection and retention of fiduciaries can themselves be considered fiduciaries by reason of that authority.

A plan fiduciary often designates an investment manager to manage the plan's assets. If the investment manager is chosen through a careful and prudent process and the manager's performance is monitored regularly and continually, the plan fiduciary may not be liable for any acts or omissions by that manager.

A fiduciary may receive reasonable compensation for services rendered, unless the fiduciary is already being paid a full-time salary from the employer, employee association, or union.

A fiduciary may also be reimbursed for expenses incurred in the performance of duties for the plan.

All fiduciaries and persons who handle funds or other assets must be bonded for 10 percent of the aggregated amount handled, with a minimum bond of $1,000 and a maximum bond of $500,000.

Responsibilities

The fiduciary's responsibility is to manage the assets of an employee benefit plan so that those assets are used exclusively to provide benefits for employees and beneficiaries and to defray administrative costs of the plan. The fiduciary is charged with using the care and skill in managing the plan that a prudent person would use in similar circumstances. The fiduciary must diversify the investments of the plan to minimize the risk of large losses. Finally, the fiduciary must discharge his or her duties in accordance with the documents and instruments governing the employee benefit plan.

In a 1988 case, a U.S. district court said that the trustees of a union-administered welfare fund had breached their fiduciary duties through their actions in choosing a law firm to provide prepaid legal services to participants. That firm charged $20,000 per month for services to 2,000 participants, but handled only 262 cases in a 15-month period.

The court said the trustees failed to take bids from other firms before awarding the contract and then allowed the law firm to charge unreasonably high fees for the services performed (*Benvenuto v. Schneider*, 678 F. Supp. 51 (E.D.N.Y. 1988)).

Prohibitions

The fiduciary may not

- Deal with assets of the plan for his or her own benefit
- Receive compensation from any person in connection with any action involving plan assets
- Act on behalf of a party whose interests are adverse to the plan or to its participants

- Invest in assets outside the jurisdiction of U.S. district courts

Prudence Rule

The standard to which ERISA holds fiduciaries in the exercise of their duties is the standard that has been used for years for the management of trusts—the prudence rule (also known as the "prudent expert" rule or the "prudent man" rule).

The rule calls for a fiduciary to act "with the care, skill, prudence, and diligence under the circumstances then prevailing that a prudent man acting in a like capacity and familiar with such matters would use in the conduct of an enterprise of a like character and with like aims."

The management trustees of a professional football players' pension fund breached their fiduciary responsibilities, a U.S. district court ruled, by failing to vote on proposals submitted by player trustees to deal with management's failure to make full contributions to the plan. The management trustees violated their fiduciary responsibility to safeguard the plan when they were confronted with a conflict of interest as club officials as well as plan trustees (*Bidwell v. Garvey*, 12 EBC 1521 (D. Md. 1990)).

Department of Labor Regulations

The prudence rule and its relation to the investment of pension plan assets became an extremely controversial feature of ERISA soon after the law's enactment. Investment managers in particular were extremely wary about what ERISA required of them.

A final regulation concerning the investment duties of fiduciaries under the rule was not issued until June 26, 1979. Even then, the regulation was couched in general terms, as the Labor Department emphasized that the regulation did not prescribe the only way to satisfy the rule and that a determination of whether a fiduciary met the standard often would turn on the facts of each case.

The Labor Department made clear that the relative riskiness of a specific investment or course of action in making investments was not the sole determining factor as to whether the action was prudent. The Department also would not provide a list of appropriate investment vehicles or investment techniques. Use of funds for even real estate venture capital or purchases of precious metals might be appropriate investments under certain circumstances or within certain portfolios, it was noted.

Fiduciaries would satisfy the prudence rule, the Labor Department said, if they had given "appropriate consideration" to those facts and circumstances that, given the scope of their investment duties, they knew or should have known were relevant to the particular investment course of action.

"Appropriate consideration" includes a determination by the fiduciary that an investment is reasonably designed to further the purposes of the benefit plan, taking into account the risk of loss and the opportunity for gain associated with the investment. The "facts and circumstances" would include the role of the investment in the overall portfolio for which the fiduciary was responsible. An investment thus is to be judged on the basis of the role it played in the portfolio, not as an investment standing alone.

A case that illustrates the requirements of fiduciaries with regard to investments of plan assets is *Marshall v. Glass Metal Association* (507 F. Supp. 378, 2 EBC 1006 (D. Hawaii 1980)). The trustees of a pension plan in Hawaii committed the plan to a $1.2 million loan to a single real estate venture. The Department of Labor sued the trustees to stop the loan on the grounds that the trustees failed to act prudently in their roles as fiduciaries and failed to diversify the assets of the plan. The trustees later amended the loan commitment to $750,000, but the court ordered that the loan not be made.

In *Brock v. Citizens Bank of Clovis* (841 F.2d 322 (10th Cir. 1988)), an appellate court found violations of the prudence rule by a defined benefit pension plan of a bank that invested 82 percent of total plan assets in first mortgages secured by commercial property in a New Mexico county and lent money to the pension fund so that the plan could participate in the mortgages. This investment subjected the plan to the risk of default, the court said.

"Total Return" Concept

The prudence rule does not require that every item in a portfolio be income-producing under all circumstances, as the Department of Labor accepts the "total return" concept of portfolio management. The overall investment performance of the portfolio is to be judged, not the performance of specific portfolio holdings.

A fiduciary is supposed to consider the following factors as they relate to an investment:

- Diversification of the portfolio
- Liquidity and current return of the portfolio relative to the anticipated cash flow requirements of the plan
- Projected return from the portfolio relative to the funding objectives of the plan

When taking over an employee benefit plan from another fiduciary, a fiduciary who finds unproductive investments must liquidate those holdings. Further, if there have been breaches of responsibility by the previous fiduciary resulting in losses to the plan, the new fiduciary is expected to attempt to recover those amounts from the previous fiduciary.

"Nontraditional" Investments

Since the 1970s, controversy has developed over a movement, particularly strong among labor unions, for nontraditional investing or targeted investing of pension funds. Also called "social investing," this is the practice of investing pension funds in housing, small businesses, local economic development projects, and jobs programs instead of in the more traditional investments of stocks, bonds, and government securities. The terms also refer to efforts to prevent investments of pension funds in companies whose practices and policies might be inimical to the interests of workers covered by the fund. (A union based in the Northwest might, for example, oppose investment in companies planning to move operations to the Southwest.)

Advocates of nontraditional investing have argued that it is possible to achieve social and political goals—such as helping to promote housing and jobs for workers—by using the money that is accumulating to pay for their own future pensions without sacrificing traditional financial goals.

Opponents of nontraditional investing maintain that professional investment managers must seek the highest rate of return at acceptable levels of risk, a standard that they say nontraditional investments fail to meet.

Several multiemployer pension funds have offered below-market interest rates on mortgages for employees in their pension plans. However, the Labor Department position has been that the investment must have equal merit to other possible investments and that the social purposes are incidental.

In the case of *Donovan v. Walton* (609 F. Supp. 1221 (S.D. Fla. 1985)), the Labor Department filed an action in May 1981 against the trustees of a union pension plan for failing to manage pension plan assets prudently when they invested in loans for the construction of an office building and auditorium complex designed for occupancy by the union. The department said the loans were improper because they were made at below-market interest rates unfavorable to the plan.

PROHIBITED TRANSACTIONS

The prohibited transaction provisions of ERISA have caused as much controversy among pension managers, trustees, and fiduciaries as has the prudence rule.

Party-in-Interest

Prohibited transaction provisions are included in essentially the same language in both the labor and tax sections of ERISA. The main difference is the use of the term "party-in-interest" in the labor section and the term "disqualified person" in the tax section. The terms cover the same group of persons, as follows:

- Fiduciaries
- Persons providing services to a plan
- Administrators, officers, and employees of the plan
- Persons who are 10-percent shareholders or partners
- Directors or indirect owners of 50 percent of the stock of a corporation or partnership
- Relatives of people in the above group

A party-in-interest or disqualified person found to be engaged in a prohibited transaction is subject to a civil penalty—in the form of an excise tax—of 5 percent of the amount involved in the transaction. If no action is taken to correct or end the prohibited transaction within 90 days of the assessment of the excise tax, an additional tax of 100 percent of the amount involved may be charged against the party-in-interest.

Activities Covered

ERISA lists the following activities as prohibited between a party-in-interest and an employee benefit plan:

- Sale, exchange, or leasing of property
- Lending money or other extension of credit
- Furnishing goods, services, or facilities
- Use of plan assets for the benefit of the party-in-interest
- Acquisition of qualifying employer securities and real property in excess of allowable limits

In 1982, a U.S. district court found that an employer's sale of its jet aircraft to the company pension plan constituted a prohibited transaction (*McDougall v. Donovan*, 552 F. Supp. 1206 (N.D. Ill. 1982)). Another district court found in a 1987 case that a plan's investment manager had engaged in prohibited transactions by investing assets of the plan in companies from which he received over $1 million in fees and commissions for services he performed for those companies (*Lowen v. Tower Asset Management, Inc.*, 653 F. Supp. 1542 (S.D.N.Y. 1987)).

Loans

A case that illustrates the prohibition against loans is *Marshall v. Kelly* (465 F. Supp. 341, 1 EBC 1850 (W.D. Okla. 1978)). The Labor Department alleged that the owner of a construction company violated his fiduciary obligations as sole trustee of the profit-sharing plan of his company by making loans and payments from the pension fund to the company. The district court ordered the defendant to repay the loans and payments and removed him as trustee until the repayments were made.

Employer Securities

Defined benefit pension plans are prohibited from acquiring qualifying securities or qualifying real property of the employer if, after the acquisition, the fair market value of those securities would exceed 10 percent of the assets of the plan.

Qualifying employer securities include stock and marketable obligations. Qualifying real property includes parcels of real property, a substantial number of which are geographically dispersed and that are suitable or adaptable to more than one use. The 10-percent limit does not apply to profit-sharing, employee stock ownership, or stock bonus pension plans, as long as the pension plan provides that assets can be invested in employer securities and indicates the extent to which they can be so invested.

The Pension Protection Act adds certain additional requirements that have to be met for stock to be considered "qualifying employer security." No more than 25 percent of the aggregate amount of stock of the same class issued and outstanding at the time of acquisition may be held by the plan. In addition, at least 50 percent of the stock must be held by outsiders.

Also, for purposes of the 10-percent limit, individual account plans previously exempt will be subject to the limit if they are part of a "floor-offset arrangement." These are arrangements of defined benefit plans and individual account plans in which the benefits provided by the latter are taken into account in determining the benefits payable from the defined benefit plan.

Plans that on February 19, 1987, held employer securities that did not meet the new requirements had until January 1, 1993, to dispose of those securities.

Statutory Exemptions

ERISA also describes specific circumstances and situations when prohibited transaction rules will not apply and allows the Labor Department to grant additional exemptions.

The statutory exemptions include the following:

- Loans to participants or beneficiaries if they are made in accordance with specific provisions in the benefit plan, bear a reasonable rate of interest, and are adequately secured
- Furnishing of office space and service by the benefit plan to a party-in-interest as long as reasonable compensation is received
- Providing of ancillary services by a bank as long as the interests of the plan are not disturbed
- Use by banks and insurance companies of their own facilities or contracts for employee benefit plans covering their own employees
- Investment of plan funds by a trustee bank in its own pooled investment fund under certain circumstances

The Labor Department issues the following two types of exemptions:

- Class exemptions to cover a particular type or class of transaction
- Individual exemptions to provide relief for specific applicants

A class exemption was given for insurance agents and brokers, pension consultants, insurance companies, investment companies, and investment company principal underwriters. They are allowed to continue servicing employee benefit plans, including receiving fees and commissions for the sale of insurance, annuity contracts, and securities. The transactions have to be conducted on arm's-length terms and for fees and commissions that are reasonable.

Other class exemptions include the following:

- The purchase of securities when the proceeds from the sale of the securities may be used to pay off indebtedness to persons who are parties-in-interest to the plan
- The lease or purchase by a collectively bargained multiple employer apprenticeship or training plan of personal or real property from a participating employer or from a wholly owned subsidiary of such an employer
- The sale of life insurance, health insurance, or annuity contracts to employee benefit plans, under certain circumstances, by insurance companies having substantial stock or partnership affiliation with employers maintaining the plans
- The extension of interest-free loans or other credit to pension and welfare plans from employers or unions sponsoring the plans or from other parties-in-interest (This exemption provides a means for a plan's operating expenses to be met when the plan has a temporary cash shortage. No interest or fees may be charged by the employers or unions.)
- Investments by employee benefit plans in real estate mortgage pools sponsored, trusteed, or insured by a party-in-interest to the plans, including a plan fiduciary

Individual Exemptions

At first, individual exemptions were most commonly granted in what were called "plan disentanglement" cases involving property that was acquired by a plan before ERISA and that the plan now wanted to sell to a party-in-interest, usually the employer. Since the passage of ERISA, that kind of sale has required the granting of an exemption. The Labor Department conditions approval on a plan demonstrating that the transaction is fair, with no pattern of abuse present. The Department must be satisfied that the plan is getting the best deal possible for its property, which necessitates at least one independent appraisal of the property and a sale at fair market value.

The Labor Department moved from the "plan disentanglement" type of individual exemption to the two following types in 1979:

- Transactions of an ongoing nature such as loans from plans to employers
- Contributions in kind from employers to plans

For these exemptions, the Labor Department requires additional evidence of safeguards to protect the plans, particularly the presence of an independent fiduciary.

REPORTING REQUIREMENTS

Each pension and welfare plan (unless exempted) must report certain detailed financial and actuarial data annually to the Treasury Department. Each plan is required to submit an audited financial statement. Defined benefit pension plans must also submit a certified actuarial report. Other reports are required when a pension plan merges with another or is terminated. (See Appendix 2.)

The 5500 Series of Forms

A group of forms known as the "Form 5500 family" or "5500 series" makes up the annual reports that must be filed with the IRS. The IRS provides copies of each annual report to the Labor Department and gives the PBGC specific information from the form. Depending on the type of employee benefit plan, one or another in the following series will be used:

- Form 5500: the basic form for employee benefit plans with more than 100 participants (See Appendix 3.)
- Form 5500-C: a short form to be used at least every third year by small plans—those with fewer than 100 participants at the beginning of a plan year (If the number of participants increases or decreases only slightly around

the 100 mark from one year to the next, the plan can continue to use the short form.)

- Form 5500-R: an abbreviated short form that can be used two out of three years by plans using Form 5500-C the third year, unless the plans find it simpler to continue using Form 5500-C every year. (This abbreviated form is the result of a simplification of the reporting requirements made in 1980 for small plans.)

Annual Report Contents

The annual report requirements of ERISA are lengthy; however, the 5500 series of forms lists all the required information. The details required include the following:

- A statement of assets and liabilities at current value, aggregated by categories such as cash or common stock
- A statement of income and expenses
- A schedule of assets held for investment purposes
- A schedule of certain transactions between the plan and a party-in-interest, including the nature of the transaction and the money involved
- A schedule of loans of fixed-income obligations and a list of all leases or loans in default or uncollectible at year-end
- A list of transactions involving amounts greater than 3 percent of the current value of the assets of the plan
- The names and addresses of the plan fiduciaries and others who render services to the plan for which they are compensated, such as trustees, accountants, and insurance carriers
- A breakdown of the number of employees showing how many are covered by the plan and how many are not

An employer who fails to file an annual report may be fined up to $1,000 per day by the Secretary of Labor, beginning with the date the report was due.

Schedule A

Every pension or welfare plan that provides benefits through insurance companies, with the exception of sole proprietors and partnerships, must also complete Schedule A and file it with the related annual report. (See Appendix 3.)

The following information must be filed on Schedule A:

- Insurance premiums and benefits paid
- Number of persons covered
- Administrative charges and commissions to agents and brokers
- Dividends credited

Schedule B

A defined benefit pension plan subject to ERISA minimum funding requirements must file Schedule B with its annual report. This schedule describes the actuarial assumptions used to determine costs for the plan and includes a facsimile of the funding standard account showing that the plan is maintaining the level of funding necessary to cover its benefit obligations. (See Appendix 3.) Schedule B must be signed by an enrolled actuary.

OTHER REPORTING REQUIREMENTS

ERISA requires pension plans to file the following additional reports when specific events take place:

- Schedule SSA must be filed with the IRS in any year during which employees with vested benefits end their employment, listing the employees and the amount of their benefits.
- Form 5310 must be filed with the IRS by any pension plan involved in a merger, consolidation, or transfer of assets or liabilities.
- An administrator of a single-employer pension plan that is being terminated must file a "notice of intent to termi-

nate'' with the PBGC at least 10 days before the effective date of the termination.

Reportable Events

Pension plan administrators must file information with the PBGC about certain developments that can mean the plan is running into financial trouble and thus risks termination. ERISA requires notice within 30 days of an occurrence of this nature, but it allows the PBGC to waive the 30-day requirement in specific cases.

To simplify the reporting requirements, the PBGC decided to permit plans to report a number of these events on their annual reports instead of within 30 days. Events that still must be reported within 30 days include the following:

- A decrease of at least 20 percent in the number of active participants in the plan since the beginning of the current plan year or of at least 25 percent since the beginning of the previous plan year (This requirement applies only to plans with over 100 participants.)
- Inability to pay benefits when due
- Failure to meet minimum funding standards

ERISA also authorized the PBGC to add to the list of reportable events; the following three events, added by regulation, must also be reported within 30 days:

- Bankruptcy, insolvency, or similar creditor settlement proceedings
- Liquidation or dissolution
- Transactions involving a change of employer for single-employer plans with unfunded benefit obligations of $1 million or more

Reportable events that must be included in a plan's annual report include the following:

- Loss of tax-qualified status
- Noncompliance with Title I provisions

- A distribution of $10,000 or more to a "substantial owner" within a 12-month period for a reason other than death when the plan has unfunded liabilities or the distribution would create unfunded liabilities (A substantial owner is a person who owns the entire interest in a business or is a partner or shareholder owning 10 percent of a business.)

Multiemployer Plans

Multiemployer pension plans have their own reporting requirements, as follows:

- If an employer contributing to the pension plan completely or partially withdraws from the plan, the plan sponsor must notify every other employer in the plan of the benefit obligations of the withdrawing employer.
- If a multiemployer pension plan undergoes reorganization as a result of financial difficulties, the plan sponsor must notify each employer contributing to the plan of any increased contributions that may be needed. This information must also be provided to any unions representing employees covered by the plan.
- If a multiemployer plan becomes insolvent, the plan sponsor must notify the Treasury Department, the PBGC, plan participants and beneficiaries, employers contributing to the plan, and affected unions.

DISCLOSURE REQUIREMENTS

The disclosure requirements of ERISA apply generally to all employee benefit plans. Information about the plans and how benefits are distributed must be communicated to employees in a form and in language that is both comprehensive and understandable to the employees. A model statement of employee rights under ERISA appears in Labor Department regulations. (See Exhibit 1.)

Employers must provide summary plan descriptions and summaries of annual financial reports to all employees who are

EXHIBIT 1
Model Statement of ERISA Rights

As a participant in (name of plan) you are entitled to certain rights and protections under the Employee Retirement Income Security Act of 1974. ERISA provides that all plan participants shall be entitled to:

- Examine, without charge, at the plan administrator's office and at other specified locations, such as worksites and union halls, all plan documents, including insurance contracts, collective bargaining agreements and copies of all documents filed by the plan with the U.S. Department of Labor, such as detailed annual reports and plan descriptions.

- Obtain copies of all plan documents and other plan information upon written request to the plan administrator. The administrator may make a reasonable charge for the copies.

- Receive a summary of the plan's annual financial report. The plan administrator is required by law to furnish each participant with a copy of this summary annual report.

- Obtain a statement telling you whether you have a right to receive a pension at normal retirement age (age***) and if so, what your benefits would be at normal retirement age if you stop working under the plan now. If you do not have a right to a pension, the statement will tell you how many more years you have to work to get a right to a pension. This statement must be requested in writing and is not required to be given more than once a year. The plan must provide the statement free of charge.

In addition to creating rights for plan participants, ERISA imposes duties upon the people who are responsible for the operation of the employee benefit plan. The people who operate your plan, called "fiduciaries" of the plan, have a duty to do so prudently and in the interest of you and other plan participants and beneficiaries. No one, including your employer, your union, or any other person, may fire you or otherwise discriminate against you in any way to prevent you from obtaining a (pension, welfare) benefit or exercising your rights under ERISA. If your claim for a (pension, welfare) benefit is denied in whole or in part you must receive a written explanation of the reason for the denial. You have the right to have the plan review and reconsider your claim. Under ERISA, there are steps you can take to enforce the above rights. For instance, if you request materials from the plan and do not receive them within 30 days, you may file suit in a federal court. In such a case, the court may require the plan administrator to provide the materials and pay you up to $100 a day until you receive the materials, unless the materials were not sent because of reasons beyond the control of the administrator. If you have a claim for benefits which is denied or ignored, in whole or in part, you may file suit in a state or federal court. If it should happen that plan fiduciaries misuse the plan's money, or if you are discriminated against for asserting your rights, you may seek assistance from the U.S. Department of Labor, or you may file suit in a federal court. The court will decide who should pay court costs and fees. If you are successful the court may order the person you have sued to pay these costs and fees. If you lose, the court may order you to pay these costs and fees, for example, if it finds your claim is frivolous. If you have any questions about your plan, you should contact the plan administrator. If you have questions about this statement or about your rights under ERISA, you should contact the nearest Area Office of the U.S. Pension and Welfare Benefits Administration.

Source: 29 C.F.R. §2520.102-3(t)(2).

or will be covered by the benefit plan. Employees must also be notified if any major modifications are made to the plan.

Other documents must be provided to employees when certain events take place, such as when a claim for benefits is denied. In addition, when an employee requests other information, he or she must either be given the material or be allowed to examine it.

Plans Exempt From Disclosure

Basically all employee benefit plans have to meet the disclosure requirements of Title I. The following are the only exemptions:

- Plans established by governmental agencies
- Church plans
- Plans maintained to comply with workers' compensation, unemployment compensation, or disability insurance laws
- Plans maintained outside the United States primarily for the benefit of nonresident aliens
- Unfunded excess benefit plans

Department of Labor regulations also exempt Keogh plans whose only participants are partners and spouses or sole proprietors and spouses.

Summary Plan Description

The summary plan description (SPD) is the basic document for providing the details of a pension or welfare plan to the persons covered by that plan. Its purpose is to explain how the plan works, what benefits it provides, and how the benefits can be obtained. (See Exhibit 2.)

Contents

The SPD must include the following information:

- Names and addresses of all key officials, such as the plan administrator, legal agent, and trustee administering the plan and its assets

EXHIBIT 2
Summary Plan Description Checklist

In order to assure that each SPD is prepared in accordance with the regulations, the following checklist is provided. The checklist should be used only as a guide.

☐ Have you included the name of your plan?

☐ Have you included the name and address of the employer or employee organization that maintains the plan, or a representative of the parties which established or maintain the plan?

Note: Collectively bargained plans involving one or more employers, and employee organizations and plans involving at least two employers, must include a statement that a complete list of employers and employee organizations may be obtained by participants and beneficiaries upon written request to the plan administrator and is available for examination. Such plans must also include in their SPDs a statement that participants and beneficiaries may request to know if a particular employer or employee organization is a sponsor, and the sponsor's address.

☐ Have you recorded your Employer Identification Number (EIN) and Plan Number?

☐ Have you indicated the type of pension or welfare plan?

☐ Have you indicated the type of administration of the plan, e.g., contract administration, sponsor administration, insurer administration, etc.?

☐ Have you included the name, business address and business telephone number of the plan administrator?

☐ Have you listed the name and address of the person designated as the legal agent?

☐ Have you indicated that service of legal process may be made upon a plan trustee or the plan administrator?

☐ Have you included the name, title and address of the principal place of business of each plan trustee (if the plan has trustees)?

☐ If the plan is maintained pursuant to one or more collective bargaining agreements, have you indicated that copies of such agreements are available upon written request and may be examined by participants and beneficiaries?

☐ Have you included a statement of the requirements for eligibility for participation and for benefits?

For pension plans:

☐ Does it define the plan's normal retirement age?

☐ Does it describe any conditions which must be met for a participant to be eligible to receive benefits?

☐ Does it describe the benefits provided by the plan?

☐ Does it describe any joint and survivor benefits provided under the plan, including any requirement that an election must be made to accept or reject the joint and survivor annuity?

SPD Checklist—Contd.

□ Does it state the service required for full benefit accrual and how benefit accrual is prorated for employers who do not have a full year of benefit accrual service?

□ Does it state whether or not plan benefits are insured by the Pension Benefit Guaranty Corporation (PBGC)?

If your plan is a defined benefit pension plan, you must summarize the pension benefit insurance program of the PBGC and give its address. It also must indicate that further information may be obtained through the plan administrator or the PBGC. An optional statement on the PBGC insurance program is provided in the regulations.* If plan benefits are not insured, state why not.

For welfare benefit plans:

□ Does it describe or summarize the benefits provided? (In the case of a welfare benefit plan, such as a medical care plan which provides an extensive schedule of benefits, only a general description of benefits is required if participants are informed that a detailed schedule of benefits is available free of charge.)

For pension and welfare plans:

□ Have you indicated the sources of contributions to the plan and the method by which the amount of contributions is calculated?

□ Have you identified any institution or organization used for the accumulation of assets, e.g., insurance company or trust fund?

□ Have you included the date on which the plan's fiscal year ends?

□ Have you listed the procedures to be followed in presenting (1) claims for benefits and (2) requests for review of denied claims?

□ Have you included the ERISA rights statement as described in section 29 CFR 2520.102-3(t) of the regulations?**

□ Have you considered any options for filing different summaries and checked out any alternative methods that may be applicable to your situation?

Source: Pension and Welfare Benefits Administration, U.S. Department of Labor, "Guide to Summary Plan Description Requirements" (Washington, D.C., 1991).

*See Exhibit 3.

**See Exhibit 1.

- A description and explanation of plan benefits
- A statement of participants' rights under ERISA
- A description of the requirements for eligibility for benefits
- A description of the circumstances that could result in a worker's disqualification or in denial, loss, or suspension of benefits
- The procedure for presenting claims for benefits and for appealing denials of those claims
- A statement indicating whether or not the pension plan is insured by the PBGC (See Exhibit 3. If the plan is not insured, the SPD must explain the reason for the lack of coverage.)

In addition, if a pension plan is funded at less than 70 percent of current liability, the annual report must include a statement of the extent to which the plan is funded.

The SPD must be written in easily understood language with no technical terms or legal jargon. The Labor Department in its regulations on the subject suggests the use of examples, illustrations, and other aids such as a table of contents. Also, the Department requires that the SPD not be slanted so as to create a favorable impression of the employer by emphasizing the benefits of a plan while playing down terms or conditions that might cause an employee to lose benefits or fail to qualify for benefits.

The importance of an SPD was described by an appellate court in a 1985 case involving a dispute about breaks in service and vesting credit. At issue was the interpretation of the language in the plan itself versus the SPD. The U.S. Court of Appeals for the Eleventh Circuit said: "It is of no effect to publish and distribute a plan summary booklet designed to simplify and explain a voluminous and complex document, and then proclaim that any inconsistencies will be governed by the plan. Unfairness will flow to the employee for reasonably relying on the summary booklet" (*McKnight v. Southern Life and Health Insurance Co.*, 758 F.2d 1566 (1985)).

If a given percentage of plan participants speak a language other than English, there must be in the SPD a notice in their

EXHIBIT 3
Model Pension Guaranty Statement

Benefits under this plan are insured by the Pension Benefit Guaranty Corporation (PBGC) if the plan terminates. Generally, the PBGC guarantees most vested normal age retirement benefits, early retirement benefits, and certain disability and survivor's pensions. However, the PBGC does not guarantee all types of benefits under covered plans, and the amount of benefit protection is subject to certain limitations.

The PBGC guarantees vested benefits at the level in effect on the date of plan termination. However, if a plan has been in effect less than five years before it terminates, or if benefits have been increased within the five years before plan termination, the whole amount of the plan's vested benefits or the benefit increase may not be guaranteed. In addition, there is a ceiling on the amount of monthly benefit that the PBGC guarantees, which is adjusted periodically.

For more information on the PBGC insurance protection and its limitations, ask your Plan Administrator or the PBGC. Inquires to the PBGC should be addressed to the Office of Communications, PBGC, 2020 K Street N.W., Washington, D.C. 20006. The PBGC Office of Communications may also be reached by calling (202) 778-8840.

Source: 29 C.F.R. §2520.102-3(m)(3).

language that assistance will be given to help them understand their benefits and obligations.

When an employee benefit plan merges with another plan, employees who remain eligible under the old plan must be given the SPD of the new plan and a description of how the merger affects them. The participants must be informed of their right to inspect and obtain copies of the old plan documents.

Abbreviated SPDs

Labor Department regulations provide that a pension plan may furnish an abbreviated SPD to retirees, beneficiaries receiving benefits, and former employees with vested rights to a pension. For former employees, the SPD must contain a statement that includes the amount of their vested benefit or the method of computing the benefit. If this information has already been provided, the SPD must still indicate that the information may be obtained on request.

The following other information should be included in the SPD for former employees:

- Duration of payment
- Optional forms of payment
- Any reduction, change, termination, forfeiture, or suspension of benefit provisions that may apply

Distribution of the SPD

When an employee benefit plan is established, the SPD must go out to employees and be furnished to the Labor Department within 120 days of the time when the plan becomes subject to the reporting and disclosure requirements of ERISA. (Generally, a plan becomes subject to ERISA on the first day on which an employee is credited with an hour of service.)

An employee must be given a copy of the SPD within 90 days of becoming a participant in or a beneficiary of an employee benefit plan. The plan administrator also has an obligation to furnish participants every five years with updated SPDs that integrate all plan amendments made within the five-year period. If no amendments have been made to the plan, administrators need not provide an updated version any more frequently than once every 10 years.

Summary of Material Modifications

When a "material modification" is made to a plan, all persons affected by the change have to be notified in a summary of material modification, as does the Department of Labor. This summary must also be written in easily understood language and provide a reasonable and adequate summary of the change made to the plan.

Examples of material modifications include changes in

- Persons administering the plan
- Eligibility or vesting provisions
- Procedures for presenting claims

The summary of material modifications must be furnished no later than 210 days after the end of the plan year in which the change becomes effective.

Summary Annual Report

The summary annual report is an abbreviated version of the yearly financial report (Form 5500) filed by pension and welfare plans. The annual financial report must be filed with the IRS within seven months after the end of the plan year; the summary must be distributed to employees no later than two months after the filing.

The Labor Department has prescribed forms to be used for summary annual reports—one for pension plans and another for welfare plans. The forms have blanks to be filled in with information from the most recent annual report.

Health Care Continuation Coverage

The health care continuation coverage mandated by the 1985 Consolidated Omnibus Budget Reconciliation Act (COBRA) includes certain disclosure requirements for employers, employees, and dependents. When a plan becomes subject to COBRA, an employer must notify employees and spouses when they first become covered under the plan. In the event of certain "qualifying events," such as the termination or death of an employee, the following notification deadlines must be met:

- An employer must notify the welfare plan within 30 days of the qualifying event.
- The plan administrator must notify qualified beneficiaries within 14 days of their election rights.
- Employees or qualified beneficiaries have at least 60 days in which to decide to elect coverage.
- Employees, retirees, or family members must notify the plan administrator within 60 days of certain events, such as divorce or legal separation. (See Exhibit 4.)

An employer faces a penalty of $100 per day for failure to provide the required COBRA notices.

Other Information for Participants

Other information that employee benefit plans have an obligation to provide in the following indicated situations include:

- For persons ending their employment, retiring, or taking a leave of absence: a statement of benefits earned under their pension plan and the percentage of such benefits that are vested
- For persons denied a pension or welfare benefit: a written explanation of the denial of the claim for benefits
- For any employee upon request no more than once each year: an account of the total pension benefit accrual and percentage vested
- For married employees under a pension plan: a written explanation of both the joint and survivor retirement annuity and the pre-retirement survivor benefit, including the effect these forms of payment will have on the amount of the benefit and an explanation of the right to reject the survivor provisions
- To all pension plan participants and beneficiaries: notification if their pension plan is funded below 70 percent of

EXHIBIT 4
Notification Procedures Under COBRA

Your Rights:
Notice And Election Procedures

COBRA outlines procedures for employees and family members to elect continuation coverage and for employers and plans to notify beneficiaries. The qualifying events contained in the law create rights and obligations for employers, plan administrators and qualified beneficiaries.

Qualified beneficiaries have the right to elect to continue coverage that is identical to the coverage provided under the plan. Employers and plan administrators have an obligation to determine the specific rights of beneficiaries with respect to election, notification and type of coverage options.

Notice Procedures

General Notices

An initial general notice must be furnished to covered employees, their spouses and newly hired employees informing them of their rights under COBRA and describing provisions of the law.

COBRA information also is required to be contained in the summary plan description (SPD) which participants receive. ERISA requires that SPDs containing certain plan information and summaries of material changes in plan requirements be furnished to participants in modified and updated SPDs. Plan administrators must automatically furnish the SPD booklet 90 days after a person becomes a participant or beneficiary or within 120 days after the plan is subject to the reporting and disclosure provisions of the law.

Specific Notices

Specific notice requirements are triggered for employers, qualified beneficiaries and plan administrators when a qualifying event occurs. Employers must notify plan administrators within 30 days of an employee's death, termination, reduced hours of employment, entitlement to Medicare or a bankruptcy. Multiemployer plans may provide for a longer period of time.

The employee, retiree or family member should notify the plan administrator within 60 days of events consisting of divorce or legal separation or a child's ceasing to be covered as a dependent under plan rules.

Disabled beneficiaries must notify plan administrators of Social Security disability determinations. A notice must be provided within 60 days of a disability determination and prior to expiration of the 18-month period of COBRA coverage. These beneficiaries also must notify the plan administrator within 30 days of a final determination that they are no longer disabled.

Plan administrators, upon notification of a qualifying event, must automatically provide a notice to employees and family members of their election rights. The notice must be provided in person or by first class mail within 14 days of receiving information that a qualifying event has occurred.

There are two special exceptions to the notice requirements for multiemployer plans. First, the time frame for providing notices may be extended beyond the 14- and 30-day requirements if allowed by plan rules. Second, employers are relieved of the obligation to notify plan administrators when employees terminate or reduce their work hours. Plan administrators are responsible for determining whether these qualifying events have occurred.

Election

The election period is the time frame during which each qualified beneficiary may choose whether to continue health care coverage under an employer's group health plan. Qualified beneficiaries have a 60-day period to elect whether to continue coverage. This period is measured from the later of the coverage loss date or the date the notice to elect COBRA coverage is sent. COBRA coverage is retroactive if elected and paid for by the qualified beneficiary.

A covered employee or the covered employee's spouse may elect COBRA coverage on behalf of any other qualified beneficiary. Each qualified beneficiary, however, may independently elect COBRA coverage. A parent or legal guardian may elect on behalf of a minor child.

A waiver of coverage may be revoked by or on behalf of a qualified beneficiary prior to the end of the election period. A beneficiary may then reinstate coverage. Then, the plan need only provide continuation coverage beginning on the date the waiver is revoked.

current liability, if the employer has failed to make required quarterly installment for the plan before the 60th day after the due date, if a funding waiver has been requested, or if the pension plan is being terminated.

BENEFIT RIGHTS

In addition to the protection of pension rights created by the vesting and benefit accrual provisions of ERISA, the law contains other safeguards for all employee benefit plans. A claim for benefits cannot be denied, for instance, without a written explanation and an opportunity for review of the denial. (See Exhibit 5.)

ERISA itself does not spell out what constitutes a claim for benefits under an employee benefit plan, nor does it describe procedures that employees or beneficiaries must follow to file claims. However, the law requires benefit plans to establish "reasonable" procedures for the settlement of disputed claims. In addition, Labor Department regulations require employee benefit plans to describe claims procedures in the SPD. The procedures have to include giving participants and beneficiaries timely written notice of any time limits for filing claims. The claim procedures cannot interfere with an employee's rights under ERISA.

If a claim for benefits is denied, ERISA requires an employee benefit plan to

- Provide adequate notice in writing to the employee explaining the reasons for the denial in language that can be easily understood by the employee
- Offer the employee a reasonable opportunity for a full and fair review of the decision

The claimant must be given at least 60 days after the claim has been denied in which to request a review. If the denial is not reversed after the employee has exhausted all administrative procedures, the employee may bring suit in a federal district court for enforcement of the claim.

EXHIBIT 5
Instructions for Filing Pension Claims

What the Law Does

The Employee Retirement Income Security Act of 1974 (ERISA) protects the interests of participants and their beneficiaries who depend on benefits from private employee benefit plans. ERISA sets standards for administering these plans, including a requirement that financial and other information be disclosed to plan participants and beneficiaries and requirements for the processing of claims for benefits under the plans.

Although some employee benefit plans are not covered by the Act (such as church or government plans, etc.), if you are one of the millions of participants and beneficiaries in employee benefit plans that fall under the Act's protection, you have certain rights if your claim for benefits is denied. Your plan must give you the reason for denial in writing and in a manner you can understand. It also must give you a reasonable opportunity for a fair and full review of the decision.

This folder outlines the steps you may take to file a claim and what to do if you are denied benefits.

Obtain a Copy of Your Summary Plan Description

The first step you should take is to carefully read your plan's summary plan description. This is a document which your plan administrator must furnish you. It gives you a detailed summary of your plan—how it works, what benefits it provides, how they may be obtained and how they may be lost. The summary plan description also is required to spell out your rights and protections under ERISA.

Filing Your Claim

You or your beneficiary may be required to first file a claim to receive the benefits you are entitled to under an employee welfare benefit plan or a pension plan. An employee welfare benefit plan is a plan, fund, or program which provides medical, surgical, hospital, sickness, accident, disability, death, severance, unemployment, vacation, apprenticeship, day care center, scholarship funds, pre-paid legal benefits, etc. A pension plan is a fund or program which provides retirement income to employees, or results in a deferral of income by employees for periods extending to the termination of covered employment or beyond. Each plan covered by ERISA must have procedures for filing a claim and must tell you what those procedures are. This information must be included in the summary plan description. If for any reason information concerning the filing of a claim has not been provided, you may give notification that you have a claim by writing to an officer of your employer, or the unit where claims are normally filed, or the plan administrator.

What Your Plan Requires

All plans have standards you must meet to qualify for benefits. Your pension plan will probably say that you must have worked a certain number of years and/or be a certain age before you can start receiving benefits. Some employee welfare benefit plans may require you to file a claim or notify plan administrator immediately when you enter a hospital or see a doctor. Some plans may require that you pay a medical bill and the plan will repay you when it is presented with a copy of the bill marked "paid."

But be sure to contact your plan administrator or other plan official for complete information on filing a claim for your benefits.

Waiting Period

Within 90 days after you have filed a claim for benefits, your plan must tell you whether or not you will receive

Instructions for Claims—Contd.

Instructions for Claims—Contd.

the benefits. Also, if because of special circumstances your plan needs more time to examine your request, it must tell you within the 90 days that additional time is needed, why it is needed and the date by which the plan expects to render a final decision. If your claim is denied, the plan administrator must notify you in writing and explain in detail why it was denied. If you receive no answer at all in 90 days—or 180 days when an extension of time was needed—the claim is considered a denial and you can use the plan's rules for appealing the denial.

What to Do If Your Claim Is Denied

Your claim may have been denied because you are not eligible for benefits under the plan. Perhaps you haven't been a participant long enough, or you are not the required age. Perhaps you needed to file additional information about your claim.

When you have been notified that your claim has been denied, your plan administrator also must tell you how to submit your denied claim for a full and fair review. You have at least 60 days (the plan may provide you with more time) in which to do this. Be sure to include all related information, particularly any additional information or evidence, and get it to the specified person and address.

Reviewing Your Appeal

If review of your appeal is going to take longer than 60 days, you must be notified in writing of the delay. Except where the review is made by a committee or board of trustees which meets at least quarterly, a decision on your appeal must be made within 120 days of your appeal.

Once the final decision has been made, you must be told the reason and the plan rules upon which the decision was based. This explanation must be written in a manner that you can understand. If you do not receive a notice within the waiting time, you can assume that your claim has been denied after it was reviewed.

What to Do If Your Appeal Is Denied

If you disagree with the final decision upon appeal, you may seek legal assistance. You also may wish to get in touch with the Department of Labor concerning your rights under ERISA.

Know Your Plan

By carefully reading your summary plan description and understanding your relationship to your plan, you can be an informed participant. So know your plan, what it requires of you, how to become eligible for its benefits, and what steps you can take to assure that you will receive your earned benefits.

Source: Pension and Welfare Benefits Administration, U.S. Department of Labor, "How to File a Claim for Your Benefits" (Washington, D.C., 1991).

5

ADMINISTRATION
AND ENFORCEMENT

The administration and enforcement of ERISA is almost as complicated as the Act itself. Jurisdiction is divided among the Department of Labor, the Department of the Treasury (IRS), and the PBGC.

The legislative history of ERISA is at least partially responsible for the fragmented administrative arrangement. Four legislative and three nonlegislative congressional committees were involved in various stages of the development of ERISA—Senate Labor and Public Welfare and Senate Finance, House Ways and Means and House Education and Labor, the Joint Economic Committee, the Senate Special Committee on Aging, and the Joint Committee on Internal Revenue Taxation. Each committee had its own ideas about which agency should handle various parts of the law.

The compromise was to give the Labor and Treasury Departments dual jurisdiction over participation, vesting, and funding. When pension plans sought tax-qualified status for deduction purposes, they were to submit information on the participation, vesting, and funding provisions both to the IRS and to the Labor Department. The IRS would determine whether the plan qualified, although the Secretary of Labor could comment on the application if requested by participants in the plan. The IRS also would audit tax-qualified plans when deciding whether a plan should be disqualified.

In 1978 a presidential reorganization plan sought to improve the administration of ERISA by reducing jurisdictional overlap between the Labor Department and the Treasury Department. The plan assigned to the Treasury Department primary jurisdiction over pension plan minimum standards and to the Labor Department primary jurisdiction over pension plan fiduciary obligations. Both departments retained their enforcement powers without change.

The reorganization did not completely quiet doubts about split jurisdiction: legislation has been introduced in Congress several times since 1978 to establish a single agency to enforce ERISA, but without success.

In January 1986, President Reagan established the ERISA Coordinating Committee under the Economic Policy Council to coordinate national retirement income policy and employee benefit issues. The Committee is made up of officials (at assistant secretary level) from the Departments of Justice, Treasury, Commerce, and Health and Human Services. Other federal offices represented include the Office of Management and Budget and the Council of Economic Advisers. The chair is the Assistant Secretary of Labor for Pension and Welfare Benefits.

DEPARTMENT OF LABOR

Department of Labor responsibilities under ERISA are handled by the Office of Pension and Welfare Benefit Programs.

The Labor Department has a broad range of powers to administer and enforce the reporting, disclosure, and fiduciary standards of ERISA. If the plan administrator fails to file one of the reports required by the law, for instance, or files a report rejected by the Department as being inadequate or incomplete, the Department can take a number of actions; it may, for example, retain an independent qualified public accountant to perform an audit, retain an enrolled actuary to prepare actuarial statements, or bring a civil action to enforce the reporting provisions.

Similarly, if a plan administrator has failed to furnish statements to employees on accrued and vested benefits, the Labor Department can compel the administrator to provide the statements.

If a plan fiduciary has breached his or her responsibilities, the Department can sue the fiduciary to make good any losses to the plan or can remove the fiduciary from office.

The Labor Department also has the authority to assess a civil penalty against a person involved with the plan (a "party-in-interest") who engages in a prohibited transaction.

On the other hand, the Labor Department cannot act against plans that violate the participation, vesting, or funding standards of Title I unless requested to do so by the Secretary of the Treasury or by participants, beneficiaries, or fiduciaries of the plan.

The Labor Department can investigate alleged violations of Title I through on-site reviews at the offices of the plan. The Department can also require plans to submit books, reports. and records during such investigations.

The Labor Department also acts on applications for exemptions from the fiduciary rules on prohibited transactions and variances from the reporting requirements.

DEPARTMENT OF THE TREASURY

Compliance with the tax provisions of ERISA is coordinated through the Treasury Department's Office of Employee Plans and Exempt Organizations in the IRS.

Tax-Exempt Status

For pension plan contributions to qualify as tax deductions for the employer and for the benefits to be tax-exempt or tax-deferred to employees, plans must obtain the approval of the IRS. Generally, when a plan seeks tax-qualified status, it submits an "advance determination letter" application to the

IRS. By seeking advance approval, plans have the opportunity to make any changes the IRS requires and still obtain tax deductions for that taxable year.

The Treasury Department gives the Labor Department and the PBGC 45 days in which to comment on the application. The Department of Labor can comment, however, only if requested by the PBGC or 10 employees or 10 percent of the employees affected by the plan, whichever is less.

If the Treasury Department approves the pension plan, the Department of Labor must accept that determination as prima facie evidence of initial compliance by the plan with the participation, vesting, and funding requirements of Title I.

Disqualification

The Treasury Department also has to notify the Labor Department if it intends to disqualify a plan for violations of the participation or vesting standards, and it must allow the Labor Department 60 days in which to comment on the proposed disqualification. If a plan has failed to meet the minimum funding standards of ERISA, the Treasury Department can impose a 10-percent excise tax on the amount of the deficiency, but it also must notify the Labor Department of its intention to impose the tax and allow it to comment on the intended action.

Annual reports are filed with the IRS but serve as a combined report for the IRS, Labor Department, and PBGC.

PENSION BENEFIT GUARANTY CORPORATION

Administration

The PBGC is a self-financing government corporation, headed by a board of directors consisting of the Secretaries of Labor, Treasury, and Commerce. The Secretary of Labor is permanent chair of the board. An executive director appointed by the board of directors oversees the operation and personnel of the PBGC.

ERISA also provides for an advisory committee to be set up to advise the PBGC on policies and procedures, particularly the investment of funds. It also advises on the appointment of trustees in termination procedures and on the question of whether terminated pension plans should be liquidated immediately or continued in operation under a trustee. The advisory committee has seven members appointed from a group of individuals recommended by the board of directors and the President. Two of the members represent employee organizations, two represent employers who maintain pension plans, and three are individuals from the general public.

Purpose

The PBGC was established to carry out the purposes of Title IV, which are as follows:

- Encourage the continuation and maintenance of voluntary pension plans for the benefit of their participants
- Provide for the timely and uninterrupted payment of pension benefits under plans to which Title IV applies
- Maintain insurance premiums established by the PBGC at the lowest level consistent with carrying out its obligations

The PBGC administers the following two pension protection programs:

- A single-employer program covering 31 million people in over 110,000 plans
- A multiemployer program covering 8.2 million people in about 3,000 plans

The premiums collected by the PBGC go into separate "revolving funds"—one for single-employer plans and the other for multiemployer plans. The assets of each revolving fund and of the trust funds made up of assets from terminated plans are managed by investment managers selected by the PBGC through competitive bidding. The investment managers follow guidelines set up by the PBGC.

Terminations

The termination of a pension plan in which the PBGC becomes involved can occur either by the initiative of the plan sponsor or through court action by the PBGC to force an involuntary termination when the PBGC believes such action is necessary to protect either its own interests or those of the plan participants.

Pension plan administrators must notify the PBGC if they intend to terminate their plan. The PBGC then determines whether the pension plan has sufficient assets to meet its obligations.

For plans with sufficient assets, the PBGC authorizes and oversees the distribution of those assets to participants and beneficiaries in accordance with the priorities established by ERISA. Pension plans that cannot meet their benefit obligations are brought under the control of a "termination trustee," which is almost always the PBGC. When the PBGC becomes a trustee, it handles all the administrative details of a plan, such as processing applications for benefits as well as issuing checks to benefit recipients and maintaining records.

The PBGC also has authority to make loans to multiemployer plans whose resources will not support the payment of all basic benefits. If such a plan becomes solvent again, it must begin repaying the loans.

CRIMINAL PENALTIES AND CIVIL ENFORCEMENT

ERISA imposes severe penalties on employers or other employee benefit plan sponsors who violate employee benefit rights safeguarded in the law. ERISA also broadened the opportunities for employees themselves to take actions to protect their benefit rights.

Criminal Penalties

The reporting and disclosure requirements in ERISA are intended to ensure that participants and beneficiaries have considerable information about their plans and benefits and that the federal government has a means of monitoring the plans. Any person willfully failing to comply with these requirements can be fined as much as $5,000, face a prison term of up to one year, or both. A corporation or a union can be fined up to $100,000 for similar violations.

ERISA also seeks to prevent intimidation of employees who might try to protect or enforce their rights under the law. Any person who through coercion or intimidation attempts to stop a participant from exercising his or her rights can be fined $10,000, imprisoned for up to one year, or both.

Civil Actions

A plan administrator who fails to meet the 30-day deadline for responding to a written request for information to which an employee is entitled can be held personally liable to that individual for up to $100 per day in fines for each day over the deadline. The employee or beneficiary can sue to enforce his or her right to information.

Participants in and beneficiaries of employee benefit plans have the right to sue

- To recover benefits
- To enforce or clarify benefit rights
- To enjoin any act violating Title I provisions or the terms of an employee benefit plan
- To obtain relief from violations of Title I

Except for a suit to recover benefits, when a person brings a private action under Title I, he or she must notify the Department of Labor, which has the power to intervene in the case. In deciding whether to intervene in a particular case, the Department considers

- The significance of the issues presented
- The degree to which the Department can contribute to the litigation
- How the case fits in with other Department priorities and responsibilities

Participants and beneficiaries can also sue a fiduciary for a breach of fiduciary duty. If the fiduciary is found guilty of such a breach, the court may require the fiduciary to make good to the plan any losses resulting from the breach and to restore to the plan any profits made through use of the plan's assets. The Department of Labor also has authority to bring an action against a fiduciary for an alleged breach of fiduciary responsibility.

The IRS has the authority to assess a civil penalty against a party-in-interest involved in a prohibited transaction. The penalty, in the form of an excise tax, cannot exceed 5 percent of the amount involved in the transaction. If there is no correction of the transaction within 90 days, however, an additional penalty of up to 100 percent of the amount involved can be assessed.

The IRS is authorized under ERISA to fine an employer $25 per day for failure to file an annual return for pension plans, cafeteria plans, and group legal and educational assistance plans. The maximum penalty that can be levied is $15,000. In addition, the Omnibus Budget Reconciliation Act of 1987 authorized the Department of Labor to assess a penalty of up to $1,000 per day (with no maximum) on any employer that fails to file the required plan information. Also subject to the Department of Labor fine is any plan that has been rejected because its annual report contains insufficient information.

Annual reports (Form 5500s) are filed with the IRS, which forwards the information to the Department of Labor. Thus, each agency can levy a penalty for failure to report.

ERISA Preemption Clause

A major congressional goal in the enactment of ERISA was the replacement of an often confusing and inconsistent system of state-by-state regulation of employee benefit plans with a comprehensive federal law covering such benefit programs. This intent is expressed in Section 514(a), ERISA's preemption clause. Section 514(a) states, in part: "The provisions of this title . . . shall supersede any and all state laws insofar as they may now or hereafter relate to any employee benefit plan."

However, another clause of Section 514 exempts or "saves" from preemption those state laws that regulate insurance, the so-called "savings clause" (Section 514(b)(2)(A)). Another clause, Section 514(b)(2)(B), states that employee benefit plans will not be deemed to be in the business of insurance and thus subject to state insurance regulation (the "deemer clause").

In deciding a number of cases that hinge on the issue of ERISA preemption, the U.S. Supreme Court has broadly interpreted the provision. In 1985, the Court distinguished between insured plans (for which state regulation was *not* preempted by ERISA) and self-funded plans that are subject only to ERISA. The Court said that self-insured plans would be subject to state regulation only if they were deemed part of the insurance industry (*Metropolitan Life Insurance Co. v. Massachusetts*, 471 U.S. 724).

In 1987, in *Pilot Life Insurance Co. v. Dedeaux* (481 U.S. 41), the U.S. Supreme Court unanimously ruled that with the passage of ERISA, Congress intended for all legal disputes over employee benefits to be decided in the federal courts. The Court said: "The policy choices reflected in the inclusion of certain remedies and the exclusion of others under the federal scheme would be completely undermined if ERISA-plan participants and beneficiaries were free to obtain remedies under state law that Congress rejected in ERISA."

The ruling meant health insurers were exempt from state laws that permit juries to assess punitive damages against an insurer that was found to have improperly denied a claim. If an employee was successful in contending that a denied medical claim should have been reimbursed, under ERISA that employee could recover only the cost of the treatment, not punitive damages. The effect of the decision was to make it more difficult for workers to obtain legal counsel to challenge denied claims.

Also in 1987, in a 5-to-4 decision, the U.S. Supreme Court said that ERISA preempts any state laws that "relate" to an employee benefit plan. The Court held that a Maine law requiring severance payments to workers in the event of a plant closing was *not* preempted by ERISA. The reasoning was that the severance was paid out in a one-time lump sum and thus was not an employee benefit plan as defined by ERISA. The payment did not constitute an employee benefit plan—ongoing benefits on a continuous basis (*Fort Halifax Packing Co. v. Coyne,* 482 U.S. 1).

These decisions hardly closed the door on further litigation testing this concept, although the Court has held to its basic position on ERISA preempting state laws for most employee benefit situations.

APPENDIX 1

PBGC Form 1*

<table>
<tr><td>

PBGC Form 1
Pension Benefit
Guaranty Corporation
1992
</td><td>

Annual Premium Payment
For Plan Years Beginning in Calendar Year 1992
See the 1992 Premium Payment Package for the Instructions for Form 1
</td><td>

Approved OMB 1212-0009
Expires 6/30/93
For PBGC Use Only
</td></tr>
</table>

1. Plan Sponsor   *Check for Address Change* ☐ | **2. Plan Administrator**

(a) Name | *(a) Name*

(b) Address | *(b) Address*

(c) City   *(d) State*   *(e) Zip* | *(c) City*   *(d) State*   *(e) Zip*

3. *Plan Sponsor's Employer Identification Number (EIN)*   *Plan Number (PN)*
(a) ☐☐☐☐☐☐☐☐☐ (b) ☐☐☐
Enter 9 Digit EIN   Enter 3 Digit PN
(c) Does EIN/PN match entry on 1991 Form 5500?
   Yes ☐   *No* ☐ *If no, attach explanation.*

4. *If* either the EIN or PN in item 3 is *NOT* the same as on prior premium filing, enter both prior EIN and prior PN.
(a) ☐☐☐☐☐☐☐☐☐ (b) ☐☐☐
Enter 9 Digit EIN   Enter 3 Digit PN
(c) ☐ EIN/PN Change *or* (d) ☐ Change Due to Merger
(e) ☐ Effective Date (*Month/Day/Year*) ☐☐☐

5. Coverage Status
(Check only one)
(a) ☐ Covered
(b) ☐ Uncertain

(If uncertain you must file. See instructions.)

6. Filing Status *(Check any applicable)*
(a) First plan filing................................. ☐ *Yes* ☐ *No*
(b) Terminated Plan .... ☐ *Yes* ☐ *No*
   If yes, enter applicable month/day/year of:
(1) *Date assets distributed* .... ☐☐
(2) *Date trustee appointed under ERISA section 4042* ...... ☐☐

7. Plan Date
Month/Day/Year

8. Industry Code
☐☐☐☐
Enter 4 digits

9. Name of Plan

10. Name and telephone number of plan contact

(a) Name

(b) Area code and phone number

* This form is revised yearly.

135

PBGC Form 1—Contd.

11. Plan type: *(Check appropriate box to indicate type of plan and type of filing.)*

    (a) ☐ Multiemployer Plan   (b) ☐ Single-Employer Plan *(includes Multiple Employer Plan)*

12. This premium is for the plan year beginning (Month/Day/Year) .... ⬚   92

    If the plan year has changed since last filing with PBGC, check here ☐

13. Enter PARTICIPANT COUNT for plan year specified in Line 12 .... | 13 |

    (If this count does not equal the count on your 1991 Form 5500,

    enter the count from your 1991 Form 5500 .... ————)

14. MULTIEMPLOYER plans: *Multiply line 13 by the $2.60 premium rate and enter amount* .... | 14 |

15. SINGLE-EMPLOYER plans: *Compute your premium as indicated below:*

    (a) Flat rate portion: *Multiply the participant count on line 13 by $19* .... | 15a |

    (b) Variable rate portion: *From Schedule A, line 9* .... | 15b |

    (c) Total Premium: *Add lines 15(a) and 15(b). Enter amount* .... | 15c |

16. Premium credits: *(See instructions)* .... | 16 |

17. Enter net amount of premium due. *If amount on line 14 or 15(c) is LARGER than the amount*
    on line 16, SUBTRACT line 16 from line 14 or 15(c) and enter amount due on line 17 ..... | 17 |

    Enter *amount of check payable to Pension Benefit Guaranty Corporation:* .... $ _____

    Mail Form 1 (including Schedule A for single-employer plans) and check to:

    Pension Benefit Guaranty Corporation, P.O. Box 105655, Atlanta, GA 30348-5655

        Note: Each plan requires a separate Form 1 and a separate check. Put the EIN/PN shown in item 3 on the check.

        (For delivery services requiring street address, see Part D1 of instructions.)

18. Overpayment. *If amount on line 16 is LARGER than the amount on line 14 or 15(c),*
    enter amount of overpayment: .... $ _____

    Do you want overpayment refunded to you or credited against next year's premium? Check one: ☐ *refund* ☐ *credit.*

19. *If you have any attachments, other than Schedule A, check here:* ☐   *Put plan name (item 9) and EIN/PIN (item 3) on each sheet.*

20. Multiemployer Plan Declaration. *(NOTE: <u>All</u> SINGLE-EMPLOYER Plan Administrators MUST sign the certification in Item 10 of Schedule A.)* Under penalties of perjury (18 U.S.C. 1001), I declare that I have examined this filing, and to the best of my knowledge and belief it is true, correct and complete.

_____   _____

Signature of Multiemployer Plan Administrator   *Date*

PBGC Form 1—Contd.

Part A INTRODUCTION

1. What Are PBGC Form 1 And Form 1-ES?

The Form 1 (including Schedule A to Form 1) and Form 1-ES are forms used to pay premiums to the Pension Benefit Guaranty Corporation (PBGC) as required by sections 4006 and 4007 of the Employee Retirement Income Security Act, as amended (ERISA), and the PBGC's Payment of Premiums regulation (29 CFR Part 2610).

The Form 1-ES is used by all plans that reported 500 or more participants on their 1991 PBGC Form 1 to make their initial 1992 premium payments (only the flat rate portion of the premium for single-employer plans) and permits the initial premium calculation to be based on an estimated participant count. These plans use the Form 1 to make a subsequent reconciliation filing and, for single-employer plans, to pay the variable rate portion of the premium, both based on an actual participant count. (NOTE: If all the information needed to file Form 1 is known before the First Filing Due Date, you should file a Form 1 instead of a Form 1-ES. If you file a Form 1-ES, you will still be required to file a Form 1 by the Final Filing Due Date.) Plans with fewer than 500 participants file the Form 1 only, with their total premium payment, by the Final Filing Due Date.

It is the responsibility of the plan administrator to obtain and complete the Form 1 and Form 1-ES, as applicable, and make the premium payment each year. The PBGC will permit the use of re-typed or other facsimile forms. However, any such forms must present the same information in the same location as on the PBGC forms. (Any signatures or initials required from the plan administrator or enrolled actuary must be filed in original form.) The instructions in this pamphlet describe how to complete Form 1 and Form 1-ES and make the premium payment due.

2. Definitions

In these instructions -

"ERISA" means the Employee Retirement Income Security Act of 1974, as amended (29 U.S.C. 1001, et seq.).

"Code" means the Internal Revenue Code of 1986, as amended.

"First Filing Due Date" means the last day of the 2nd full calendar month following the close of the preceding plan year, except that, in the case of plans changing plan years, it is the later of the last day of the 2nd full calendar month following the close of the preceding plan year or 30 days following the date on which a plan amendment was adopted changing the

plan year. See Part C for plans that must file a Form 1-ES on a "First Filing Due Date".

"Final Filing Due Date" means the 15th day of the 8th full calendar month following the month in which the plan year began except:

a. In the case of plans filing for the first time it is the latest of the following dates-

(i) the 15th day of the 8th full calendar month following the month in which the plan year began, or if later, in which the plan became effective for benefit accruals for future service,

(ii) 90 days after the date of the plan's adoption,

(iii) 90 days after the date on which the plan became covered under ERISA section 4021.

b. In the case of plans changing plan years, it is the later of the 15th day of the 8th full calendar month following the month in which the plan year began, or 30 days after the date on which a plan amendment was adopted changing the plan year.

See Part C for plans that must file a Form 1 on a "Final Filing Due Date".

"Filing Due Date" means either of the filing dates defined above.

"Form 1" means the Annual Premium Payment Form 1 issued by the PBGC and, includes, for single-employer plans, the Schedule A.

"Form 1-ES" means the Estimated Premium Payment Form 1-ES issued by the PBGC for estimating the flat rate portion of the premium for single-employer plans   and the total premium for multiemployer plans.

"Schedule A" means the schedule to the Form 1 which is used by single-employer plans only to calculate unfunded vested benefits and compute the variable rate portion of the premium.

"Flat rate portion of the premium" means the portion of the single-employer premium determined by multiplying the flat rate premium charge by the number of participants in the plan on the last day of the preceding plan year or, for a new or newly covered plan, the first day of the current plan year. The flat rate charge for single-employer plans for plan years beginning in 1992 is $19 per participant.

"Variable rate portion of the premium" means the portion of the single-employer premium based on a plan's unfunded vested benefits and determined by multiplying the variable rate charge by the number of plan participants. The variable rate charge for plan years beginning in 1992 is $9 for every $1,000 (or fraction thereof) of unfunded vested benefits, with that product divided by the number of plan participants. The variable rate charge is subject to a cap of, generally, $53 per participant for plan years beginning in 1992.

PBGC Form 1—Contd.

"Premium payment year" means the plan year for which the premium is being paid.

"Premium regulation" means the PBGC's regulation on Payment of Premiums (29 CFR Part 2610). The Form 1-ES and Form 1 and these instructions are issued under and implement the premium regulation.

"Form 5500 series" means Form 5500 and 5500C/R, Annual Return/Report of Employee Benefit Plan, jointly developed by the Internal Revenue Service, the Department of Labor and the PBGC. (Copies of this form may be obtained from the Department of Labor or the Internal Revenue Service.)

"We" or "us" means the Pension Benefit Guaranty Corporation.

"You" or "your" means the administrator of a pension plan.

"Plan administrator" means: (a) the person specifically so designated by the terms of the instrument under which the plan is operated; or (b) if an administrator is not so designated, the plan sponsor.

"EIN" means Employer Identification Number. It is always a 9-digit number assigned by the Internal Revenue Service for income tax purposes.

"PN" means Plan Number. This is always a 3-digit number. The plan sponsor assigns this number to distinguish among employee benefit plans established or maintained by the same plan sponsor. A plan sponsor usually starts numbering pension plans at "001" and uses consecutive Plan Numbers for each additional plan. Once a PN is assigned, always use it to identify the same plan. If a plan is terminated, retire the PN - do not use it for another plan.

3. Recordkeeping Requirements; PBGC Audits

Plan administrators are required to retain all plan records that are necessary to support or validate PBGC premium payments. The records must include calculations and other data prepared by the plan's actuary or, for a plan described in section 412(i) of the Internal Revenue Code, by the insurer from which the insurance contracts are purchased. The records are to be kept for six years after the premium due date.

Records that must be retained include, but are not limited to, records that establish the number of plan participants, that reconcile the calculation of the plan's unfunded vested benefits with the actuarial valuation upon which the calculation was based, and, for plans that assert entitlement to the reduction in the cap on the variable rate portion of the premium, that demonstrate the methods and assumptions used by the plan during the base period with respect to calculating its maximum deductible contribution pursuant to section 404 of the Code. Records retained pursuant to this paragraph must be made available to the PBGC upon request for inspection and photocopying.

The PBGC may audit any premium payment. If PBGC determines upon audit that the full amount of the premium due was not paid, late payment interest charges under § 2610.7 of the premium regulation and the late payment penalty charges under § 2610.8 of the premium regulation shall apply to the unpaid balance from the premium due date to the date of payment. If, in the judgment of the PBGC, the plan's records fail to establish the number of participants with respect to whom premiums were required for any premium payment year, the PBGC may rely on data it obtains from other sources (including the Internal Revenue Service and the Department of Labor) for presumptively establishing the number of plan participants for premium computation purposes. Similarly, if, in the PBGC's judgment, the plan's records fail to establish that the unfunded vested benefits were the amount reported in the premium filing, the variable rate portion of the premium owed with respect to that premium payment may be deemed to be the maximum $53 per participant charge.

Part B   WHO MUST FILE

1. General Rule

The plan administrator of each single-employer plan and multiemployer plan covered under section 4021 of ERISA is required annually to file the Form 1 and, if applicable, Form 1-ES, and pay the premium due. If you are uncertain whether your plan is covered under section 4021, you should promptly request a coverage determination by writing to us at the address shown in Part D. A request for a coverage determination does not extend the due date for any premium that is finally determined to be due. If we determine that the plan is not a covered plan, we will review the plan's premium payments to determine whether any refunds may be made.

2. Terminating Plans

a. <u>Obligation To File</u>. The obligation to file the PBGC Form 1 and Form 1-ES and make the required premium payments continues until the end of the plan year in which all plan assets are distributed pursuant to the plan's termination, or a trustee for the terminating plan is appointed under ERISA section 4042, whichever occurs first.

b. <u>Refunds</u>. Any required premium payments are for a full plan year. You may not prorate the premium for the plan's final (short) plan year. However, you may request a refund for that plan year. The PBGC will determine the amount of the refund by prorating the premium for the short plan year on a monthly basis (treating a part of a month as a full month). For this purpose, the PBGC will treat the short plan year as ending on --

PBGC Form 1—Contd.

(i) for a multiemployer plan that distributed all its assets pursuant to section 4041A of ERISA, the date the distribution is completed; or

(ii) for a single-employer plan, the earlier of the dates described in (A) or (B) below:

(A) the date on which the distribution of the plan's assets was completed, or, if later, the date 30 days prior to the date the PBGC received the plan's post-distribution certification;

(B) the date that a trustee for the terminating plan was appointed under ERISA section 4042.

To request a refund, write promptly, under separate cover, to the address shown in Part D, Item 2. Enclose a copy of the Form 1 that you filed. We will calculate the amount of your refund.

If a plan terminates and a new plan is established, premiums are due for the terminated plan as described above, and premiums are also due for the new plan from the first day of its first plan year (see Part C, Item 2).

Example 1

A plan with a plan year beginning January 1, 1991, and ending December 31, 1991, terminates in a standard termination on September 30, 1991. On April 8, 1992, all assets are distributed and the PBGC is notified within 30 days. Since the terminating plan is sufficient to pay all benefit liabilities, no trusteeship is involved. The plan administrator must file and make the premium payments for the 1991 plan year and for the 1992 plan year. However, the plan administrator may request a refund for the short 1992 plan year, January 1, 1992 - April 7, 1992. A refund will be made for the period of May - December 1992.

Example 2

A plan with a plan year beginning July 1, 1991 and ending on June 30, 1992, terminates in a distress termination on April 29, 1992. On July 31, 1992, a trustee is appointed to administer the plan under ERISA section 4042. This plan is required to file and make premium payments for both the 1991 and 1992 plan years, because a trustee was not appointed until after the beginning of the 1992 plan year. However, the plan administrator may request a refund for the short 1992 plan year, July 1, 1992 - July 31, 1992. A refund will be made for the period of August 1992 - June 1993.

Part C   WHEN TO FILE

1. General Rule

The following table shows the filing due dates for the 1992 premium payment year.

Filing Due Dates

Premium Payment Year Begins	Form 1-ES Due Date (By Day of Month Plan Year Begins)		Form 1 Filing Due Date
	1st Day	2nd-End	
Jan 1992	03/02/92	03/31/92	09/15/92
Feb 1992	03/31/92	04/30/92	10/15/92
Mar 1992	04/30/92	06/01/92	11/16/92
Apr 1992	06/01/92	06/30/92	12/15/92
May 1992	06/30/92	07/31/92	01/15/93
Jun 1992	07/31/92	08/31/92	02/16/93
Jul 1992	08/31/92	09/30/92	03/15/93
Aug 1992	09/30/92	11/02/92	04/15/93
Sept 1992	11/02/92	11/30/92	05/17/93
Oct 1992	11/30/92	12/31/92	06/15/93
Nov 1992	12/31/92	02/01/93	07/15/93
Dec 1992	02/01/93	03/01/93	08/16/93

Your due date for filing the Form 1 and, if applicable, Form 1-ES and paying the premium owed depends on the number of plan participants as of the last day of the second plan year preceding the premium payment year. This number is the participant count required to be reported on the Form 1 for the plan year preceding the year for which you make the filing (i.e., for 1992 premiums, the participant count on the 1991 Form 1). NOTE: The participant count date for purposes of determining your Filing Due Date is different from the participant count date used for computing the premium (see Part G).

Plans that were required to report 500 or more participants on the preceding year's Form 1 must generally file a Form 1-ES by the last day of the second full calendar month following the close of the preceding plan year ("First Filing Due Date") and a Form 1 by the 15th day of the eighth full calendar month following the month in which the plan year began ("Final Filing Due Date"). For single-employer plans, only the flat rate portion of the premium is due by the First Filing Due Date; the variable rate portion is due by the Final Filing Due Date. For multiemployer plans, the entire premium is due by the First Filing Due Date.

Plans that reported fewer than 500 participants on the preceding year's Form 1 are required to file the Form 1 and pay the entire premium due by the 15th day of the 8th full calendar month following the month in which the plan year began.

The premium owed for a plan year is based on the number of plan participants as of the last day of the preceding plan year. However, plans may not have an accurate participant count before the First Filing Due Date. For this reason, the Form 1-ES permits plans to compute the amount owed on the basis of an estimated participant count. However, we remind you that for plans with 500 or more participants, the total flat rate portion of the premium, in the case of a single-

PBGC Form 1—Contd.

employer plan, or the entire premium, in the case of a multiemployer plan, is due by the First Filing Due Date. If the full amount due is not paid by that date, the plan will be subject to late payment interest and penalty charges (see Part F).

You may avoid a late payment penalty charge (but not the interest) (see Part F) for the flat rate portion of the premium if you do two things:

a. First, you must pay 100 percent of the premium amount due on the plan's Final Filing Due Date for the $19 per participant flat rate portion of the single-employer premium or the $2.60 per participant multiemployer total premium; and

b. Second, the premium based on an estimated participant count that you pay with the Form 1-ES by the First Filing Due Date must equal at least the *lesser* of:

(i) 90 percent of the premium amount due on the plan's Final Filing Due Date for the $19 per participant flat rate portion of the single-employer premium or the $2.60 per participant multiemployer premium, or

(ii) an amount equal to the participant count for the PBGC Form 1 for the year before this premium payment year multiplied by $19 for single-employer plans and $2.60 for multiemployer plans.

If you have an accurate participant count by the First Filing Due Date, you should pay the amount owed by that date. If you do this, you will avoid the interest and penalty charges. If you have all the information needed to file Form 1 on or before the First Filing Due Date, you should file a Form 1. If you file a Form 1-ES, you will still be required to file a Form 1 by the Final Filing Due Date. (A single-employer plan that files a Form 1 with its first payment but does not include the variable rate portion of the premium, will have to file another Form 1, identified as an "Amended Filing," with that payment by the Final Filing Due Date.)

2. Plans Filing For The First Time

a. First Filing Due Date. New and newly covered plans are not required to pay an estimated premium by a First Filing Due Date.

b. Final Filing Due Date. For all new and newly covered plans, regardless of the number of plan participants, that have NOT previously been required to file a Form 1 and pay premiums to us, the Final Filing Due Date is the latest of the following dates:

(i) the 15th day of the 8th full calendar month following the month in which the plan year began, or if later, following the month in which the plan first became effective for benefit accruals for future service (see Examples 1 and 2),

(ii) 90 days after the date of the plan's adoption (see Example 3), or

(iii) 90 days after the date on which the plan became covered under ERISA section 4021 (see Example 4).

c. Refunds. Any required premium payments are for a full plan year. Thus, you must pay a full year's premium payment for the plan's first plan year, even if it is a short plan year (e.g., a new plan maintained on a calendar year basis becomes effective for benefit accruals for future service on July 1, 1992). However, you may request a refund for the plan's first (short) plan year by writing promptly, under separate cover, to the address shown in Part D, Item 2. Enclose a copy of the Form 1 that you filed. We will calculate the amount of the refund by prorating the premium for the short plan year on a monthly basis (treating a part of a month as a full month.)

| Example 1 | A new plan has a plan year beginning January 1, 1992, and ending December 31, 1992. |

The plan was adopted October 1, 1991, and became effective for benefit accruals January 1, 1992. The Final Filing Due Date is September 15, 1992.

| Example 2 | A new plan is adopted on December 1, 1992, and has a July 1 - June 30 plan year. |

The plan became effective for benefit accruals for future service on December 1, 1992. The Final Filing Due Date for the plan's first year, July 1, 1992, through June 30, 1993, is August 16, 1992, because August 15 is a Sunday. The plan owes a premium for all of 1992, and may request a refund for the period of July 1992 through November 1992.

| Example 3 | A new plan has a plan year beginning January 1, 1992, and ending December 31, 1992. |

The plan was adopted on September 15, 1992, with a retroactive effective date of January 1, 1992. The Final Filing Due Date is December 14, 1992.

| Example 4 | A professional service employer maintains a plan with a plan year beginning on January 1, 1992, and |

ending December 31, 1992. If this type of plan has always had fewer than 25 participants it is not a covered plan under ERISA section 4021. On October 15, 1992, the plan, which always had under 25 participants, has 26 participants. It is now a covered plan and will continue to be a covered plan regardless of the plan's future participant count. The Final Filing Due Date is January 13, 1993.

3. Plans Filing For the Second Time

The due date rules for plans filing for their second (or second covered) plan year are the same as the General Rule under Item 1, with one exception. For these plans, the determination of whether the plan has

PBGC Form 1—Contd.

500 or more participants is made as of the first day of the preceding plan year, i.e., the first day of the plan's first (or first covered) plan year. For plans in their second premium payment year, this is the participant count required to be reported on the preceding year's Form 1.

| Example 1 | A single-employer plan has a plan year beginning on July 1st and ending on June 30th. It had a participant |

count of 950 as of the first day of its first year, July 1, 1991. The First Filing Due Date for the plan's 1992 (its second) plan year is August 31, 1992, and the plan must generally file a Form 1-ES by that date, using an estimated participant count for determining the flat rate portion of the premium. The plan must file its Form 1 and pay any outstanding balance of the flat rate portion of the premium plus the variable rate portion by the Final Filing Due Date, which is March 15, 1993.

| Example 2 | A multiemployer plan has a plan year beginning on July 15th and ending on July 14th. It had a participant count |

of 1,500 as of the first day of the plan' first year, July 15, 1991. The First Filing Due Date for the plan's 1992 (its second) plan year is September 30, 1992, and the plan must generally file a Form 1-ES on that date, using an estimated participant count for determining the amount of the premium. The plan must make a final, reconciliation filing on Form 1 by the Final Filing Due Date, which is March 15, 1993.

| Example 3 | A plan had a participant count of 300 as of the first day of the plan's first year. This plan has a plan year |

beginning on April 1st and ending on March 31st. For the plan year beginning April 1, 1992 (its second plan year), the plan must file Form 1 by the Final Filing Due Date, which is December 15, 1992.

4. Plans Changing Plan Years

a. <u>Due Dates</u>. Plans that change their plan year as the result of a plan amendment must, for the short plan year, follow the due date rules described in Items 1, 2, and 3 above, as applicable.

(i) For the plan year following the short plan year, the First Filing Due Date is the later of:

(A) the last day of the second full calendar month following the close of the short plan year, or

(B) 30 days after the date on which the plan amendment changing the plan year is adopted.

(ii) For the plan year following the short plan year, the Final Filing Due Date is the later of:

(A) the 15th day of the 8th full calendar month following the month in which the plan year begins, or

(B) 30 days after the date on which the plan amendment changing the plan year is adopted.

b. <u>Refunds</u>. Each plan year's premium filing(s) and payment(s) must reflect and be based on a full 12-month plan year. You may not prorate the premium for the short plan year. When a change in plan year resulting from a plan amendment results in a duplicate or overlapping premium payment, you may request a refund. To request a refund, write promptly, under separate cover, to the address shown in Part D, Item 2. Enclose copies of the relevant Forms 1 that you filed. We will then calculate the amount of your refund by prorating the premium for the short plan year on a monthly basis (treating a part of a month as a full month).

| Example 1 | By plan amendment adopted on December 1, 1991, a plan changes from a plan year beginning January 1 |

to a plan year beginning June 1. This results in a short plan year beginning January 1, 1992, and ending May 31, 1992. The plan always has fewer than 500 participants. The Final Filing Due Date for the short plan year is September 15, 1992. The Final Filing Due Date for the new plan year beginning on June 1, 1992, is February 15, 1993. The plan owes a full year's premium for the short plan year, and may request a refund for the period June through December of 1992.

| Example 2 | By plan amendment adopted on October 1, 1992, and made retroactively effective to February 1, |

1992, a plan changes from a plan year beginning on January 1 to a plan year beginning on February 1. The plan always has fewer than 500 participants. The Final Filing Due Date for the plan year that began on January 1, 1992, is September 15, 1992. The Final Filing Due Date for the new plan year, which began February 1, 1992, is November 2, 1992, since October 31st is a Saturday. The plan owes a full year's premium for the short plan year, and may request a refund for the period February through December of 1992.

| Example 3 | By plan amendment adopted on June 1, 1992, and made retroactively effective to April 1, 1992, a plan |

changes from a plan year beginning January 1 to a plan year beginning April 1. The plan always has 500 or more participants. The First Filing Due Date for the short plan year is March 2, 1992, because February 29, 1992, is a Saturday, and the Final Filing Due Date is September 15, 1992. The First Filing Due Date for the new plan year, which began April 1, 1992, is July 1, 1992, which is the later of the end of the second full calendar month after the close of the short plan year or 30 days after adoption of the plan amendment. The Final Filing Due Date is December 15, 1992. The plan

PBGC Form 1—Contd.

owes a full year's premium for the short plan year, and may request a refund for the period April through December of 1992.

5. Saturday, Sunday And Federal Holiday

a. Filing Due Dates. In computing any period of time described in the premium regulation and these instructions, the day of the event or default from which the period of time begins to run is not counted. The last day of the period is counted, unless it falls on a Saturday, Sunday or Federal holiday, in which event the period runs until the end of the next day which is not a Saturday, Sunday or Federal holiday.

> Example | Plans with plan years beginning on March 1, 1992, normally would have a Final Filing Due Date of November 15, 1992. Because that day is a Sunday, the due date is Monday, November 16, 1992.

b. Interest and Penalty Charges. When computing late payment interest and penalty charges, Saturdays, Sundays and Federal holidays are included.

6. Postmark Date Is Controlling

We will consider that you filed Form 1 or Form 1-ES and your premium payment on the date on which the mailing envelope is postmarked by the United States Postal Service. If the envelope does not contain a legible Postal Service postmark, we will consider that you filed the form and payment on the date that is three days before the date on which we receive it. We will disregard any private postage meter date.

7. Relationship Between Form 1 And Form 5500 Series

a. Due Dates. For many plans, the deadline for filing the Form 1 and the Form 5500 series may coincide. This occurs when a corporate plan sponsor takes the automatic 6-month extension for filing its corporate tax return. This extension automatically extends the due date for filing the Form 5500 series to the tax due date.

> Example | A calendar year plan has a Final Filing Due Date for the Form 1 of September 15th. The corporate tax deadline for a calendar year tax year is March 15th and the corporate plan sponsor takes the automatic extension to September 15th. This would make the due date for the Form 5500 series (which is normally July 31st for a calendar year plan) also September 15th. NOTE: Extensions of time to file the Form 5500 series do not extend the Filing Due Dates for the PBGC forms.

b. Participant Count. Further, the participant count for premium computation purposes for the PBGC Form 1 and the participant count for the Form 5500 series filed in the same year (1992 Form 1 and 1991 Form 5500) are generally determined as of the

same date, i.e., the last day of the plan year preceding the year of the filing, and therefore, these numbers should generally be the same. (But see Part G, Item 13.c.)

c. Plan Years Covered By Forms. However, there is a CRITICAL DIFFERENCE between the two filings. The Form 1 is filed for the current plan year and the Form 5500 series is filed for the previous plan year.

Part D   ADDRESSES

1. Where To File Form 1 And Form 1-ES

a. Mail Service. Mail Form 1 and Form 1-ES with your premium payment(s) to:

Pension Benefit Guaranty Corporation
P.O. Box 105655
Atlanta, GA 30348-5655

Do not use this address for any purpose except to mail Form 1 and Form 1-ES and your premium payment(s).

b. Delivery Service. Alternatively, if you use a delivery service that does not deliver to a P.O. Box, the Form 1 and Form 1-ES, along with your premium payment, may be hand-delivered to:

NationsBank Retail Lockbox Processing Center
PBGC Lockbox 105655
6000 Feldwood Road
5 Southside East
College Park, GA 30349

2. Where To Obtain Form 1 And Form 1-ES

a. PBGC Mailing. We will mail a Premium Payment Package containing a Form 1-ES and Form 1 and a Schedule A to the plan sponsor of each plan that filed a Form 1 the previous year. We will mail these forms to the address shown in Item 1 of the Form 1, at least 45 days before the expected Filing Due Date.

b. Form Requests.

(i) *Plan Administrator.* If you do not receive a package, it is your responsibility to obtain it. To do so or if you need extra copies, contact:

Pension Benefit Guaranty Corporation
FOD/Premium Operations Division (33700)
2020 K Street, NW
Washington, DC 20006-1860
Phone: (202) 778-8825

This is not a toll-free number. We cannot accept collect calls.

You may also obtain extra copies of the Premium Payment Package and forms from the Pension and Welfare Benefits Administration of the U.S. Department of Labor (see addresses following the instructions).

(ii) *Pension Practitioner.* If you are a pension practitioner serving many covered plans, you may

PBGC Form 1—Contd.

wish to receive a single copy (for duplicating) or a bulk shipment of the Premium Payment Package and forms. If so, complete the order blank at the end of this Premium Payment Package. Check the appropriate box at the bottom of the order blank.

c. Facsimile. You may photocopy Form 1 and Schedule A, and Form 1-ES. If you send us a photocopy, it must be signed in ink. We will not accept a photocopy of your signature. The PBGC will permit the use of re-typed or other facsimile forms. However, any such forms must present the same information in the same location as on the PBGC forms.

d. Forms For Prior Years. If you are filing for previous years, you may use the current Form 1 and other premium forms, but at the top of the form, you should write the year for which you are filing. However, if the forms are not the same, be sure to include all information required on the previous form.

3. Where To Get Help In Filing The Form 1 Or Form 1-ES

If you have any questions concerning your filing, including questions about the variable rate portion of the single-employer premium, you should contact us at the address or phone number given in Item 2 above.

4. Where To Get A Coverage Determination

If you have any questions concerning whether your plan is covered or wish to obtain a coverage determination, promptly contact:

Pension Benefit Guaranty Corporation
CO/CD Administrative Review and Technical Assistance Division (45400)
2020 K Street, NW
Washington, DC 20006-1860
Phone: (202) 778-8800

This is not a toll-free number. We cannot accept collect calls.

Part E   HOW TO CORRECT A FILING

1. Check Without A Form 1 Or Form 1-ES

If you inadvertently sent in your check without the Form 1 or Form 1-ES, as applicable, send the correct form to the address shown in Part D, Item 2.

2. Form Without A Check

If you inadvertently sent us Form 1 or Form 1-ES without enclosing your check, we will return your form to you. Enclose your check with the returned form and mail them to the address shown in Part D, Item 1.

3. Amended Filing-Premium Underpayment

If you discover after you have filed a Form 1 and Schedule A with us that you have inadvertently made an error in your participant count or in the calculation of the variable rate portion of the premium due, you may use the extra forms in this booklet (or use a photocopy of the forms in this booklet) to file an amended Form 1 and Schedule A. (Multiemployer plans need to file only an amended Form 1.) Print or type at the top of the Form 1 and Schedule A "AMENDED FILING". Fill in the Form 1 and Schedule A as you would for your annual filing. Enter the correct total in Item 15(a) for the flat rate portion of the premium and the correct variable rate amount in Item 15(b) and enter the total of Items 15(a) and 15(b) in Item 15(c). (For multiemployer plans, enter the corrected premium amount in Item 14.) Subtract from this result the amount previously paid as shown in Item 16 and enter the difference in Item 17. Write the amount of your check for the net amount of the premium due in the space provided for "CHECK for $____" on the Form 1. Mail your amended Form 1 and Schedule A and check to the address shown in Part D, Item 1.

4. Amended Filing-Premium Overpayment

If you discover after you have filed a Form 1 and Schedule A with us that you overpaid your premium, follow the instructions in Item 3, except that the difference between the amount owed and the amount previously paid should be entered in Item 18. Also, you must check the appropriate box indicating whether you want this amount refunded to you or credited against your premium for next year. If you fail to check either of the boxes, we will automatically credit the overpayment against next year's premium. Mail your amended Form 1 and Schedule A promptly to the address shown in Part D, Item 2.

5. How to Correct An Address

See Part G, Item 1 if you need to correct your address and are doing so at the same time you are making your premium filing.

However, to keep our records current and to ensure that your forms will be mailed to the correct address, you should provide us with your current address as soon as a change has occurred. You may do so by contacting us either in writing or by phone using the information found in Part D, Item 2.

Part F   LATE PAYMENT CHARGES

If we receive a premium payment after the Filing Due Date, we will bill the plan for the appropriate Late Payment Charges. The charges include both interest and penalty charges. The charges are based on

PBGC Form 1—Contd.

the outstanding premium amount due at the Filing Due Date.

1. Interest Charges

The Late Payment Interest Charge is set by ERISA and cannot be waived by us. The interest rate charged is established periodically (currently on a quarterly basis) and the interest rates are published in Appendix A to the premium regulation.

Late Payment Interest Charges will be assessed for any premium amount not paid when due, whether because of an estimated participant count or an erroneous participant count or other mistake in computing the premium owed.

2. Penalty Charges

The Late Payment Penalty Charge is established by us, subject to ERISA's restriction that the penalty not exceed 100 percent of the unpaid amount. Currently, the Late Payment Penalty Charge is the greater of:

a. 5 percent per month (or fraction thereof) of the unpaid premium, or

b. $25.00,

but not more than 100 percent of the unpaid premium. (Penalty charges for premiums due for plan years prior to 1984 may be found in § 2610.8 of the premium regulation.)

3. PBGC Waivers

Prior to the Filing Due Date, if you can show substantial hardship and that you will be able to pay the premium within 60 days after the Filing Due Date, you may request us to waive the Late Payment Penalty Charge. If we grant your request, we will waive the Late Payment Penalty Charge for up to 60 days.

To request a waiver, write separately to:

Pension Benefit Guaranty Corporation
FOD/Financial Programs Division (33600)
2020 K Street, NW
Washington, DC 20006-1860

Waivers may also be granted based on any other demonstration of good cause. If you wish to request such a waiver, write to the address above *after* you receive a statement of account assessing penalties.

It is YOUR responsibility as plan administrator to obtain the necessary forms and submit filings on time. (You should ensure that you maintain an updated address with the PBGC so that we can mail to you your next Premium Payment Package. See Part G, Item1.) We will NOT waive late payment charges resulting from your failure to obtain the necessary forms.

4. IRS Extension For Form 5500

NOTE: If the Internal Revenue Service has granted the plan an extension of the due date for filing the Form 5500 series, this does NOT extend the Filing Due Date for Form 1.

5. Minimizing Late Payment Charges

If you are having difficulty determining the actual participant count prior to the First Filing Due Date, see Part C, Item 1 "Participant Count," on how to file using an estimated participant count. This will minimize the assessment of Late Payment Charges to the plan.

If you are having difficulty determining your plan's premium prior to the Final Filing Due Date, you can file the Form 1 and Schedule A using an estimate. You can then file an amended Form 1 and Schedule A reflecting the actual figure (see Part E for procedure). This will minimize the assessment of Late Payment Charges to the plan.

If you file a Form 1-ES for your plan by its First Filing Due Date, you may be able to avoid a Late Payment Penalty Charge with respect to that payment (see Part C). However, if the flat-rate amounts paid with your Form 1 and Form 1-ES total less than the flat rate portion of your premium for a single-employer plan (or the total premium for a multiemployer plan), then you will be charged a Late Payment Penalty Charge (as well as an Interest Charge) on the shortfall from the Form 1-ES First Filing Due Date until the shortfall is paid.

Part G LINE-BY-LINE INSTRUCTIONS FOR FORM 1

The "Item" numbers below refer to the Item or Line numbers on the Form 1.

Item 1 Name Of Plan Sponsor

Enter the name and address of the plan sponsor.

If the address or name printed on the cover of the PBGC Premium Payment Package has changed since your last filing, enter the correct address in the space provided and check the box in the upper right hand corner of Item 1.

It is very important that the address shown in Item 1 be correct, since this is the address we will use to mail your next Premium Payment Package.

The term "plan sponsor" means:

a. the employer(s), in the case of a single-employer pension plan;

b. the employee organization, in the case of a plan established or maintained by an employee organization; or

c. in the case of a plan established or maintained by two or more employers and one or more employee organizations, the association, committee, joint board of trustees, or other similar group of representatives of the parties who establish or maintain the plan.

Item 2 Name of Plan Administrator

Enter the name and address of the plan administrator.

PBGC Form 1—Contd.

Item 3   Plan Sponsor's EIN and PN

Item 3(a) EIN For The Plan Sponsor

Enter the EIN for the plan sponsor. Be sure that the EIN entered here is the same as the EIN entered on the Form 5500 series for the plan year preceding the premium payment year.

For plans with more than one employer that meet the definition of a multiemployer plan, enter the EIN assigned to the joint board of trustees. In the case of a plan to which more than one employer contributes (other than a multiemployer plan), enter the EIN of the plan sponsor identified in Item 1. In the case of a controlled group plan, enter the EIN of the parent or, if there is no parent, of the largest employer.

Item 3(b) Plan Number

Enter the Plan Number (PN) for the plan. Be sure that the PN entered here is the same as the PN entered on the Form 5500 series for the plan year preceding the premium payment year.

Item 3(c) Does EIN/PN Match Form 5500?

Does the EIN in Item 3(a) and the PN in Item 3(b) match exactly the EIN and PN entered on the Form 5500 series for the plan year preceding the premium payment year? Check the "Yes" or "No" box. If no, attach an explanation including the EIN/PN used for the Form 5500 filing, and for single-employer plans, enter that EIN/PN on the top of the Schedule A.

Item 4   Change In EIN Or PN

This item should be completed to report a change in EIN or PN since your last Form 1 or Form 1-ES filing. The EIN of the plan sponsor or the PN may change for a number of reasons, including the acquisition of a division or of an entire company, or because of a mistake in your previous Form 1 filing.

Item 4(a) Change In EIN

Enter the previous EIN in the space provided.

Item 4(b) Change In PN

Enter the previous PN in the space provided.

Item 4(c) EIN/PN Change

If the EIN or PN has changed for any reason other than a plan merger, check the box in Item 4(c), "EIN/PN Change."

Item 4(d) Merger Change

If the EIN or PN has changed because your plan merged with another plan, check the box in Item 4(d), "Change Due to Merger." (If more than one plan has merged into the plan whose EIN/PN is entered in Item 3, attach a separate sheet listing the EIN/PN's that were merged and provide any necessary explanation.)

Item 4(e) Effective Date

Enter the effective date of the change in EIN/PN.

Item 5   Coverage Status

If the plan is covered under section 4021 of ERISA, check 5(a) "Covered."

If you are not certain if the plan is covered, check 5(b) "Uncertain." See Part B, Item 1, and Part D, Item 4, of these instructions.

If you check "Uncertain," you *must* complete Form 1 and pay the appropriate premium as if the plan were covered. Attach a separate sheet to explain the reason why you checked "Uncertain."

Item 6   Filing Status

Item 6(a) First Plan Filing

Check the "Yes" box if you are filing for the first time, and the "No" box if you are filing for a second or subsequent time.

Item 6(b) Terminated Plan

Check the "Yes" box if you have issued notices of intent to terminate to affected parties (with respect to a single-employer plan), or you have filed a Notice of Termination with PBGC (with respect to a multiemployer plan).

If you check "Yes," enter, on line 6(b)(1), the date the assets were distributed, or, on line 6(b)(2), the date a trustee was appointed under section 4042 of ERISA, whichever occurred earlier. If neither event has occurred then enter "UNKNOWN" in the space provided for the dates; and

NOTE: You must continue to file Form 1 and, if applicable, Form 1-ES, and pay premiums through and including the plan year in which all assets are distributed or a trustee for the plan is appointed under section 4042. See Part B, Item 2.

Item 7   Plan Date

Enter the plan date. For new or continuing plans covered under section 4021 of ERISA, enter the later of -

a. the date on which the plan was formally adopted (see Example 1), or

b. the date on which the plan became effective with respect to benefit accruals for future service (see Example 2).

For existing plans not previously covered under section 4021 of ERISA, enter the date on which the plan became covered (see Example 3).

If the plan has been amended or completely restated, show the original plan date.

| Example 1 | A plan with a calendar year plan year was adopted on October 1, 1992, with benefit accruals for future service |

PBGC Form 1—Contd.

retroactively effective to January 1, 1992. The plan date is October 1, 1992.

| Example 2 | A new plan with a calendar year plan |

year was adopted on November 3, 1991. The plan became effective for benefit accruals for future service on January 1, 1992. The plan date is January 1, 1992.

| Example 3 | A professional service employer |

maintains a plan that always has had 20 participants. This type of plan is not a covered plan under ERISA section 4021, provided it never has had more than 25 participants. However, on October 10, 1992, the plan for the first time has 26 participants. As of that date, it is a covered plan and will continue to be a covered plan regardless of the plan's future participant count. The plan date is October 10, 1992.

Item 8   Industry Code
Enter the 4 digit code that best describes the nature of the employer's business. If more than one employer is involved, enter the industry code for the predominant business activity of all employers. Choose one code from the list at the back of this package.

Item 9   Name of Plan
Enter the complete name of the plan as stated in the plan document. For example, "The ABC Company Pension Plan for Salaried Personnel."

Item 10   Name And Phone Number
of Plan Contact
Enter the name and phone number of the person we may contact if we have any questions concerning this filing. If Form 1 was completed by a plan consultant, you may enter the consultant's name and phone number.

Item 11   Plan Type
Check the appropriate box to show plan type. For purposes of determining plan type, all trades or businesses (whether or not incorporated) that are under common control are considered to be one employer.

Item 11(a)   Multiemployer Plans
Check Item 11(a), "Multiemployer Plan", if the plan is a multiemployer plan.

All plans that file the Form 5500 series for the preceding plan year as a "Multiemployer Plan" should file the PBGC Form 1 for the current plan year as a multiemployer plan. If the two filings do not both report a multiemployer plan, you must provide an explanation on a separate sheet attached to the Form 1. All other Form 5500 series plan type

categories are considered as single-employer plans for the PBGC Form 1 filing.

For any plan year beginning on or after September 26, 1980, a multiemployer plan is a plan -

a. to which more than one employer is required to contribute,

b. which is maintained pursuant to one or more collective bargaining agreements between one or more employee organizations and more than one employer, and

c. which satisfies such other requirements as the Secretary of Labor may prescribe by regulation.

(The above definition does not apply to a plan that elected on or before September 26, 1981, with PBGC's approval, not to be treated as a multiemployer plan (see ERISA section 4303). Such a plan is treated as a single-employer plan.)

The plan administrator of a multiemployer plan MUST file a Form 1 and, if applicable, Form 1-ES and pay a premium for the plan as a whole. The administrator CANNOT file a separate Form 1 (or Form 1-ES) and pay a premium for each individual employer.

Item 11(b)   Single-Employer Plans
Check Item 11(b), "Single-Employer Plan", if the plan does not meet the above definition of multiemployer plan.

A single-employer plan includes a "multiple employer plan", A multiple employer plan is a plan -

a. to which more than one employer contributes, and

b. that does NOT satisfy the definition of multiemployer plan, or that elected on or before September 26, 1981, with PBGC's approval, not to be treated as a multiemployer plan (see ERISA section 4303).

If several employers participate in a program of benefits wherein the funds attributable to each employer are available only to pay benefits to that employer's employees, then the plan administrator MUST file a separate Form 1, and, if applicable, Form 1-ES and pay a separate premium for each individual employer.

If several employers participate in a program of benefits wherein the funds attributable to each employer are available to pay benefits to all participants, then the plan administrator MUST file a Form 1, and, if applicable, Form 1-ES and pay a premium for the plan as a whole. Separate filings and premiums CANNOT be submitted for each individual employer.

If separate plans are maintained for different groups of employees, regardless of whether each has the same sponsor or the sponsors are part of the same controlled group, then the plan administrator(s) MUST file a separate Form 1, and if applicable, Form 1-ES and pay a separate premium for each plan.

PBGC Form 1—Contd.

Item 12   Plan Year

Enter the beginning date of the plan year for which you are making the premium payment.

If the month and day on which the plan year begins is not the same as that shown on the last Form 1 you filed with us, then check the box in Item 12. Attach a separate sheet with a brief explanation for the change.

Item 13   Participant Count

Enter the total number of participants covered by the plan. This is the number on which the plan's premium is based.

   a. Participant Definition

For the purposes of Item 13, a "participant" is an individual who is included in one of the categories below:

   (i) *Active.*

     (A) Any individual who is currently in employment covered by the plan and who is earning or retaining credited service under the plan. This category includes any individual who is considered covered under Code minimum coverage rules but does not have any accrued benefit.

     (B) Any non-vested individual who is not currently in employment covered by the plan but who is earning or retaining credited service under the plan. This category does not include a non-vested former employee who has incurred a break in service the greater of one year or the break in service period specified in the plan.

   (ii) *Inactive.*

     (A) Inactive Receiving Benefits. Any individual who is retired or separated from employment covered by the plan and who is receiving benefits under the plan. This category does not include an individual to whom an insurer has made an irrevocable commitment to pay all the benefits to which the individual is entitled under the plan.

     (B) Inactive Entitled to Future Benefits. Any individual who is retired or separated from employment covered by the plan and who is entitled to begin receiving benefits under the plan in the future. This category does not include an individual to whom an insurer has made an irrevocable commitment to pay all the benefits to which the individual is entitled under the plan.

   (iii) *Deceased.*

Any deceased individual who has one or more beneficiaries who are receiving or entitled to receive benefits under the plan. This category does not include an individual if an insurer has made an irrevocable commitment to pay all the benefits to which the beneficiaries of that individual are entitled under the plan.

   b. Participant Count

Count the number of plan participants as of the LAST DAY OF THE PRECEDING PLAN YEAR (see Examples 1 and 2), *except* as follows:

   (i) *New or Newly Covered Plans.* If this is a new plan or a newly covered plan, count participants as of the first day of the plan year for which you are making the premium payment, or the first day the plan became effective for benefit accruals for future service, if that is later (see Example 3).

   (ii) *Certain Mergers or Spinoffs.* If the plan is the transferee plan in a merger or the transferor plan in a spinoff and the transaction meets the conditions described in (A) and (B) below, count participants as of the first day of the plan year for which you are making the premium payment (see Examples 4 and 5). A plan merger or spinoff (as defined in the regulations under section 414(l) of the Code) is covered by this rule if -

     (A) a merger is effective on the first day of the transferee (the continuing) plan's plan year, or a spinoff is effective on the first day of the transferor plan's plan year, and

     (B) the merger or spinoff is not de minimis, as defined in the regulations under section 414(l) of the Code with respect to single-employer plans, or under the PBGC's regulation under section 4231 of ERISA (29 CFR Part 2672) with respect to multiemployer plans.

| Example 1 | A continuing plan has a plan year beginning September 1, 1992, and ending August 31, 1993. Determine the participant count as of August 31, 1992. |

| Example 2 | A continuing plan changes its plan year from a calendar year to a plan year that begins June 1, 1992. For the plan year beginning January 1, 1992, determine the participant count as of December 31, 1991. For the plan year beginning June 1, 1992, determine the participant count as of May 31, 1992. |

| Example 3 | A new plan has a plan year beginning January 1, 1992, and ending December 31, 1992. Determine the participant count as of January 1, 1992. |

| Example 4 | Plan A has a calendar year plan year and Plan B has a July 1-June 30 plan year. Effective January 1, 1992, Plan B merges into Plan A (and the merger is not de minimis). Plan A determines its participant count as of January 1, 1992. (Since Plan B did not exist at any time during 1992, it does not owe a premium for the 1992 plan year.) |

PBGC Form 1—Contd.

Example 5

Plan A has a calendar year plan year. Effective January 1, 1992, Plan A spins off assets and liabilities to form a new plan, Plan B (and the spinoff is not de minimis). Plan A determines its participant count as of January 1, 1992. (Plan B also determines its participant count as of January 1, 1992, since it is a new plan that became effective on that date.)

c. Relationship To Form 5500

You must also enter the participant count reported on the plan's Form 5500 series for the plan year preceding the premium payment year, if it is different from the entry in the box in Item 13. This does not apply to new plans since they are not required to file a Form 5500 series for the year preceding their first plan year.

The participant count you enter in Item 13 of the PBGC Form 1 is usually the same as the participant count reported on the plan's Form 5500 series for the preceding plan year.

If the Form 5500 participant count is higher than the premium participant count, you may enter in Item 13 the participant count you reported in the Form 5500 series. Entering the higher participant count will increase the flat rate portion of the premium for all plans and the variable rate portion of the premium payable by single-employer plans at the per participant cap (see Part I, Subpart 2, line 7).

Item 14　Premium For Multiemployer Plans

Multiply the participant count you entered in Item 13 by $2.60. Enter the result in Item 14. This is the total premium due.

Item 15　Premium For Single-Employer Plans

Item 15(a)　Flat Rate Portion

Multiply the participant count you entered in Item 13 by $19 and enter the result in Item 15(a). This is the flat rate portion of the premium.

Item 15(b)　Variable Rate Portion

In Item 15(b) enter the amount entered in line 9 of Schedule A. This is the amount you must pay for the variable rate portion of the premium.

Item 15(c)　Total Premium

Add Items 15(a) and 15(b) and enter the result in Item 15(c) of the Form 1. This is the total premium.

Item 16　Premium Credit

Include on line 16 the following:

a. Credit for 1992 Premium Amount Previously Paid. Amounts you previously paid for the 1992 plan year. (In most cases, this will be the amount you paid when you filed your 1992 Form 1-ES.)

b. Credit from 1991 Form 1 line 18. Amount of any credit you claimed on line 18 of your 1991 Form 1 or amended 1991 Form 1 (see Part E).

Item 17　Premium Due The PBGC

If this is a multiemployer plan and the amount you entered in Item 14 exceeds the amount entered in Item 16, subtract the amount entered in Item 16 from the amount entered in Item 14 and enter the result in Item 17 of Form 1. This is the amount you owe the PBGC.

If this is a single-employer plan and the amount you entered in Item 15(c) exceeds the amount entered in Item 16, subtract the amount entered in Item 16 from the amount entered in Item 15(c) and enter the result in Item 17 of the Form 1. This is the amount you owe the PBGC.

Enclose with the Form 1 a check for the amount shown in Item 17 payable to the Pension Benefit Guaranty Corporation. Enter the amount of the check payable in the space provided. Write the EIN/PN you entered in Item 3 on the check. To assure proper crediting of your premium payment, each Form 1 for each EIN/PN must be filed with a check for the exact amount due for the plan. Do not combine payments for different plans in one check.

Item 18　Amount Of Overpayment

If this is a multiemployer plan and the amount you entered in Item 14 is less than the amount entered in Item 16, subtract the amount entered in Item 14 from the amount entered in Item 16 and enter the result in Item 18. This is the amount of your overpayment.

If this is a single-employer plan and the amount you entered in Item 15(c) is less than the amount entered in Item 16, subtract the amount entered in Item 15(c) from the amount entered in Item 16 and enter the result in Item 18. This is the amount of your overpayment.

You may either request a refund of the overpayment or have that amount credited against your plan's premium for the next plan year. Check the appropriate box indicating your choice beneath Item 18. If you do not check a box, PBGC will automatically credit your overpayment against next year's premium for the plan. An overpayment on one plan cannot be applied to offset an underpayment on one or more other plans.

Item 19　Additional Information

If you have used attachments other than the Schedule A to explain any of your answers, check the box. Be sure to show the plan name and the EIN/PN at the top of each sheet.

Item 20　Certification of Multiemployer Plan Administrator

PBGC Form 1—Contd.

As plan administrator of a multiemployer plan, you must sign the Form 1 in this space. We may return any filing that does not have your signature. Single-employer plans - see Items 10 and 11 of Schedule A to Form 1.

Part H   GENERAL INSTRUCTIONS FOR SCHEDULE A

The instructions in this part give you the general instructions and requirements for filling out the Schedule A that must be attached to each Form 1 for each single-employer plan.

A key point to filling out the Schedule A is the requirement for you to select a "Filing Method" for your plan. Your plan may be eligible for more than one filing method. However, you may select only one filing method. Under some filing methods, it may take more time to complete the Schedule A than under others. Some methods require the services of an enrolled actuary.

In order that you may take advantage of the filing method that best suits your needs, we urge you to review this part carefully before completing the Schedule A.

The specific instructions for each line of the Schedule A are in Part I, Line-By-Line Instructions for Schedule A.

1. General Requirements

All single-employer plans must complete Schedule A of the PBGC Form 1. You will use Schedule A to determine the amount of the variable rate portion of the premium. For some plans, the amount will be $0. The variable rate portion, including a $0 amount, must be entered on both the Schedule A, line 9, and on the Form 1, Line 15(b). You, and in some cases an enrolled actuary, must certify that the variable rate portion is correct, even if the amount is $0.

The per participant variable rate portion of the premium is $9 per $1,000, or fraction thereof, of unfunded vested benefits as of the last day of the plan year preceding the premium payment year, divided by the number of plan participants. The vested benefits must be valued using an interest rate required by ERISA. (See Part H.7.)

The variable rate portion may not exceed $53 per participant. The $53 maximum figure is reduced by $3 for each of the five plan years preceding the plan year beginning in 1988 for which the maximum deductible contributions to the plan were made.

2. Failure To File Schedule A

If you fail to file a completed and signed Schedule A, the variable rate amount due will be the maximum $53 per participant charge and you will be billed for that amount plus penalties and interest, as applicable.

3. Computation Date For The Variable Rate Portion of The Premium

The date for the computation or determination of the variable rate portion of the premium is generally the last day of the plan year preceding the premium payment year and is the same date as the participant count date.

However, for new or newly covered plans, plans that are transferee plans in a merger (other than a de minimis merger) that is effective on the first day of the plan's premium payment year, and plans that are transferor plans in a spinoff (other than a de minimis spinoff) that is effective on the first day of the plan's premium payment year, the "first day of the premium payment year (or, in the case of a new or newly covered plan, the date on which the plan became effective for benefit accruals for future service, if later)" should be substituted for the "last day of the plan year preceding the premium payment year" whenever that latter date is used in Parts H and I of these instructions or in the Schedule A. This exception is the same as the exception for the participant count date for the same situations; see Part G, Item 13, for additional information and examples.

4. Filing Methods

You determine the variable rate portion of the premium on Schedule A under the "General Rule" or under an optional filing method.

All single-employer plans are eligible to use the "General Rule." The General Rule requires a determination of vested benefits and assets and a determination of unfunded vested benefits by an enrolled actuary as of the last day of the plan year preceding the premium payment year. (For a more complete description of the requirements, see 5.a. below.)

To avoid the expense that might be involved in using the General Rule, you may wish to consider using an optional filing method. Review the requirements for each method to see if you can or wish to use it.

The first optional filing method - the Alternative Calculation Method - requires only an adjustment of amounts determined as of the first day of the plan year preceding the premium payment year that were reported in the plan's Form 5500, Schedule B.

If you file under optional filing methods on lines 1(c)(1) through 1(c)(5), you do not have to determine or calculate unfunded vested benefits and you do not have to pay a variable rate portion of the premium.

The optional filing method on line 1(d) is a variation of the Alternative Calculation Method for plans terminating in distress or involuntary terminations. It uses the Schedule B for the termination plan year or, if unavailable, for the preceding plan year.

PBGC Form 1—Contd.

If you use the optional filing method on line 1(e) for the Maximum Variable Rate premium, you do not need to complete lines 2 through 6 of the Schedule A. You also generally do not need an enrolled actuary certification. (The only instance in which an enrolled actuary certification is required is where a plan pays the maximum premium based on a claimed entitlement to the cap reduction under the special rule for nonprofit entities. See Part I, Subpart 2, line 7.)

The optional filing methods are listed below with the line numbers on Schedule A.

LINE	OPTIONAL FILING METHODS
1(b)	Alternative Calculation Method (See 5.b. below.)
1(c)(1)	Plans with no vested participants (See 5.c.(i) below.)
1(c)(2)	Section 412(i) plans (See 5.c.(ii) below.)
1(c)(3)	Fully funded small plans (under 500 participants) (See 5.c.(iii) below.)
1(c)(4)	Plans terminating in standard termination (See 5.c.(iv) below.)
1(c)(5)	Plans at full funding limit (See 5.c.(v) below.)
1(d)	Plans terminating in distress or involuntary termination (See 5.d. below.)
1(e)	Small plans (under 500 participants) paying maximum variable rate premium (See 5.e. below.)

5. Requirements For Filing Method Selection

Listed below are the requirements for the filing methods and the location of the line-by-line instructions for completing Schedule A under each of the filing methods.

All the filing methods require the plan administrator to certify to the correct completion of Form 1 and Schedule A, and that any information given to the enrolled actuary is true, correct and complete. Additional certifications are noted below.

a. General Rule. Under the General Rule, an enrolled actuary determines the amount of unfunded vested benefits as of the last day of the plan year preceding the premium payment year, in accordance with generally accepted actuarial principles and practices. A plan's unfunded vested benefits equal the excess of: (1) the plan's current liability (within the meaning of ERISA section 302(d)(7)) determined by taking into account only vested benefits and valued at the Required Interest Rate described in Part H.7. of these instructions, over (2) the actuarial value of the plan's assets determined in accordance with ERISA

section 302(c)(2) without a reduction for any credit balance in the plan's funding standard account.

(i) *General Requirements*: The determination under the General Rule must reflect the plan's population and provisions as of the last day of the plan year preceding the premium payment year. The enrolled actuary must make the determination using the same actuarial assumptions and methods used by the plan for purposes of determining the minimum funding contributions under section 302 of ERISA and section 412 of the Code for the plan year preceding the premium payment year (or, in the case of a new or newly covered plan, for the premium payment year), except to the extent that other actuarial assumptions are specifically prescribed by these instructions or are necessary to reflect the occurrence of a significant event described in Part H.6. below, between the date of the funding valuation and the last day of the plan year preceding the premium payment year. (If the plan does a funding valuation as of the last day of the plan year preceding the premium payment year, no separate adjustment for significant events is needed.)

The value of vested benefits must be determined using an interest rate prescribed by ERISA. This interest rate is 80% of the annual yield on 30-year Treasury constant maturities, as reported in Federal Reserve Statistical Release G.13 or H.15, for the calendar month preceding the calendar month in which the plan year begins. (See Part H.7. of these instructions for further information on the Required Interest Rate.)

Under this rule, the determination of the unfunded vested benefits may be based on a plan funding valuation done as of the first day of the premium payment year, provided that --

(A) the actuarial assumptions and methods used are those used by the plan for purposes of determining the minimum funding contributions under section 302 of the Act and section 412 of the Code for the premium payment year, except to the extent that other actuarial assumptions are specifically prescribed by these instructions or are required to make the adjustment described in paragraph (B) below; and

(B) if an enrolled actuary determines that there is a material difference between the values determined under the valuation and the values that would have been determined as of the last day of the preceding plan year, the valuation results are adjusted to reflect appropriately the values as of the last day of the preceding plan year. (This adjustment need not be made if the unadjusted valuation would result in greater unfunded vested benefits.)

PBGC Form 1—Contd.

(ii) *Certification Requirement (in addition to general plan administrator certification)*: In all cases under the General Rule, an enrolled actuary must certify to the determination of the variable rate portion of the premium. In addition --

(A) in the case of a large plan (500 or more participants), if the enrolled actuary
-- determines that the actuarial value of plan assets equals or exceeds the value of all accrued benefits (valued at the Required Interest Rate described in Part H.7. of these instructions); and
-- elects to report the value of accrued benefits in lieu of the value of vested benefits on line 2(a) of Schedule A, the enrolled actuary must certify to having done so on line 11(a) of Schedule A.

(B) If
-- each interest rate used by the plan to value current liability was not greater than the Required Interest Rate described in Part H.7.; and
-- the enrolled actuary reports the value of vested benefits at the plan's interest rate(s) on line 2(b) of Schedule A, the enrolled actuary must certify to the above on line 11(c) of Schedule A.

(C) In the case of a plan maintained by a nonprofit entity, if an enrolled actuary determines that the plan qualifies for the per participant cap reduction under the special rule for nonprofit entities, the enrolled actuary must so certify on line 11(d) of Schedule A.

(iii) *Size Requirement*: Plans with any number of participants may use this method.

(iv) *Instructions*: For line-by-line instructions for completing Schedule A, see Part I, Subpart 1 of these instructions.

(v) *Schedule A Filing Method*: Check the box on line 1(a).

b. Alternative Calculation Method. This method is a simplified method intended to approximate the more precise determinations of the General Rule. It uses two formulae to calculate unfunded vested benefits as of the last day of the plan year preceding the premium payment year.

The first formula adjusts the value of vested benefits for participants in pay status and deferred vested participants, as reported on Schedule B of the Form 5500 as of the first day of the plan year preceding the premium payment year, using the Required Interest Rate prescribed by ERISA. Part H.7. of these instructions tells you where to find the Required Interest Rate.

The second formula adjusts the resulting unfunded vested benefits figure for the passage of time from the first day of the plan year preceding the premium payment year to the last day of the plan year preceding

the premium payment year. The adjustment is necessary because, for premium purposes, unfunded vested benefits are determined as of the last day of the plan year preceding the premium payment year. See the line-by-line instructions in Part I, Subpart 2, lines 2(b) and 4, for the two formulae.

If the Alternative Calculation Method is used by a plan that has 500 or more participants as of the last day of the plan year preceding the premium payment year, an enrolled actuary must adjust the unfunded vested benefits to reflect the occurrence of any significant event during the plan year preceding the premium payment year. See Part H.6. for a list of significant events.

(i) *General Requirements*: To use the Alternative Calculation Method, a plan must have filed a Form 5500, Schedule B, for the plan year preceding the premium payment year, that has -

(A) vested benefit values reported on lines 6d(i), 6d(ii), and 6d(iii);

(B) the interest rates used to determine the vested benefit values reported on line 12c(i);

(C) the assumed retirement age reported on line 12d; and

(D) assets reported on line 8b or 6c.

(ii) *Certification Requirements (in addition to general plan administrator certification)*: If -

(A) each interest rate used to determine the entries in lines 6d(i), 6d(ii) and 6d(iii) of the Schedule B was no greater than the interest rate described in Part H.7. of these instructions; and

(B) the plan administrator reports the value of vested benefits at the plan's rate(s) on line 2(b) of Schedule A, the plan administrator must certify to the above on line 10(c) of Schedule A.

For plans with 500 or more participants, an enrolled actuary must certify on line 11(e) that the unfunded vested benefits have been adjusted for the occurrence, if any, of a significant event and that the adjustment is consistent with generally accepted actuarial principles and practices.

In the case of a plan maintained by a nonprofit entity that is claiming entitlement to the cap reduction, an enrolled actuary must certify on line 11(d) that the plan meets the requirements for doing so, as described under the instructions for line 7 in Subpart 2 of Part I.

(iii) *Size Requirements*: Plans with any number of participants may use this method. However, plans with 500 or more participants that use this method must report unfunded vested benefits that reflect the occurrence, if any, of significant events listed in Part H.6..

(iv) *Instructions*: For line-by-line instructions for completing Schedule A, see Part I, Subpart 2, of these instructions.

PBGC Form 1—Contd.

(v) *Schedule A Filing Method*: Check the applicable box on line 1(b). If your plan has fewer than 500 participants, check the box on line 1(b)(1). If your plan has 500 or more participants, check the box on line 1(b)(2).

c. Plans Exempt From Variable Rate Portion of Premium. Certain categories of plans are not required to determine or report vested benefits, assets or unfunded vested benefits on Schedule A, or to pay a variable rate portion of the premium. These plans are required only to complete lines 1 and 9 on the Schedule A indicating that the plan comes within one of the exempted categories and to provide the appropriate plan administrator or enrolled actuary certification.

(i) *Plans with No Vested Participants*. If a plan has no vested participants as of the last day of the plan year preceding the premium payment year, the plan administrator may use this filing method and report $0 unfunded vested benefits on the Schedule A.

(A) General Requirements: To use this rule a plan must have had no vested participants as of the last day of the plan year preceding the premium payment year. PBGC will accept that if there are no vested participants, there are no vested benefits and no unfunded vested benefits.

(B) Certification Requirement (in addition to general plan administrator certification): The plan administrator must certify that there were no vested participants.

(C) Size Requirement: Plans with any number of participants may use this method.

(D) Instructions: For line-by-line instruction for completing Schedule A, see Part I, Subpart 3, of these instructions.

(E) Schedule A Filing Method: Check the box on Schedule A, Line 1(c)(1).

(ii) *Section 412(i) Plans*. Plans described in section 412(i) of the Internal Revenue Code and regulations thereunder are not subject to the variable rate premium charge and report $0 unfunded vested benefits on Schedule A.

(A) General Requirements: To use the section 412(i) plan rule, a plan must be a plan described in section 412(i) of the Code and the regulations thereunder at all times during the plan year preceding the premium payment year. If the plan is a new or newly covered plan, it must be a 412(i) plan at all times during the premium payment year through the due date for the variable rate portion of the premium.

(B) Certification Requirement (in addition to general plan administrator certification): The plan administrator must certify that the plan is a 412(i) plan.

(C) Size Requirement: Plans with any number of participants may use this method.

(D) Instructions: For line-by-line instructions for completing Schedule A, see Part I, Subpart 4, of these instructions.

(E) Schedule A Filing Method: Check the box on Schedule A, Line 1(c)(2).

(iii) *Fully Funded Small Plans*. Under this rule, an enrolled actuary certifies that the plan has no unfunded vested benefits. No computations of unfunded vested benefits need be reported. The enrolled actuary simply reports $0 unfunded vested benefits on Schedule A.

(A) General Requirements: To use this rule, a plan must have fewer than 500 participants as of the last day of the plan year preceding the premium payment year and no unfunded vested benefits as of that date (valued at the Required Interest Rate described in Part H.7. of these instructions).

(B) Certification Requirements (in addition to general plan administrator certification): The enrolled actuary must certify on line 11(b) that the plan had fewer than 500 participants and that the plan had no unfunded vested benefits as of the last day of the plan year preceding the premium payment year (valued at the Required Interest Rate described in Part H.7. of these instructions).

(C) Size Requirement: Only plans with fewer than 500 participants on the last day of the plan year preceding the premium payment year may use this method.

(D) Instructions: For line-by-line instructions for completing Schedule A, see Part I, Subpart 5, of these instructions.

(E) Schedule A Filing Method: Check the box on Schedule A, Line 1(c)(3).

(iv) *Plans Terminating in Standard Terminations*. Under this exemption, plans terminating in standard terminations are not subject to the variable rate premium charge and report $0 unfunded vested benefits on Schedule A.

(A) General Requirements: Plans that issued a notice of intent to terminate in a standard termination in accordance with section 4041(a)(2) of ERISA, setting forth a proposed date of termination (i.e., the 60-day prospective date) that is on or before the last day of the plan year preceding the premium payment year may use this method.

If the plan does not ultimately make a final distribution of assets in full satisfaction of its obligations under the standard termination, the right to use this filing method will be revoked and the premium(s) that would otherwise have been required will be due retroactive to the applicable due date(s).

PBGC Form 1—Contd.

(B) Certification Requirement (in addition to general plan administrator certification): None. Only the general plan administrator certification is required.

(C) Size Requirement: Plans with any number of participants may use this method.

(D) Instructions: For line-by-line instructions for completing Schedule A, see Part I, Subpart 6, of these instructions.

(E) Schedule A Filing Method: Check the box on Schedule A, line 1(c)(4).

(v) *Plans at the full funding limit.* As provided below, plans at the full funding limit for the plan year preceding the premium payment year are exempt from the variable rate portion of the premium and should report $0 unfunded vested benefits on Schedule A.

(A) General Requirements: Plans may use this method if, on or before the earlier of the due date for payment of the variable rate portion of the premium (see Part C) or the date that portion is paid, the plan's contributing sponsor or contributing sponsors made contributions to the plan for the plan year preceding the premium payment year in an amount not less than the full funding limitation for that preceding premium payment year under section 412(c)(7) of the Internal Revenue Code.

The determination of whether contributions for the preceding plan year were in an amount not less than the full funding limitation under section 412(c)(7) of the Code for the preceding plan year is based on the methods of computing the full funding limitation, including actuarial assumptions and funding methods, used by the plan (provided these assumptions and methods met all requirements, including the requirements for reasonableness, under section 412 of the Code) with respect to the preceding plan year. In the event of a PBGC audit, the plan administrator may be required to provide documentation to establish both the computation methods used and the conformance of those methods with the requirements of Code section 412. The PBGC will report to the Internal Revenue Service any plans using assumptions and methods that appear not to meet the requirements of Code section 412.

A plan may be entitled to this exemption if contributions were rounded down slightly from the amount of the full funding limitation. Thus, any contribution that is rounded down to no less than the next lower multiple of one hundred dollars (in the case of full funding limitations up to one hundred thousand dollars) or to no less than the next lower multiple of one thousand dollars (in the case

of full funding limitations above one hundred thousand dollars) is deemed for purposes of this exemption to be in an amount equal to the full funding limitation. (**NOTE:** Relief may also be available where the plan's actuary rounded off *de minimis* amounts to determine the full funding limit. Whether the exemption applies in such circumstances would be determined under the rule discussed in the preceding paragraph, based on a review of the plan's practice with respect to the computation methods used.)

A plan may be entitled to this exemption if the sum of the contributions for the plan year preceding the premium payment year was less than the full funding limit and the contributions plus the interest credit under the Code is at least equal to the full funding limit as of the end of the plan year preceding the premium payment year.

(B) Certification Requirement (in addition to general plan administrator certification): The enrolled actuary must certify on line 11(f) that the plan has met the general requirements described above.

(C) Size Requirement: Plans with any number of participants may use this method.

(D) Instructions: For line-by-line instructions for completing Schedule A, see Part I, Subpart 7, of these instructions.

(E) Schedule A Filing Method: Check the box on Schedule A, line 1(c)(5).

d. Plans Terminating In Distress Or Involuntary Terminations. Under this special rule, plans terminating in distress or involuntary terminations may use a modified version of the Alternative Calculation Method.

(i) *General Requirements*: The following plans may use this method:

-- Plans that issue notices of intent to terminate in a distress termination in accordance with ERISA section 4041(a)(2) setting forth a proposed termination date that is on or before the last day of the plan year preceding the premium payment year; or

-- Plans for which the PBGC has initiated proceedings for an involuntary termination and has sought a termination date on or before the last day of the plan year preceding the premium payment year.

Some plans terminating in distress or involuntary terminations may not have filed the Schedule B for the plan year preceding the premium payment year and therefore would not be able to use the Alternative Calculation Method to calculate unfunded vested benefits. This filing method allows such plans to calculate unfunded vested benefits under a variation of the Alternative

PBGC Form 1—Contd.

Calculation Method that uses vested benefit values and asset values from an earlier Schedule B than under the Alternative Calculation Method. The Schedule B used under this special rule must be for the plan year that includes (in the case of a distress termination) the proposed date of termination or (in the case of an involuntary termination) the termination date sought by the PBGC, or, if no Schedule B is filed for that plan year, the Schedule B for the preceding plan year. The Schedule B must have the entries required for the Alternative Calculation Method, as described in Part H.5.b.(i) of these instructions. (NOTE: Line item references are to the 1989 through 1991 Schedule B's. If your Schedule B is for an earlier year with different line numbers, use the corresponding entries.)

NOTE: This method assumes (in the case of a distress termination) that the PBGC has not disapproved the termination or (in the case of an involuntary termination) that the PBGC's petition for involuntary termination has not been denied, dismissed or withdrawn. At such time as any of these events occurs, the plan will be treated as an ongoing plan and must file amended premium forms using another permitted filing method.

(ii) *Certification Requirement (in addition to general plan administrator certification)*: Same as for Alternative Calculation Method. (See Part H.5.b.(ii) of these instructions.)

(iii) *Size Requirement*: Same as for Alternative Calculation Method. (See Part H.5.b(iii) of these instructions.)

(iv) *Instructions*: For line-by-line instructions for completing Schedule A, see Part I, Subpart 8, of these instructions.

(v) *Schedule A Filing Method*: Check the box on Schedule A, line 1(d).

e. Small Plans Paying Maximum Variable Rate Premium. Plans that are required to pay the maximum variable rate portion of the premium or that choose to do so, rather than compute their unfunded vested benefits under the General Rule or the Alternative Calculation Method, can use this filing method. Plans choosing this method do not need to complete lines 2 through 6 of the Schedule A.

(i) *General Requirements:* Plans may use this method if they pay the maximum per participant variable rate amount. That amount is generally $53, but may be less if the plan qualifies for a reduction in the cap on the variable rate amount (see Part I, Subpart 2, Line 7.)

(ii) *Certification Requirement (in addition to general plan administrator certification):* Generally none. However, an enrolled actuary certification is required on line 11(d) where a plan pays the maximum variable rate amount based on a claimed entitlement to the cap reduction under the special

rule for nonprofit entities. (See Part I, Subpart 2, Line 7.) In all other instances, only the general plan administrator certification is required.

(iii) *Size Requirements:* Plans with fewer than 500 participants may use this method.

(iv) *Instructions:* For line-by-line instructions for completing Schedule A, see Part I, Subpart 9 of these instructions.

(v) *Schedule A Filing Method:* Check the box on Schedule A, Line 1(e).

6. Significant Events

a. General Rule. Plans filing under the General Rule must use actuarial assumptions and methods that reflect the occurrence, if any, of a significant event listed below between the date of the funding valuation for the plan year preceding the premium payment year and the last day of the plan year preceding the premium payment year.

b. Alternative Calculation Method. Plans with 500 or more participants filing under the Alternative Calculation Method are required to reflect in the value of unfunded vested benefits as of the last day of the plan year preceding the premium payment year the occurrence, if any, of a significant event listed below during the plan year preceding the premium payment year.

c. Distress Or Involuntary Terminations. Plans with 500 or more participants filing under the method for plans terminating in distress or involuntary terminations are required to reflect in the value of unfunded vested benefits as of the last day of the plan year preceding the premium payment year the occurrence, if any, of a significant event listed below between the first day of the plan year for which the Schedule B being used was filed and the last day of the plan year preceding the premium payment year.

d. Significant Events. In each of the above circumstances, the plan's enrolled actuary must make appropriate adjustments to reflect the occurrence of any significant event.

The Significant Events are:

(1) an increase in the plan's actuarial costs (consisting of the plan's normal cost under section 412(b)(2)(A) of the Code, amortization charges under section 412(b)(2)(B) of the Code, and amortization credits under section 412(b)(3)(B) of the Code) attributable to a plan amendment, unless the cost increase attributable to the amendment is less than 5% of the actuarial costs determined without regard to the amendment;

(2) the extension of coverage under the plan to a new group of employees resulting in an increase of 5% or more in the plan's liability for accrued benefits;

(3) a plan merger, consolidation or spinoff that is not de minimis pursuant to the regulations under section 414(l) of the Code;

(4) the shutdown of any facility, plant, store, etc., that creates immediate eligibility for benefits that

PBGC Form 1—Contd.

would not otherwise be immediately payable for participants separating from service;

(5) the offer by the plan for a temporary period to permit participants to retire at benefit levels greater than that to which they would otherwise be entitled;

(6) a cost-of-living increase for retirees resulting in an increase of 5% or more in the plan's liability for accrued benefits; and

(7) any other event or trend that results in a material increase in the value of unfunded vested benefits.

7. Required Interest Rate For Valuing Vested Benefits

The following table - taken from Appendix B to the PBGC's premium regulation - lists the Required Interest rates to be used in valuing a plan's vested benefits under the General Rule, the Alternative Calculation Method, and the method for plans terminating in distress or involuntary terminations. The table contains all interest rates available when these instructions were printed.

For Premium Payment Years Beginning In	The Required Interest Rate is [1]
January 1992	6.16
February 1992	6.06
March 1992	6.28

[1] The required interest rate listed above is equal to 80% of the annual yield for 30-year Treasury constant maturities, as reported in Federal Reserve Statistical Release G.13 and H.15, for the calendar month preceding the calendar month in which the premium payment year begins.

Example If the first month of the premium payment year is January 1992, use the Appendix B required interest rate for January 1992, of 6.16 percent.

PBGC updates Appendix B in the Federal Register on a quarterly basis, by publishing the rates for November through January on or about January 15, for February through April on or about April 15, for May through July on or about July 15, and for August through October on or about October 15. PBGC makes interest rate information available through a telephone hot line, (202) 778-8899.

For further information contact:
Pension Benefit Guaranty Corporation
Communications and
    Public Affairs Department
2020 K Street, NW
Washington, DC 20006-1860
Telephone (202) 778-8840

Additionally, the National Technical Information Service provides the Required Interest Rates and other PBGC interest rates through a subscription service.

For further information, contact:
U.S. Department of Commerce
National Technical Information Service
5285 Port Royal Road
Springfield, VA 22161
    Telephone: (703) 487-4630
    Facsimile: (703) 321-8547
    Order No.: PB92-924400-ACM

Plan administrators are also notified of the Required Interest Rate for the premium payment year on the mailing label on these instructions. The top line of the mailing label on your premium payment package shows the Required Interest Rate for your plan. The rate is determined by the month in which your plan year begins. Check the month on the mailing label to make sure it corresponds to the first month of your plan year.

Reporting Calendar

Information to be Filed Annually with IRS, DOL or PBGC for Pension and Profit-Sharing Plans*

Form	Title/Description	Who Must File	When Filed	Where Filed
5500	Annual Return/Report of Employee Benefit Plan (with 100 or more participants at beginning of plan year)**	Plan administrator or sponsor of an employee pension benefit plan (defined benefit or defined contribution) covered by ERISA. Includes frozen plans, §408(c) IRAs, some SEPs and §403(b) TSAs.	On or before last day of seventh month after close of plan year. A 2½ month extension may be granted if Form 5558 is filed early enough for the IRS to act before the regular due date of the annual return.***	IRS service center indicated in instructions to Form 5500.
5500-C/R	Return/Report of Employee Benefit Plan (with fewer than 100 participants at beginning of plan year)**	Plan administrator or sponsor of a pension benefit plan covered by ERISA. Includes frozen plans, §408(c) IRAs, some SEPs and §403(b) TSAs. The shorter version, Form 5500-R, may be filed instead of the longer Form 5500-C provided Form 5500-C has been filed for one of the prior two plan years, and this is not the first or final plan year.	Same as Form 5500.	Same as Form 5500.
5500EZ	Annual Return of One-Participant (Owners and Their Spouses) Pension Benefit Plan	Employer who has a pension benefit plan that covers only the individual or individual and spouse who wholly own a business. May also be filed for partnership plans that cover only partners or partners and their spouses.****	Same as Form 5500.	Internal Revenue Service Center Andover, MA 05501
Schedule A (Form 5500 Series)	Insurance Information	Plan administrator or sponsor of employee pension benefit plan where any plan benefits are provided by an insurance company, insurance service or similar organization.	Attachment to Form 5500 or 5500-C/R, whichever is appropriate. Schedule A need not be filed for plans filing Form 5500EZ.	Same as Form 5500.
Schedule B (Form 5500 Series)	Actuarial Information	Plan administrator or sponsor of a defined benefit plan subject to minimum funding standards.	Attachment to Form 5500, 5500-C/R or 5500EZ, whichever is appropriate.	Same as Form 5500.
Schedule C (Form 5500)	Service Provider and Trustee Information	Form 5500 filers.	Attachment to Form 5500.	Same as Form 5500.
Schedule E (Form 5500 Series)	ESOP Annual Information	Plan administrator or sponsor of a pension benefit plan that contains ESOP benefits.	Attachment to Form 5500, 5500-C/R or 5500EZ, whichever is appropriate.	Same as Form 5500.
Schedule P (Form 5500 Series)	Annual Return of Fiduciary of Employee Benefit Trust	Trustee or custodian of a tax-exempt qualified trust or custodial account that wants the statute of limitations to begin as provided in §6501.	Attachment to Form 5500, 5500-C/R or 5500EZ, whichever is appropriate, for the trust year ending with or within the plan year.	Same as Form 5500.

* Whenever a tax return/report deadline or other act required by the internal revenue laws falls on a Saturday, Sunday or legal holiday, the act will be considered timely if it is performed on the next business day.

** If the plan had between 80 and 120 participants at the beginning of the plan year, the plan may file the same series of forms (Form 5500 or Form 5500-C/R) that it filed for the previous year (29 CFR §2520.103-1(d)).

*** For a single employer plan, or plans of a controlled group of corporations filing a consolidated return, with the same plan year as the employer's tax year, any extension granted for filing the employer's tax return beyond the due date of the annual report automatically applies to the annual report filing.

**** Form 5500EZ need not be filed for a one-participant plan that has $100,000 or less in assets, or by an employer that has more than one one-participant plan that, in the aggregate, have $100,000 or less in assets. However, Form 5500EZ should be filed for a final plan year, even if the plan has less than $100,000 in assets.

Reporting Calendar—Contd.

Information to be Filed Annually with IRS, DOL or PBGC for Pension and Profit-Sharing Plans (continued)

Form	Title/Description	Who Must File	When Filed	Where Filed
Schedule SSA (Form 5500 Series)	Annual Registration Statement Identifying Separated Participants with Deferred Vested Benefits	Plan administrator for any plan year having a separated participant with a deferred vested benefit under the plan.	Attachment to Form 5500 or 5500-C/R, whichever is appropriate, no later than the plan year following the plan year in which separation occurs.	Same as Form 5500.
None prescribed	Financial statements, schedules and accountant's opinion (for plans that file Form 5500)*	Plan administrator or sponsor of an employee pension benefit plan covered by ERISA.	Attachment to Form 5500.	Same as Form 5500.
Form 5500 Series	Notification of change of status (i.e., name of the plan, name or address of plan administrator, termination, merger or consolidation of the plan)	Plan administrator of employee pension benefit plan.	Same as Form 5500.	Same as Form 5500.
8453-E	Return/Report of Employee Benefit Plan (with fewer than 100 participants) Electronic/Magnetic Media	Participants in the electronic/magnetic media program who want to file Forms 5500-C/R or 5500EZ, and related schedules via magnetic media.	See IRS Pub. 1507.	Internal Revenue Service P.O. Box 4050 Attn: EFU (EPMF) Stop 983 Woburn, MA 01888-4050
990-T	Exempt Organization Business Income Tax Return	Trustees of trusts used to hold qualified plan and IRA assets with gross income from an unrelated trade or business of $1,000 or more.	By the 15th day of the fourth month after the close of the taxable year.	IRS service center indicated in instructions.
PBGC Form 1-ES	Estimated Premium Payment (Base premiums for plans with 500 or more participants)	Plan administrator of single employer defined benefit pension plan subject to termination insurance provisions of Title IV of ERISA.	Within two months after the end of the prior plan year. (Must use PBGC Form 1 for subsequent reconciliation filing and for variable rate portion of premium.)	Pension Benefit Guaranty Corporation P.O. Box 105655 Atlanta, GA 30348-5655
PBGC Form 1	Annual Premium Payment (Base premiums for plans with fewer than 500 participants and for variable rate premiums)	Plan administrator of defined benefit pension plan subject to termination insurance provisions of Title IV of ERISA.	Within 8½ months after the plan year begins.	Pension Benefit Guaranty Corporation P.O. Box 105655 Atlanta, GA 30348-5655
Schedule A (PBGC Form 1)	Single Employer Plan Variable Rate Portion of the Premium	All single-employer defined benefit pension plans subject to the termination insurance provisions of Title IV of ERISA.	Attachment to PBGC Form 1.	Same as PBGC Form 1.
5329	Return for Additional Taxes Attributable to Qualified Retirement Plans (including IRAs), Annuities and Modified Endowment Contracts	An individual owing taxes for excess contributions to an IRA, or for failure to receive required minimum distributions from a qualified plan or IRA; an individual who receives an excess retirement plan distribution (whether or not tax is owed), or an early distribution from an IRA, SEP, §403(b) TSA, §457 deferred compensation plan, or qualified plan unless entire distribution is rolled over or an exception to the tax applies (unless Form 1099-R incorrectly fails to indicate that an exception applies).	Attachment to Form 1040.	IRS service center indicated in instructions to Form 1040.

* Plans with more than 100 but fewer than 120 participants that file Form 5500-C/R under the 80/120 rule are not required to file financial statements, schedules and an accountant's opinion.

Reporting Calendar—Contd.

Information to be Filed Annually with IRS, DOL or PBGC for Pension and Profit-Sharing Plans (continued)

Form	Title/Description	Who Must File	When Filed	Where Filed
5330	Return of Excise Taxes Related to Employee Benefit Plans	Employer failing to meet minimum funding standards for pension plans; disqualified person participating in a prohibited transaction; individual for whom excess contribution was made to a §403(b)(7) custodial account; sponsor of an ESOP that disposes of qualified securities within three years; employer making nondeductible contributions to qualified plans; employer failing to timely distribute excess contributions or excess aggregate contributions from a 401(k) plan; employer making a prohibited allocation of qualified securities of an ESOP; and an employer receiving an asset reversion.	For funding deficiency, on or before the later of 7 months after the end of the employer's tax year, or 8½ months after the end of the plan year that ends with or within the employer's tax year (a 6-month extension of time to file may be granted if Form 5558 is filed by the regular due date); for failure to timely distribute excess contributions or excess aggregate contributions, on or before the last day of the 15th month after the close of the plan year to which they relate; for excise tax on asset reversions, the last day of the month following the month in which reversion occurs. For all other reasons, within 7 months after the end of the tax year (an extension of time to file may be granted).	IRS service center where income tax return is filed.
W-2	Wage and Tax Statement	Employers. (In addition to reporting wages and withholding, used to report distributions from nonqualified plans, elective deferrals, dependent care assistance and §457 plans, certain group-term life insurance coverage, and to indicate active participant status.)	Last day of February	Social Security Administration Office indicated in instructions to Form W-3 (transmittal form).
1099-R	Distributions from Pensions, Annuities, Retirement or Profit-Sharing Plans, IRAs, Insurance Contracts, Etc.	Trustees of plan or other payor of designated distributions (including corrective distributions and death benefit payments).	February 28	IRS service center indicated in instructions (transmitted with Form 1096).
1099-DIV	Dividends and Distributions	Plan administrator or other payor for cash dividends paid on employer stock held by an ESOP that are distributed to participants.	February 28	IRS service center indicated in instructions (transmitted with Form 1096).
5498	Individual Retirement Arrangement Information	Trustees or issuers of IRAs and SEPs to report IRA contributions and rollovers, and the fair market value of IRAs and SEPs.	May 31	IRS service center indicated in instructions (transmitted with Form 1096).
941 941E	Employer's Quarterly Federal Tax Return (to report income tax withholding on distributions)	Trustees of plan or other payor of distribution. (Form 941 used where payor also pays wages subject to FICA.)	For quarter ending Due date March 31 April 30 June 30 July 31 September 30 October 31 December 31 January 31	IRS service center indicated in instructions.
5558	Application for Extension of Time to File Certain Employee Plan Returns	May be used to apply for an extension of time to file Form 5500 Series or Form 5330. If extension filed for Form 5330, estimated tax must be paid with Form 5558.	In sufficient time for the IRS to consider and act on it before the return's regular due date (not including extensions).	IRS service center where Form 5500 Series or Form 5330 is filed.

Reporting Calendar—Contd.

Forms to be Filed for Establishment, Amendment, Merger or Termination of Pension and Profit-Sharing Plans

Form	Title/Description	Who May/Must File	When Filed	Where Filed
5300* 5303	Application for Determination for Employee Benefit Plan (Form 5300), Collectively Bargained Plan (Form 5303)	Employer or plan administrator may file to request a determination letter concerning the qualified status of a new or amended plan, the partial termination of a plan, affiliated service group status, the effect of §414(m) on the plan, or to give notice of merger, consolidation or transfer of plan assets and simultaneously request determination on remaining plan(s).	See Rev. Proc. 89-65, IRS Notice 90-73 and IRS Announcement 92-29 for extended filing deadlines for plans seeking a determination letter with respect to TRA 1986 and subsequent tax laws. If used to provide notice of merger, etc., must be filed at least 30 days before event. See Rev. Proc. 91-66 and IRS Announcement 91-171 for temporary procedures for determination letter requests.	IRS Key District Office for employer's principal place of business.
5307*	Application for Determination for Adopters of Master or Prototype, Regional Prototype or Volume Submitter Plans	May be used by employer that has adopted an IRS approved master or prototype plan, a regional prototype plan or volume submitter plan. May not be used for collectively bargained plans, multiple employer plans, ESOPs, or for affiliated group status.	For volume submitters, same as Form 5300. For adopters of master or prototype plans and regional prototype plans, see Rev. Procs. 89-9 and 89-13 for extended filing deadlines. See Rev. Proc. 91-66 and IRS Announcement 91-171 for temporary procedures for determination letter requests.	Same as Form 5300.
5309	Application for Determination of an ESOP	Corporate sponsor of an ESOP intended to satisfy the requirements of §4975(e)(7).	Attachment to Form 5300 or 5303, whichever is appropriate.	Same as Form 5300.
6406*	Short Form Application for Determination for Amendment of Employee Benefit Plan	Employer or plan administrator may file to request a determination letter concerning the qualification of a plan amendment. May not be used for TRA 1986 amendments, restated plans, or for plan terminations, mergers, consolidations or transfers of assets.	Any time a determination letter for a plan amendment is desired, provided the plan has an outstanding determination letter.	Same as Form 5300.
Schedule T** (Form 5300 Series)	Supplemental Application for Approval of Employee Benefit Plans Under TEFRA, TRA 1984, REA and TRA 1986.	Must be filed with Form 5300, 5301, 5303, 5307 or 6406 determination letter requests for TEFRA, TRA 1984, REA and certain TRA 1986 affected provisions.	Attachment to pre-Rev. 2/90 Form 5300 Series.	Same as Form 5300.
5302	Employee Census	Employer or plan administrator who files an application for determination.	Attachment to Form 5300 Series.	Same as Form 5300.
5308	Request for Change in Plan/Trust Year	Pension plans that do not meet criteria for automatic approval must file to change plan year under §412(c)(5) or trust years for trust related to plan. (User fee must accompany request.)	By the last day of the short plan year or the trust's short tax year.	Same as Form 5300.
5310* 6088	Application for Determination upon Termination; Distributable Benefits from Employee Pension Benefit Plans	Employer or plan administrator may file to request a determination letter concerning plan termination.	Any time a determination letter upon termination is desired.	Commissioner of Internal Revenue, Attn: E:EP:R P.O. Box 14073 Ben Franklin Station Washington, D.C. 20044

* A user fee is imposed on determination letter requests submitted to the IRS. The appropriate fee must accompany the request along with Form 8717.

** The revised Form 5300 Series must be used for determination letter requests with respect to TRA 1986 and subsequent tax laws. However, until the determination letter program for TRA 1986 amendments is opened for all plans, the old Form 5300 Series must continue to be used along with Schedule T for determination letter requests for plans for which the TRA 1986 program is not yet opened.

Reporting Calendar—Contd.

Forms to be Filed for Establishment, Amendment, Merger or Termination of Pension and Profit-Sharing Plans (continued)

Form	Title/Description	Who May/Must File	When Filed	Where Filed
5310-A	Notice of Merger, Consolidation, or Transfer of Plan Assets or Liabilities	Employer or plan administrator must file for certain plan mergers or consolidations, or transfers of assets or liabilities from one plan to another (each plan should file). The instructions provide four new exceptions.	At least 30 days before the plan merger or consolidation, or transfer of plan assets or liabilities.	IRS Key District Office for employer's principal place of business.
PBGC Form 500	Standard Termination Notice Single-Employer Plan Termination	Plan administrator of a defined benefit pension plan subject to the plan termination insurance provisions of ERISA must file for standard plan termination.	Within 90 days after proposed termination date.	Pension Benefit Guaranty Corp. Case Operations and Assistance Division Room 5500 (Code 25420) 2020 K Street, NW Washington, D.C. 20006-1860
Schedule EA-S (PBGC Form 500)	Standard Termination Certification of Sufficiency	Enrolled actuary must certify that terminating plan is projected to have sufficient assets to provide all benefit liabilities.	Attachment to PBGC Form 500.	Same as PBGC Form 500.
PBGC Form 501	Post-Distribution Certification for Standard Terminations	Plan administrator of defined benefit pension plan for standard termination.	Within 30 days after completion of final distribution of plan assets.	Same as PBGC Form 500.
PBGC Form 600	Distress Termination Notice of Intent to Terminate	Plan administrator of defined benefit pension plan subject to plan termination insurance provisions of ERISA must file to advise PBGC of proposed distress termination and to provide plan and sponsor data.	Between 60 and 90 days prior to the proposed termination date, and after notices of intent to terminate are sent to other affected parties.	Pension Benefit Guaranty Corp. Case Operations and Assistance Division Room 5500 (Code 25410) 2020 K Street, NW Washington, D.C. 20006-1860
PBGC Form 601	Distress Termination Notice Single-Employer Plan Termination	Plan administrator of defined benefit pension plan must file for distress termination to demonstrate satisfaction of distress criteria and to provide plan, sponsor and participant data.	Within 60 days after proposed termination date. Must complete notice by submitting detailed participant and benefit data by the later of 120 days after proposed termination date, or 30 days after PBGC determines that requirements have been satisfied unless enrolled actuary certifies plan is sufficient for guaranteed benefits.	Same as PBGC Form 600.
Schedule EA-D (PBGC Form 601)	Distress Termination Enrolled Actuary Certification	Enrolled actuary must certify the level of benefits that can be provided by plan assets.	Attachment to PBGC Form 601.	Same as PBGC Form 600.
None prescribed (notice must include information required by 29 CFR §2615.3)	PBGC reportable events (i.e., a reduction in the number of active participants, failure to meet minimum funding standards, the inability to pay benefits when due, a distribution to a substantial owner, bankruptcy or liquidation and change of employer)	Employer or plan administrator of a defined benefit pension plan subject to the plan termination insurance provisions of ERISA (other than multiemployer plans).	Within 30 days after the employer or plan administrator knows or has reason to know a reportable event has occurred.	Pension Benefit Guaranty Corporation, Office of Program Operations Room 5300-A 2020 K Street, NW Washington, D.C. 20006-1860
PBGC Form 200	Notice of Failure to Make Required Contributions	Contributing sponsor (or parent corporation, if part of "parent-subsidiary" controlled group) of a defined benefit pension plan that fails to make required minimum funding installment with unpaid balance (including interest) of more than $1 million.	Within 10 days of the due date for the required installment or other payment.	Pension Benefit Guaranty Corp., Case Operations and Compliance Department 2020 K Street, NW Washington, D.C. 20006-1860

Reporting Calendar—Contd.

Forms to be Filed for Establishment, Amendment, Merger or Termination of Pension and Profit-Sharing Plans (continued)

Form	Title/Description	Who May/Must File	When Filed	Where Filed
None prescribed	Notice to PBGC of adoption of plan amendment that results in significant underfunding	Contributing sponsor of defined benefit pension plan that is required to provide security for plan amendment that results in significant underfunding.	Within 30 days after the amendment takes effect.	Pension Benefit Guaranty Corporation 2020 K Street, NW Washington, D.C. 20006-1860
None prescribed	Notice of Substantial Cessation of Operations	Plan administrator of defined benefit pension plan to provide information regarding plant closing and its effect on plan.	Within 60 days of the plant closing.	Pension Benefit Guaranty Corporation 2020 K Street, NW Washington, D.C. 20006-1860
None prescribed	Notice of Substantial Employer Status	Plan administrator of single employer defined benefit pension plan with at least two contributing sponsors not under common control to notify contributing sponsor when it (and its controlled group members) is a substantial employer for the year.	Within 6 months after the end of the plan year.	Substantial employers (as defined in ERISA §4001(a)(2))
None prescribed	Notice of Withdrawal of a Substantial Employer	Plan administrator of single employer defined benefit pension plan with at least two contributing sponsors not under common control to notify PBGC of the withdrawal of a substantial employer and to request that PBGC determine liability of all persons with respect to withdrawal.	Within 60 days after withdrawal from plan.	Pension Benefit Guaranty Corporation 2020 K Street, NW Washington, D.C. 20006-1860

Other Reporting Material for Pension and Profit-Sharing Plans to be Filed with DOL

Item	Who Must File	When Filed	Where Filed
Summary Plan Description	Plan administrator of an employee benefit plan subject to Part 1 of Title I of ERISA.	Within 120 days after the later of when the plan becomes effective or is adopted. A new SPD must be filed once every 5 years after the initial filing date if the plan is amended; otherwise, must be filed every 10 years.	SPD, Room N-5644 Pension and Welfare Benefits Administration U.S. Department of Labor 200 Constitution Ave., NW Washington, D.C. 20210
Summary of Material Modifications	Plan administrator of an employee benefit plan subject to Part 1 of Title I of ERISA.	Within 210 days after the close of the plan year in which the modification was adopted unless changes or modifications are described in a timely filed SPD.	SMM, Room N-5644 Pension and Welfare Benefits Administration U.S. Department of Labor 200 Constitution Ave., NW Washington, D.C. 20210
Notice of Transfer of Excess Pension Assets to Retiree Health Account (Contents prescribed by ERISA §101(e)(2)(B) and ERISA Technical Release 91-1)	Employer that transfers excess pension assets from defined benefit pension plan to a §401(h) retiree health account to provide information concerning the amount of the transfer, a detailed accounting of assets projected to be held before and after the transfer, and current liabilities under the plan at the time of transfer.	At least 60 days before the transfer of excess pension assets to the retiree health account. In addition to filing with DOL, must also provide written notice to plan administrator and each employee organization representing plan participants.	Section 101(e)(2) Notice, Room N-5644 Division of Reports Pension and Welfare Benefits Administration U.S. Department of Labor 200 Constitution Ave., NW Washington, DC 20210

Reporting Calendar—Contd.

Disclosure to Pension and Profit-Sharing Plan Participants and Beneficiaries

Item	Description	Who Must Furnish	When Provided
Summary Plan Description	Summary of the provisions of the plan in language understandable to the average participant; gives details on the administrative operations of plan and statement of ERISA-protected rights.	Plan administrator of pension or profit-sharing plan.	New plans: within 120 days after the later of when the plan becomes effective or is adopted. Updated SPD must be furnished every 5 years for plans that have been amended; otherwise SPD must be redistributed every 10 years. New participants: within 90 days after becoming a participant or after benefits commence (in the case of beneficiaries).
Summary of Material Modifications	Summary of any material modification to the plan and any change in information required to be included in the SPD.	Plan administrator of pension or profit-sharing plan.	Within 210 days after the close of the plan year in which the modification was adopted unless changes or modifications are described in a timely distributed SPD.
Summary Annual Report	Summary of annual report Form 5500 or 5500-C (the shorter Form 5500-R version of Form 5500-C/R may be distributed for plans filing that version).	Plan administrator of pension or profit-sharing plan.	Nine months after end of plan year, or within two months after close of extension period for filing annual report, if applicable.
Preretirement Survivor Benefit Notification	Written explanation of qualified preretirement survivor annuity (including a description of the eligibility conditions and an explanation of the relative values of the optional forms of benefits available under the plan), the participant's right to elect to waive the annuity or revoke such waiver, the effect of such an election or revocation, and the rights of the participant's spouse.	Plan administrator of pension plans and certain profit-sharing plans if benefit is not fully subsidized.*	Written explanation: generally the later of (1) the period beginning on first day of plan year in which participant attains age 32 and ending with close of plan year in which participant attains age 34, or (2) one year after individual becomes a participant. Election must be made within the period beginning on the first day of the plan year in which the participant attains age 35 and ending with the participant's death.
Joint and Survivor Benefit Notification	Written explanation of qualified joint and survivor annuity (including a description of the eligibility conditions and an explanation of the relative values of the optional forms of benefits available under the plan), the right to elect to waive the annuity or revoke waiver, the effect of election or revocation, and the rights of the participant's spouse.	Plan administrator of pension plans and certain profit-sharing plans if benefit is not fully subsidized.*	Written explanation: no less than 30 days and no more than 90 days before annuity starting date. Election must be made no sooner than 90 days before the annuity starting date.
Notice to Terminated Vested Participants	Same information as provided to IRS on Schedule SSA (Form 5500 Series) concerning participant's accrued benefit. The statement must include a notice of any benefits that may be forfeited if the participant dies before a certain date.	Plan administrator of pension or profit-sharing plan.	No later than due date for filing Schedule SSA (Form 5500 Series).
Notice to Interested Parties	Notice of application for determination letter from IRS regarding qualification of a new or amended pension plan or upon termination to allow participants to appeal to IRS and/or DOL concerning plan's qualification.	Plan administrator of pension or profit-sharing plan.	Between 7 and 21 days before application is made if notice is given in person or posted in a location frequented by participants; between 10 and 24 days if mailed to each participant.
Notice of Transfer of Excess Pension Assets to Health Benefits Accounts	Notice to participants and beneficiaries of the transfer of excess pension assets to a §401(h) retiree health account. Notice must include the amount of excess pension assets, the portion to be transferred, the amount of health benefits liabilities expected to be provided by the transferred assets, and the amount of pension benefits of the participant that will be nonforfeitable immediately after the transfer.	Plan administrator of defined benefit pension plan that plans to transfer excess pension assets to retiree health accounts.	At least 60 days before the date of the qualified transfer of excess pension assets to retire health accounts.

* The survivor annuity rules generally do not apply to a profit-sharing or stock bonus plan or an ESOP provided the plan pays a participant's vested account balance upon death to the surviving spouse (unless the spouse agrees otherwise), and the participant does not elect to receive benefits in the form of a life annuity.

Reporting Calendar—Contd.

Disclosure to Pension and Profit-Sharing Plan Participants and Beneficiaries (continued)

Item	Description	Who Must Furnish	When Provided
Plan Terminations (a) Notice of Intent to Terminate	Notice to participants, beneficiaries, alternate payees and each employee organization representing participants of proposed termination. (Plans undergoing standard termination must inform participants that PBGC guaranty ceases with distribution of benefit liabilities.)	Plan administrator of terminating single employer defined benefit pension plan.	At least 60 days before the proposed date of termination.
(b) Notice of Plan Benefits	Notice to participants, beneficiaries and alternate payees of their full benefit under the plan calculated as of the proposed date of termination and the specific data used to compute benefit.	Plan administrator of terminating single employer defined benefit pension plan for standard plan termination.	No later than the date PBGC Form 500 is filed with the PBGC.
Notice of Future Benefit Reduction	Notice to participants, beneficiaries, alternate payees and each employee organization representing participants of a plan amendment to significantly reduce or freeze future benefit accruals and its effective date.	Plan administrator of defined benefit or money purchase pension plan.	At least 15 days before plan amendment is effective.
Notice of Minimum Funding Waiver Request	Notice to each employee organization representing participants, and to plan participants, beneficiaries and alternate payees of minimum funding waiver request. Notice must include a description of the extent plan is funded for guaranteed benefits and for benefit liabilities.	Employer that requests a minimum funding waiver for pension benefit plan.	Employer must provide evidence that notice has been provided before the IRS will grant a funding waiver or extension.
Notice of Failure to Meet Minimum Funding Standards	Notice to participants, beneficiaries and alternate payees of failure to meet required minimum funding installment or other payment (unless there is a pending funding waiver request).	Employer maintaining defined benefit plan that fails to make quarterly or other required payment within 60 days of due date.	At the time and in the manner to be prescribed by the Department of Labor.
Accrued Benefit Statement	Statement, based on the latest available data, of a participant's total benefit accrued to date, and the amount that is nonforfeitable or the earliest date on which benefits will become nonforfeitable.	Plan administrator of pension or profit-sharing plan.	Within 30 days of request from participant. Need not be provided more than once in a 12-month period.
Tax Information Returns (a) Form W-2	In addition to reporting wages and withholding, used to report distributions from nonqualified plans and §457 plans, elective deferrals, the amount of dependent care assistance provided by employer, certain group-term life insurance coverage, and to indicate active participant status.	Employer.	No later than January 31.
(b) Form 1099-R*	Reports all distributions from qualified retirement plans, IRAs, SEPs and DECs during the calendar year, including participant loans treated as distributions. Also reports certain death benefit payments.	Plan administrator or other payor of plan distribution, employer for death benefit payments.	No later than January 31.

* If corrective distributions of excess contributions or excess aggregate contributions plus related income are distributed more than 2½ months after the close of the prior plan year, the payor or plan administrator must furnish the employer either with copies of Form 1099-R or a written statement containing the information reportable on this form within 30 days of the date of distribution. The employer is subject to a 10% penalty tax for failure to timely distribute corrective distributions and must file Form 5330 to pay this tax.

Reporting Calendar—Contd.

Disclosure to Pension and Profit-Sharing Plan Participants and Beneficiaries (continued)

Item	Description	Who Must Furnish	When Provided
Tax Information Returns (continued)			
(c) Form 1099-DIV	Reports cash dividends paid on employer stock held by an ESOP that are either paid directly to participants or paid to the plan and later distributed in cash to participants.	Plan administrator or other payor of cash dividend paid on employer stock held by an ESOP.	No later than January 31.
(d) Information on IRAs and SEPs (Form 5498 may be used)	Reports IRA contributions and rollovers, and the fair market value of IRAs and SEPs. (See Rev. Proc. 89-52 for rules where IRA owner dies.)	Trustee of IRA or SEP.	Statement of value of account: January 31. Contribution information: by May 31 for the prior calendar year.
Effect of distributions of excess deferrals, excess contributions and excess aggregate contributions on individual's income tax return.	Plan participants must be advised that receipt of amounts includible in income in a prior year will require participants to file an amended income tax return if a return has already been filed for that year, and, if applicable, how to report losses on excess deferrals on Form 1040.	Payors making corrective distributions of excess deferrals, excess contributions and excess aggregate contributions.	At the time of distribution.
Notice of Rollover Treatment	Written notice to recipient of qualifying rollover distribution that the distribution will not be taxed currently to extent transferred to another qualified plan or IRA within 60 days, and explanation of lump sum treatment, if applicable. May satisfy requirement with statement describing how to determine whether distribution is a qualifying rollover distribution.	Plan administrator of pension or profit-sharing plan that makes a qualified total distribution, or a partial distribution eligible for rollover to an IRA.	Within two weeks of making any qualified total distribution (as defined in §402(a)(5)), or any partial distribution eligible for rollover to an IRA.
Notice of right to elect not to have withholding apply (Form W-4P may be used)	Notice to payee of periodic or nonperiodic distribution of right to elect not to have withholding apply (Withholding Certificate for Pension or Annuity Payments).	Plan administrator or other payor of periodic or nonperiodic distributions.	Periodic payments: no more than six months before the first payment and not later than first payment; must also be given with first payment and each year thereafter. Nonperiodic payments: no more than six months before distribution and not later than the time that will give the payee reasonable time to elect not to have withholding apply.
Qualified Domestic Relations Order	Written notice to participant and alternate payee of receipt of order and plan procedures for determining whether order is qualified; and notification whether order is qualified.	Plan administrator of pension or profit-sharing plan that receives a domestic relations order.	Notice to participants and alternate payees: promptly on receipt of court order; determination and notification whether order is qualified: within a reasonable period after receipt of order.
Notice of Suspension of Benefits	Description of specific reasons why benefit payments are being suspended, general description of plan provisions relating to the suspension of payments, a copy of plan provisions, and an explanation of plan's review procedures (contents prescribed by regulations).	Plan administrator of defined benefit pension plan that suspends payments for reemployment.	During first calendar month or payroll period in which plan withholds payments on account of reemployment of retiree or continued employment beyond normal retirement age.
IRA Disclosure Statement	Written explanation of Code requirements, tax effects of contributions and distributions, any restrictions and applicable penalty provisions. Must include financial information relating to guaranteed or projected benefits.	Sponsors of IRAs.	When an individual sets up an IRA.

Reporting Calendar—Contd.

Disclosure to Pension and Profit-Sharing Plan Participants and Beneficiaries (continued)

Item	Description	Who Must Furnish	When Provided
Claims Procedure	Procedure for claiming plan benefits. Written explanation of the reasons for denial of an application under the plan, the specific plan provisions on which the denial was based, any additional material or information needed to perfect claim and the procedure for appeal.	Plan administrator of pension or profit-sharing plan.	Procedure for claiming plan benefits must be described in SPD. Claims must be processed within 90 days of initial claim for benefits (90-day extension is permitted if participant is notified of the delay within the initial 90-day period). Participant must be given at least 60 days to appeal, and final decision must be rendered within 60 days (60-day extension is permitted).
Plan Documents and Government Reporting Forms	Copies of plan, trust agreement, summary plan description, bargaining agreement, contracts, annual report and schedules, application for IRS determination letter.	Plan administrator of pension or profit-sharing plan.	All documents, except those containing individual employee data, must be available at the principal business office(s) during normal working hours. Copies of these documents generally must be mailed within 30 days of written request from participant. No more than $.25 per page may be charged for copying. Important: Forms 5302 and 6088 are not to be made available for public inspection.

Reporting Calendar—Contd.

Reporting and Disclosure Penalty Provisions for Pension and Profit-Sharing Plans*

Item	Title/Description	Penalty
Form 5500 Series	Annual Return/Report of Employee Benefit Plan	The DOL may assess a civil penalty of up to $1,000 a day for a plan administrator's material failure or refusal to file an annual report (*ERISA §502(c)(2)*). In addition, the IRS may also assess a penalty of $25 for each day of failure to file complete annual returns (up to $15,000) unless failure is due to reasonable cause (*IRC §6652(e)*). This penalty does not apply for failure to include Schedules B or SSA.
Schedule B	Actuarial Information	A penalty of $1,000 for failure to file an actuarial statement unless failure is due to reasonable cause (*IRC §6692*).
Schedule SSA	Annual Registration Statement Identifying Separated Participants with Deferred Vested Benefits	A penalty of $1 a day for each participant for whom a registration statement is not filed (up to $5,000 for any plan year) unless failure is due to a reasonable cause (*IRC §6652(d)(1)*).
Form 5500 Series	Change of status (i.e., name of the plan, name or address of plan administrator, plan termination, merger or consolidation)	A penalty of $1 a day for not filing a notification of change of status of a plan (up to $1,000) unless failure is due to reasonable cause (*IRC §6652(d)(2)*).
PBGC Form 1 PBGC Form 1-ES	Annual Premium Payment Estimated Premium Payment	A late payment penalty (not to exceed 100% of the unpaid premium) of the greater of (1) 5% per month, or fraction thereof, of the unpaid premiums; or (2) $25. May be waived for substantial hardship or for other good cause. Late payment penalty may be avoided if estimated premium payment equals the lesser of (1) 90% of base premiums due by the reconciliation due date, or (2) the premium computed by using prior year participant count; and 100% of the base premium is paid by the reconciliation due date. A late payment interest charge will be imposed on any unpaid amount at rate determined under IRC §6621 (*29 CFR §§2610.7 and 2610.8*).
PBGC reportable events and other required information	Notices and information that must be provided to the PBGC (e.g., Notice of Failure to Make Required Contributions, reportable events, plan data relating to distress terminations, or plan amendment that results in significant underfunding).	The PBGC may assess a civil penalty of up to $1,000 a day for failure to timely provide any required notice or other material information (*ERISA §4071*).
Form 990-T	Exempt Organization Unrelated Business Income Tax Return	For late filing, a penalty of 5% of the net amount due for each month or fraction of a month the return is not filed (up to 25%); for failure to pay the tax when due, a penalty of ½ of 1% of the net amount due for each month or fraction of a month the tax is not paid (up to 25%), unless failure to file or pay was due to reasonable cause and not to willful neglect. These penalties are in addition to the interest charge imposed on the unpaid tax at a rate set by IRC §6621 (*IRC §§6601 and 6651*).
Form 5310-A	Notice of Merger, Consolidation or Transfer of Plan Assets or Liabilities	A penalty of $25 for each day Form 5310-A is late (up to $15,000) unless failure is due to reasonable cause (*IRC §6652(e)*).

* In addition to the specific penalties described in this section, any person convicted of willfully violating any provision of Part 1 of Title 1 of ERISA (relating to reporting and disclosure) will be fined not more than $5,000 or imprisoned for not more than one year or both (§501 of ERISA). For a violation by an entity, the fine imposed may not exceed $100,000. Any person knowingly making any false statement or representation of fact or knowingly concealing, covering up or failing to disclose any fact required by ERISA (18 U.S.C. §1027 as amended by §111 of ERISA) will be fined up to $10,000 or imprisoned for five years or both.

Reporting Calendar—Contd.

Reporting and Disclosure Penalty Provisions for Pension and Profit-Sharing Plans* (continued)

Item	Title/Description	Penalty
Form 5329	Return for Additional Taxes Attributable to Qualified Plans (including IRAs), Annuities and Modified Endowment Contracts	Generally, the same interest charges and penalties for late filing and for not paying taxes when due that apply to Form 990-T (*IRC §§6601 and 6651*). However, for IRAs, same penalties that apply to Form 5500 (*IRC §6652(e)*).
Form 5330	Return of Excise Taxes Related to Employee Benefit Plans	Same interest charges and penalties for late filing and for not paying taxes when due that apply to Form 990-T (*IRC §§6601 and 6651*).
Forms 1099-R, 1099-DIV**	Reports distributions from pension and profit-sharing plans, annuities and IRAs, and cash dividends from an ESOP	Same penalties that apply to Form 5500 (*IRC §6652(e)*).
Form 5498**	Individual Retirement Arrangement Information	A penalty of $50 for each failure to file reports on IRAs unless failure is due to reasonable cause (*IRC §6693*).
Notice of right to elect not to have withholding apply (Form W-4P)	Notice to payee of right to elect not to have withholding apply (Withholding for Pension or Annuity Payments)	A penalty of $10 for each failure to provide notice to payee of right to elect out of withholding (up to $5,000 per calendar year), unless failure is due to reasonable cause and not to willful neglect (*IRC §6652(h)*).
Notice of Rollover Treatment	Written explanation to recipients of distributions eligible for rollover.	A penalty of $10 for each failure to provide written explanation (up to $5,000 per calendar year), unless failure is due to reasonable cause and not to willful neglect (*IRC §6652(i)*).
Notice of Failure to Meet Minimum Funding Standards	Notice to participants, beneficiaries and alternate payees of failure to make minimum funding quarterly installment within 60 days of due date.	A penalty of up to $100 a day and any other relief that a court in its discretion may impose if notice is not provided (*ERISA §502(c)(3)*).
Notice of Transfer of Excess Pension Assets to Health Benefits Accounts	Notice to DOL, plan administrator and employee organizations representing plan participants of transfer of excess pension assets to §401(h) retiree health accounts.	A penalty of up to $100 a day and any other relief that a court in its discretion may impose if notice is not provided (*ERISA §502(c)(3)*).
Notice of Transfer of Excess Pension Assets to Health Benefits Accounts	Notice to participants and beneficiaries of transfer of excess pension assets to §401(h) retiree health accounts.	A penalty of up to $100 a day and any other relief that a court in its discretion may impose if required notice is not provided, unless the failure results from matters reasonably beyond the plan administrator's control (*ERISA §502(c)(1)*).
Notice to Terminated Vested Participants	Statement describing the vested deferred benefit to which participant is entitled.	A penalty of $50 for each willful failure to furnish statement (*IRC §6690*).
Information requested by participants or beneficiaries that must be furnished by the plan administrator	Copies of plan documents, annual reports, application for determination, accrued benefit statement, summary plan description, summary annual report.	A penalty of up to $100 a day and any other relief that a court in its discretion may impose if requested information is not mailed to last known address within 30 days of the date of the request, unless the failure or refusal by the plan administrator results from matters reasonably beyond the administrator's control (*ERISA §502(c)(1)*).
Recordkeeping Requirement	Records maintained by an employer must be detailed enough to determine benefits due or that may become due.	A penalty of $10 for each employee unless failure to maintain records or to furnish them to the plan administrator is due to reasonable cause (*ERISA §209(b)*).
Maintenance of data base sufficient to provide required reports	Adequate records must be maintained by employer or plan administrator to report plan distributions.	A penalty of $50 for each employee (up to $50,000) for each calendar year unless failure is due to reasonable cause or inability to correct previous failure (*IRC §6704*).

* In addition to the specific penalties described in this section, any person convicted of willfully violating any provision of Part 1 of Title 1 of ERISA (relating to reporting and disclosure) will be fined not more than $5,000 or imprisoned for not more than one year or both (§501 of ERISA). For a violation by an entity, the fine imposed may not exceed $100,000. Any person knowingly making any false statement or representation of fact or knowingly concealing, covering up or failing to disclose any fact required by ERISA (18 U.S.C. §1027 as amended by §111 of ERISA) will be fined up to $10,000 or imprisoned for five years or both.

** Failure to file a return on magnetic media when required to do so under IRC §6011(e) and the regulations thereunder is treated as a failure to file the return and may result in the imposition of a penalty.

Source: Reprinted with permission from Coopers & Lybrand Actuarial, Benefits and Compensation Consulting Services.

APPENDIX 3

Form 5500

Form **5500** Department of the Treasury Internal Revenue Service Department of Labor Pension and Welfare Benefits Administration Pension Benefit Guaranty Corporation	**Annual Return/Report of Employee Benefit Plan** (With 100 or more participants) This form is required to be filed under sections 104 and 4065 of the Employee Retirement Income Security Act of 1974 and sections 6039D, 6057(b), and 6058(a) of the Internal Revenue Code, referred to as the Code. ▶ See separate instructions

OMB No. 1210-0016

1991

This Form Is Open to Public Inspection.

For the calendar plan year 1991 or fiscal plan year beginning _____ , 1991, and ending _____ , 19 ____

A If *(1)* through *(4)* do not apply to this year's return/report, leave the boxes unmarked. This return/report is:

For IRS Use Only

EP–ID

(1) ☐ the first return/report filed for the plan;

(2) ☐ an amended return/report;

(3) ☐ the final return/report filed for the plan; or

(4) ☐ a short plan year return/report (less than 12 months).

Information in 1a through 6b is used to identify your employee benefit plan. Check it for accuracy and make any necessary corrections. Also complete any incomplete items in 1a through 6b. This page must accompany your completed return/report.

B IF YOU MADE ANY CHANGES TO THE PREPRINTED INFORMATION OR FILLED IN ANY INCOMPLETE INFORMATION IN 1a THROUGH 6b BELOW, CHECK HERE . ▶ ☐

C If your plan year changed since the last return/report, check this box . . . . ▶ ☐

D If you filed for an extension of time to file this return/report, check this box and attach a copy of the extension . . . . ▶ ☐

1a Name and address of plan sponsor (employer, if for a single-employer plan) (address should include room or suite no.)

1b Employer identification number

1c Sponsor's telephone number

1d Business code (see instructions, page 19)

1e CUSIP issuer number

2a Name and address of plan administrator (if same as plan sponsor, enter "Same")

2b Administrator's employer identification no.

2c Administrator's telephone number

3 If you are not filing a page one with the historical plan information preprinted and the name, address and EIN of the plan sponsor or plan administrator is different than that on the last return/report filed for this plan, enter the information from the last return/report in **a** and/or **b** and complete **c**.

a Sponsor . . . . EIN . . . . Plan number . . . .

b Administrator . . . . EIN . . . .

c If a indicates a change in the sponsor's name, address and EIN, is this a change in sponsorship only? (See instruction 3c for definition of sponsorship.) Enter "Yes" or "No."

4 Enter the applicable plan entity code listed in the instructions for line 4 on page 8. ▶

5a(1) Name of plan ▶ . . . .

. . . .

5b Effective date of plan (mo., day, yr.)

(2) Does this plan cover self-employed individuals? (Enter "Yes" or "No.") ▶

5c Enter three-digit plan number ▶

All filers must complete 6a, 6b, and 6c as applicable.

6a(1) Welfare or fringe benefit plan (Enter the applicable codes from page 8 of the instructions in the boxes.) ▶

(2) If you entered a code M, N, or **O** is the plan funded? (see instructions) . . . . ▶ ☐ Yes ☐ No

6b Pension benefit plan (Enter the applicable pension codes from page 8 of the instructions.) ▶

Be sure to include all required schedules and attachments. This page must accompany your completed return/report.

Caution: *A penalty for the late or incomplete filing of this return/report will be assessed unless reasonable cause is established.*

Under penalties of perjury and other penalties set forth in the instructions, I declare that I have examined this return/report, including accompanying schedules and statements, and to the best of my knowledge and belief, it is true, correct, and complete.

Signature of employer/plan sponsor ▶ . . . . Date ▶ . . . .

Type or print name of individual signing for the employer/plan sponsor . . . .

Signature of plan administrator ▶ . . . .

Type or print name of individual signing for the plan administrator . . . . Date ▶ . . . .

For Paperwork Reduction Act Notice, see page 1 of the instructions.   Cat. No. 13500F   Form **5500** (1991)

Form 5500—Contd.

3c Other plan features (if you check box *(1)* or *(2)*, attach Schedule E (Form 5500)):   *(1)* ☐ ESOP   *(2)* ☐ Leveraged ESOP
     (3) ☐ Participant-directed account plan   *(4)* ☐ Pension plan maintained outside the United States
     (5) ☐ Master trust (see instructions)   *(6)* ☐ 103-12 investment entity (see instructions)
     (7) ☐ Common/collective trust   *(8)* ☐ Pooled separate account

		Yes	No
d Single-employer plans enter the tax year end of the employer in which this plan year ends ▶ Month..... Day..... Year.....			
e Is the employer a member of an affiliated service group?			
f Does this plan contain a cash or deferred arrangement described in Code section 401(k)?.			

7 Number of participants as of the end of the plan year (welfare plans complete only a(4), b, c, and d):

a Active participants:*(1)* Number fully vested.	**a(1)**	
(2) Number partially vested	**a(2)**	
(3) Number nonvested	**a(3)**	
(4) Total .	**a(4)**	
b Retired or separated participants receiving benefits	**b**	
c Retired or separated participants entitled to future benefits	**c**	
d Subtotal (add **a(4), b,** and **c**).	**d**	
e Deceased participants whose beneficiaries are receiving or are entitled to receive benefits.	**e**	
f Total (add **d** and **e**).	**f**	
g Number of participants with account balances (Defined benefit plans do not complete this line item.)	**g**	

		Yes	No
h *(1)* Was any participant(s) separated from service with a deferred vested benefit for which a Schedule SSA (Form 5500) is required to be attached to this form? (See instructions.)	**h(1)**		
(2) If "Yes," enter the number of separated participants required to be reported ▶			
8a Was this plan amended in this plan year or any prior plan year? If "No," go to item 9a	**8a**		
b If **a** is "Yes," enter the date the most recent amendment was adopted. ▶ Month....... Day........ Year....... If the date in **b** is in the plan year for which this return/report is filed, complete **c** through **f**			
c Did any amendment during the current plan year result in the retroactive reduction of accrued benefits for any participants?	**c**		
d Did any amendment during the current plan year provide former employees with an additional allocation or accrual this year?	**d**		
e During this plan year did any amendment change the information contained in the latest summary plan descriptions or summary description of modifications available at the time of amendment?	**e**		
f If **e** is "Yes," has a summary plan description or summary description of modifications that reflects the plan amendments referred to in **e** been both furnished to participants and filed with the Department of Labor?	**f**		
9a Was this plan terminated during this plan year or any prior plan year? If "Yes," enter the year ▶...........	**9a**		
b Were all plan assets either distributed to participants or beneficiaries, transferred to another plan, or brought under the control of PBGC?.	**b**		
c Was a resolution to terminate this plan adopted during this plan year or any prior plan year?.	**c**		
d If **a** or **c** is "Yes," have you received a favorable determination letter from IRS for the termination?.	**d**		
e If **d** is "No," has a determination letter been requested from IRS?.	**e**		
f If **a** or **c** is "Yes," have participants and beneficiaries been notified of the termination or the proposed termination?	**f**		
g If **a** is "Yes" and the plan is covered by PBGC, is the plan continuing to file a PBGC Form 1 and pay premiums until the end of the plan year in which assets are distributed or brought under the control of PBGC?	**g**		
h During this plan year, did any trust assets revert to the employer for which Code section 4980 excise tax is due?	**h**		
i If **h** is "Yes," enter the amount of tax paid with your Form 5330 ▶ $			

10a In this plan year, was this plan merged or consolidated into another plan(s), or were assets or liabilities transferred to another plan(s)? If "No," go to item 11   ☐ **Yes** ☐ **No**
     If "Yes," identify other plan(s)

	c Employer identification number(s)	**d** Plan number(s)
b Name of plan(s) ▶		

e Has Form 5310 or 5310-A been filed?   ☐ **Yes** ☐ **No**

		Yes	No
11 Enter the plan funding arrangement code from page 9 of the instructions ▶	**12** Enter the plan benefit arrangement code from page 9 of the instructions ▶		
13a Is this a plan established or maintained pursuant to one or more collective bargaining agreements?.		**13a**	
b If **a** is "Yes," enter the appropriate six-digit LM number(s) of the sponsoring labor organization(s) (see instructions):			
(1) *(2)* *(3)*			
14 If any benefits are provided by an insurance company, insurance service, or similar organization, enter the number of **Schedules A (Form 5500),** Insurance Information, that are attached. If none, enter "-0-." ▶			

Form 5500—Contd.

Welfare Plans Do Not Complete Items 15 Through 27. Go To Item 28. Fringe Benefit Plans see page 5 of the instructions.

			Yes	No
15a	If this is a defined benefit plan, subject to the minimum funding standards for this plan year, is **Schedule** **B** (Form 5500) required to be attached? (If this is a defined contribution plan leave blank.)	**15a**		
b	If this is a defined contribution plan, i.e., money purchase or target benefit, is it subject to the minimum funding standards? (If a waiver was granted, see instructions.) (If this is a defined benefit plan leave blank.) If "Yes," complete *(1)*, *(2)*, and *(3)* below:	**b**		

(1) Amount of employer contribution required for the plan year under Code section 412 **b(1)** $

(2) Amount of contribution paid by the employer for the plan year **b(2)** $

Enter date of last payment by employer ▶ Month........ Day........ Year......

(3) If *(1)* is greater than *(2)*, subtract *(2)* from *(1)* and enter the funding deficiency here; otherwise, enter zero. (If you have a funding deficiency, file Form 5330.) **b(3)** $

			Yes	No
16	Has the plan been top-heavy at any time beginning with the 1984 plan year?	**16**		
17	Has the annual compensation of each participant taken into account under the current plan year been limited to $222,220?	**17**		
18a *(1)*	Did the plan distribute any annuity contracts this year? (See instructions.)	**a(1)**		
(2)	If *(1)* is "Yes," did these contracts contain a requirement that the spouse consent before any distributions under the contract are made in a form other than a qualified joint and survivor annuity?	**a(2)**		
b	Did the plan make distributions to participants or spouses in a form other than a qualified joint and survivor annuity (a life annuity if a single person) or qualified preretirement survivor annuity (exclude deferred annuity contracts)?	**b**		
c	Did the plan make distributions or loans to married participants and beneficiaries without the required consent of the participant's spouse?	**c**		
d	Upon plan amendment or termination, do the accrued benefits of every participant include the subsidized benefits that the participant may become entitled to receive subsequent to the plan amendment or termination?	**d**		
19	Were distributions, if any, made in accordance with the requirements under Code sections 411(a)(11) and 417(e)?	**19**		
20	Have any contributions been made or benefits accrued in excess of the Code section 415 limits, as amended by the Tax Reform Act of 1986?	**20**		
21	Has the plan made the required distributions in 1991 under Code section 401(a)(9)? (See instructions.)	**21**		
22a	Does the employer apply the separate line of business rules of Code section 414(r) when testing to see if this plan satisfies the coverage and discrimination tests of Code sections 410(b) and 401(a)(4)?	**22a**		

b If **a** is "Yes," enter the total number of separate lines of business claimed by the employer ▶ ....
If more than one separate line of business, see instructions for additional information to attach.

			Yes	No
c	Does the plan consist of more than one part that is mandatorily disaggregated under Income Tax Regulations section 1.410(b)-7(c)? If "Yes," see instructions for additional information to attach.	**c**		
d	In testing whether this plan satisfies the coverage and discrimination tests of Code sections 410(b) and 401(a), does the employer aggregate plans?	**d**		
e	Does the employer restructure the plan into component plans to satisfy the coverage and discrimination tests of Code sections 410(b) and 401(a)(4)?	**e**		

f If you meet either of the following exceptions, check the applicable box to tell us which exception you meet and do NOT complete the rest of question **22**:

(1) ☐ No highly compensated employee benefited under the plan at any time during the plan year;

(2) ☐ This is a collectively bargained plan that benefits only employees covered under a collective bargaining agreement, and no more than 2 percent of the employees who are covered under the collectively bargained agreement are professional employees.

			Yes	No
g	Did any leased employee perform services for the employer at any time during the plan year?	**g**		

			Number
h	Enter the total number of employees of the employer. Employer includes entities aggregated with the employer under Code sections 414(b), (c), or (m). The number of employees includes leased employees and self-employed individuals.	**h**	
i	Enter the total number of employees excludable because of: *(1)* failure to meet requirements for minimum age and years of service; *(2)* coverage under a collective bargaining agreement; *(3)* nonresident aliens who receive no earned income from U. S. sources; and *(4)* the 500 hours of service/last day rule	**i**	
j	Enter the number of nonexcludable employees (subtract line **i** from line **h**)	**j**	

k Do 100 percent of the nonexcludable employees entered on line **j** benefit under the plan? . ☐ **Yes** ☐ **No**
If line **k** is "Yes," do NOT complete lines **22l** through **22o**.

			Number
l	Enter the number of nonexcludable employees (line **j**) who are highly compensated employees	**l**	
m	Enter the number of nonexcludable employees (line **j**) who benefit under the plan.	**m**	
n	Enter the number of employees entered on line **m** who are highly compensated employees	**n**	

o This plan satisfies the coverage requirements on the basis of (check one):

(1) ☐ The average benefits test

(2) ☐ The ratio percentage test—Enter value ▶

Form 5500—Contd.

		Yes	No

23a Is it intended that this plan qualify under Code section 401(a)? **23a**

If "Yes," complete **b** and **c** .

  b Enter the date of the most recent IRS determination letter. . . . . ▶ Month .... Year ....

  c Is a determination letter request pending with IRS? . . . . **c**

24a If this is a plan with Employee Stock Ownership (ESOP) features, was a current appraisal of the value of the stock made immediately before any contribution of stock or the purchase of the stock by the trust for the plan year covered by this return/report? . . **24a**

(If this plan has NO ESOP features leave blank and go to item 25.)

  b If **a** is "Yes," was the appraisal made by an unrelated third party? . . . . **b**

  c If dividends paid on employer securities held by the ESOP were used to make payments on ESOP loans enter the amount of the dividends used to make the payments **24c**

25 Does the plan provide for permitted disparity? See Code sections 401(a)(5) and 401(l) **25**

26 Does the employer/sponsor listed in **1a** of this form maintain other qualified pension benefit plans?. . . **26**

If "Yes," enter the total number of plans, including this plan ▶

27 If this plan is an adoption of a master, prototype, or regional prototype plan, indicate which type by checking the appropriate box: **a** ☐ Master   **b** ☐ Prototype   **c** ☐ Regional Prototype

28a Did any person who rendered services to the plan receive directly or indirectly $5,000 or more in compensation from the plan during the plan year (except for employees of the plan who were paid less than $1,000 in each month)? . . **28a**

If "Yes," complete Part I of **Schedule C** (Form 5500).

  b Did the plan have any trustees who must be listed in Part II of **Schedule C** (Form 5500)? . . . . . . **b**

  c Has there been a termination in the appointment of any person listed in **d** below? . . . . **c**

  d If **c** is "Yes," check the appropriate box(es), answer **e** and **f**, and complete Part III of **Schedule C** (Form 5500):

    (1) ☐ Accountant   *(2)* ☐ Enrolled actuary   *(3)* ☐ Insurance carrier   *(4)* ☐ Custodian

    (5) ☐ Administrator *(6)* ☐ Investment manager   *(7)* ☐ Trustee

  e Have there been any outstanding material disputes or matters of disagreement concerning the above termination? **e**

  f If an accountant or enrolled actuary has been terminated during the plan year, has the terminated accountant/actuary been provided a copy of the explanation required by Part III of **Schedule C** (Form 5500) with a notice advising them of their opportunity to submit comments on the explanation directly to DOL?. . **f**

  g Enter the number of **Schedules C** (Form 5500) that are attached. If none, enter -0- ▶

29a Is this plan exempt from the requirement to engage an independent qualified public accountant? . . . **29a**

  b If **a** is "No," attach the accountant's opinion to this return/report and check the appropriate box. This opinion is:

    (1) ☐ Unqualified

    (2) ☐ Qualified/disclaimer per Department of Labor Regulations 29 CFR 2520.103-8 and/or 2520.103-12(d)

    (3) ☐ Qualified/disclaimer other *(4)* ☐ Adverse *(5)* ☐ Other (explain) ....

....

  c If **a** is "No," does the accountant's report, including the financial statements and/or notes required to be attached to this return/report disclose (1) errors or irregularities; (2) illegal acts; (3) material internal control weaknesses; (4) a loss contingency indicating that assets are impaired or a liability incurred; (5) significant real estate or other transactions in which the plan and (A) the sponsor, (B) the plan administrator, (C) the employer(s), or (D) the employee organization(s) are jointly involved; (6) that the plan has participated in any related party transactions; or (7) any unusual or infrequent events or transactions occurring subsequent to the plan year end that might significantly affect the usefulness of the financial statements in assessing the plan's present or future ability to pay benefits? **c**

  d If **c** is "Yes," provide the total amount involved in such disclosure ▶

30 If **29a** is "No," complete the following questions. (You may NOT use "N/A" in response to item 30):

If **a, b, c, d, e,** or **f** is checked "Yes," schedules of these items in the format set forth in the instructions are required to be attached to this return/report.

During the plan year:

  a Did the plan have assets held for investment?. **30a**

  b Were any loans by the plan or fixed income obligations due the plan in default as of the close of the plan year or classified during the year as uncollectible? . . . . **b**

  c Were any leases to which the plan was a party in default or classified during the year as uncollectible? . **c**

  d Were any plan transactions or series of transactions in excess of 5% of the current value of plan assets? **d**

  e Do the notes to the financial statements accompanying the accountant's opinion disclose any nonexempt transactions with parties-in-interest? . . . . **e**

  f Did the plan engage in any nonexempt transactions with parties-in-interest not reported in **e** ? . . . . **f**

  g Did the plan hold qualifying employer securities that are not publicly traded? . . . . **g**

  h Did the plan purchase or receive any nonpublicly traded securities that were not appraised in writing by an unrelated third party within 3 months prior to their receipt? . . . . **h**

  i Did any person manage plan assets who had a financial interest worth more than 10% in any party providing services to the plan or receive anything of value from any party providing services to the plan? . . . . **i**

31 Did the plan acquire individual whole life insurance contracts during the plan year? **31**

Form 5500—Contd.

32 During the plan year:

					Yes	No
a	(1)	Was this plan covered by a fidelity bond? If "Yes," complete a(2) and a(3)		32a(1)		
	(2)	Enter amount of bond ▶ $				
	(3)	Enter the name of the surety company ▶				
b	(1)	Was there any loss to the plan, whether or not reimbursed, caused by fraud or dishonesty?	b(1)			
	(2)	If (1) is "Yes," enter amount of loss ▶ $				

33a Is the plan covered under the Pension Benefit Guaranty Corporation termination insurance program?

☐ Yes   ☐ No   ☐ Not determined

b If **a** is "Yes" or "Not determined," enter the employer identification number and the plan number used to identify it.
Employer identification number ▶   Plan number ▶

34 Current value of plan assets and liabilities at the beginning and end of the plan year. Combine the value of plan assets held in more than one trust. Allocate the value of the plan's interest in a commingled trust containing the assets of more than one plan on a line- by-line basis unless the trust meets one of the specific exceptions described in the instructions. Do not enter the value of that portion of an insurance contract which guarantees, during this plan year, to pay a specific dollar benefit at a future date. **Round off amounts to the nearest dollar; any other amounts are subject to rejection.** Plans with no assets at the beginning and the end of the plan year, enter zero on line f.

Assets

			(a) Beginning of year	(b) End of Year
a	Total noninterest-bearing cash	a		
b	Receivables: (1) Employer contributions	b(1)		
	(2) Participant contributions	(2)		
	(3) Income	(3)		
	(4) Other	(4)		
	(5) Less allowance for doubtful accounts	(5)		
	(6) Total. Add b(1) through (4) and subtract (5) ▶	(6)		
c	General Investments: (1) Interest-bearing cash (including money market funds)	c(1)		
	(2) Certificates of deposit	(2)		
	(3) U.S. Government securities	(3)		
	(4) Corporate debt instruments: (A) Preferred	(4)(A)		
	(B) All other	(4)(B)		
	(5) Corporate stocks: (A) Preferred	(5)(A)		
	(B) Common	(5)(B)		
	(6) Partnership/joint venture interests	(6)		
	(7) Real estate: (A) Income-producing	(7)(A)		
	(B) Nonincome-producing	(7)(B)		
	(8) Loans (other than to participants) secured by mortgages: (A) Residential	(8)(A)		
	(B) Commercial	(8)(B)		
	(9) Loans to participants: (A) Mortgages	(9)(A)		
	(B) Other	(9)(B)		
	(10) Other loans	(10)		
	(11) Value of interest in common/collective trusts	(11)		
	(12) Value of interest in pooled separate accounts	(12)		
	(13) Value of interest in master trusts	(13)		
	(14) Value of interest in 103-12 investment entities	(14)		
	(15) Value of interest in registered investment companies	(15)		
	(16) Value of funds held in insurance company general account (unallocated contracts)	(16)		
	(17) Other	(17)		
	(18) Total. Add c(1) through c(17) ▶	(18)		
d	Employer-related investments: (1) Employer securities	d(1)		
	(2) Employer real property	(2)		
e	Buildings and other property used in plan operation	e		
f	**Total** assets. Add a, b(6), c(18), d(1), d(2), and e ▶	f		

Liabilities

g	Benefit claims payable	g		
h	Operating payables	h		
i	Acquisition indebtedness	i		
j	Other liabilities	j		
k	**Total** liabilities. Add g through j ▶	k		

Net Assets

l	Line f minus line k ▶	l		

Form 5500—Contd.

Form 5500 (1991)   Page **6**

5   Plan income, expenses, and changes in net assets for the plan year. *Include all income and expenses of the plan, including any trust(s) or separately maintained fund(s), and any payments/receipts to/from insurance carriers.* **Round off amounts to the nearest dollar; any other amounts are subject to rejection.**

Income		(a) Amount	(b) Total
a Contributions:			
(1) Received or receivable from:			
(A) Employers	a(1)(A)		
(B) Participants	(B)		
(C) Others	(C)		
(2) Noncash contributions	(2)		
(3) Total contributions. Add a(1)(A), (B), (C) and a(2) ▶	(3)		
b Earnings on investments:			
(1) Interest			
(A) Interest-bearing cash (including money market funds)	b(1)(A)		
(B) Certificates of deposit	(B)		
(C) U.S. Government securities	(C)		
(D) Corporate debt instruments	(D)		
(E) Mortgage loans	(E)		
(F) Other loans	(F)		
(G) Other interest	(G)		
(H) Total interest. Add b(1)(A) through (G) ▶	(H)		
(2) Dividends: **(A)** Preferred stock	b(2)(A)		
(B) Common stock	(B)		
(C) Total dividends. Add b(2)(A) and (B) ▶	(C)		
(3) Rents	(3)		
(4) Net gain (loss) on sale of assets: **(A)** Aggregate proceeds	(4)(A)		
(B) Aggregate carrying amount (see instructions)	(B)		
(C) Subtract (B) from (A) and enter result	(C)		
(5) Unrealized appreciation (depreciation) of assets	(5)		
(6) Net investment gain (loss) from common/collective trusts	(6)		
(7) Net investment gain (loss) from pooled separate accounts	(7)		
(8) Net investment gain (loss) from master trusts	(8)		
(9) Net investment gain (loss) from 103-12 investment entities	(9)		
(10) Net investment gain (loss) from registered investment companies	(10)		
c Other income	c		
d Total income. Add all amounts in column (b) and enter total ▶	d		
Expenses			
e Benefit payment and payments to provide benefits:			
(1) Directly to participants or beneficiaries	e(1)		
(2) To insurance carriers for the provision of benefits	(2)		
(3) Other	(3)		
(4) Total payments. Add e(1) through (3) ▶	(4)		
f Interest expense	f		
g Administrative expenses: **(1)** *Salaries and allowances*	g(1)		
(2) Accounting fees	(2)		
(3) Actuarial fees	(3)		
(4) Contract administrator fees	(4)		
(5) Investment advisory and management fees	(5)		
(6) Legal fees	(6)		
(7) Valuation/appraisal fees	(7)		
(8) Trustees fees/expenses (including travel, seminars, meetings, etc.)	(8)		
(9) Other	(9)		
(10) Total administrative expenses. Add g(1) through (9)	(10)		
h Total expenses. Add e(4), f and g(10) ▶	h		
i Net income (loss). Subtract h from d ▶	i		
j Transfers to (from) the plan (see instructions)	j		
k Net assets at beginning of year (Item 34, line I, column (a))	k		
l Net assets at end of year (Item 34, line I, column (b)) ▶	l		

		Yes	No
36 Did any employer sponsoring the plan pay any of the administrative expenses of the plan that were not reported in line 35g?			

★U.S.GPO:1991-0-285-357

Form 5500—Contd.

Department of the Treasury Internal Revenue Service	Department of Labor Pension and Welfare Benefits Administration	Pension Benefit Guaranty Corporation

19**91** Instructions for Form 5500

Annual Return/Report of Employee Benefit Plan (With 100 or more participants)

(Code references are to the Internal Revenue Code. ERISA refers to the Employee Retirement Income Security Act of 1974.)

Paperwork Reduction Act Notice.—We ask for the information on this form to carry out the law as specified in ERISA and Code section 6039D. You are required to give us the information. We need it to determine whether the plan is operating according to the law.

The time needed to complete and file the forms listed below reflects the combined requirements of the Internal Revenue Service, Department of Labor, Pension Benefit Guaranty Corporation, and the Social Security Administration. These times will vary depending on individual circumstances. The estimated average times are:

	Recordkeeping	Learning about the law or the form	Preparing the form	Copying, assembling, and sending the form to the IRS
Form 5500 (initial filers)	87 hrs., 3 min.	8 hrs., 51 min.	13 hrs., 27 min.	48 min.
Form 5500 (all other filers)	81 hrs., 19 min.	8 hrs., 51 min.	13 hrs., 22 min.	48 min.
Schedule A (Form 5500)	17 hrs., 28 min.	28 min.	1 hr., 42 min.	16 min.
Schedule B (Form 5500)	33 hrs., 58 min.	2 hrs., 19 min.	3 hrs., 3 min.	....
Schedule C (Form 5500)	5 hrs., 16 min.	18 min.	23 min.	....
Schedule E (Form 5500) (non leveraged ESOP)	1 hr., 40 min.	12 min.	14 min.	....
Schedule E (Form 5500) (leveraged ESOP)	10 hrs., 2 min.	1 hr., 41 min.	1 hr., 56 min.	....
Schedule P (Form 5500)	1 hr., 40 min.	30 min.	32 min.	....
Schedule SSA (Form 5500)	6 hrs., 42 min.	12 min.	19 min.	....

If you have comments concerning the accuracy of these time estimates or suggestions for making these forms more simple, we would be happy to hear from you. You can write to both the **Internal Revenue Service**, Washington, DC 20224, Attention: IRS Reports Clearance Officer, T:FP; and the **Office of Management and Budget,** Paperwork Reduction Project (1210-0016), Washington, DC 20503. DO NOT send this form to either of these offices. Instead, see the instructions on page 2 for information on where to file.

File 1991 forms for plan years that started in 1991. If the plan year differs from the calendar year, fill in the fiscal year space just under the form title. For a short plan year, see Section 1, instruction B on page 1.

Reminder: The return/report will be considered incomplete and penalties may be imposed if information required to be submitted on a schedule is not typed or printed on the appropriate schedule, such as the Schedule A (Form 5500). See "Schedules" on page 5. An annual return/report must be filed for employee welfare benefit plans which provide benefits wholly or partially through a Multiple Employer Welfare Arrangement (MEWA) as defined in ERISA section 3(40), unless otherwise exempt (see page 2).

In addition to filing this form with IRS, plans covered by the Pension Benefit Guaranty Corporation (PBGC) termination insurance program must file their Annual Premium Payment, PBGC Form 1, directly with that agency.

Penalties.—ERISA and the Code provide for the assessment or imposition of penalties for not giving complete information and not filing statements and returns/reports. Certain penalties are administrative; that is, they may be imposed or assessed by one of the governmental agencies delegated to administer the collection of the Form 5500 series data. Others require a legal conviction.

A. Administrative Penalties.—Listed below are various penalties for not meeting the Form 5500 series filing requirements. One or more of the following five penalties may be assessed or imposed in the event of incomplete filings or filings received after the due date unless it is determined that your explanation for failure to file properly is for reasonable cause:

1. A penalty of up to $1,000 a day for each day a plan administrator fails or refuses to file a complete return/report. See ERISA section 502(c)(2) and 29 CFR 2560.502c-2.

2. A penalty of $25 a day (up to $15,000) for not filing returns for certain plans of deferred compensation, certain trusts and annuities, and bond purchase plans by the due date(s). See Code section 6652(e). This penalty also applies to returns required to be filed under Code section 6039D.

3. A penalty of $1 a day (up to $5,000) for each participant for whom a registration statement (Schedule SSA (Form 5500)) is required but not filed. See Code section 6652(d)(1).

4. A penalty of $1 a day (up to $1,000) for not filing a notification of change of status of a plan. See Code section 6652(d)(2).

5. A penalty of $1,000 for not filing an actuarial statement. See Code section 6692.

B. Other Penalties.—

1. Any individual who willfully violates any provision of Part 1 of Title I of ERISA shall be fined not more than $5,000 or imprisoned not more than 1 year, or both. See ERISA section 501.

2. A penalty of up to $10,000, 5 years imprisonment, or both, for making any false statement or representation of fact, knowing it to be false, or for knowingly concealing or not disclosing any fact required by ERISA. See section 1027, Title 18, U.S. Code, as amended by section 111 of ERISA.

How To Use This Instruction Booklet

The instructions are divided into four main sections.

Section 1

A. Who Must File.—Any administrator or sponsor of an employee benefit plan subject to ERISA must file information about each plan **every year** (Code section 6058 and ERISA sections 104 and 4065). Also required to file, for each year, is every employer maintaining a specified fringe benefit plan as described in Code section 6039D except these plans are not required to file until further notice from IRS. The Internal Revenue Service (IRS), Department of Labor (DOL), and Pension Benefit Guaranty Corporation (PBGC) have consolidated their returns and report forms to minimize the filing burden for plan administrators and employers. The chart on page 4 gives a brief guide to the type of return/report to be filed.

B. When To File.—File all required forms and schedules by the last day of the 7th month after the plan year ends. For a short plan year, file the form and applicable schedules by the last day of the 7th month after the short plan year ends. For purposes of this return/report, the short plan year ends upon

Form 5500—Contd.

the date of the change in accounting period or upon the complete distribution of the assets of the plan. (Also see Section 3.) If the current year Form 5500 is not available before the due date of your short plan year return/report, use the latest year form available and change the date printed on the return/report to the current year. Also show the dates your short plan year began and ended.

Request for Extension of Time To File.—A one time extension of time up to 2½ months may be granted for filing returns/reports if **Form 5558,** Application for Extension of Time To File Certain Employee Plan Returns, is filed **before** the normal due date (not including any extensions) of the return/report.

Exception: *Plans are automatically granted extensions of time to file Form 5500 until the due date of the Federal income tax return of the employer if all the following conditions are met: (1) The plan year and the employer's tax year are the same. (2) The employer has been granted an extension of time to file its Federal income tax return to a date later than the income tax return to a date later than the income tax return for filing the Form 5500. (3) A copy of the IRS extension of time to file the Federal income tax return is attached to the Form 5500 filed with IRS. An extension granted by using this exception CANNOT be extended further by filing a Form 5558.* **Note:** *An extension of time to file the return/report does not operate as an extension of time to file the PBGC Form 1.*

C. Where To File.—Please file the return/report with the Internal Revenue Service Center indicated below. No street address is needed.

See page 5 for the filing address for investment arrangements filing directly with DOL.

If the principal office of the plan sponsor or the plan administrator is located at ▼	Use the following Internal Revenue Service Center address ▼
Connecticut, Delaware, District of Columbia, Foreign Address, Maine, Maryland, Massachusetts, New Hampshire, New Jersey, New York, Pennsylvania, Puerto Rico, Rhode Island, Vermont, Virginia	Holtsville, NY 00501
Alabama, Alaska, Arkansas, California, Florida, Georgia, Hawaii, Idaho, Louisiana, Mississippi, Nevada, North Carolina, Oregon, South Carolina, Tennessee, Washington	Atlanta, GA 39901
Arizona, Colorado, Illinois, Indiana, Iowa, Kansas, Kentucky, Michigan, Minnesota, Missouri, Montana, Nebraska, New Mexico, North Dakota, Ohio, Oklahoma, South Dakota, Texas, Utah, West Virginia, Wisconsin, Wyoming	Memphis, TN 37501
All Form 5500EZ filers	Andover, MA 05501

Section 2

A. Kinds of Plans.—Employee benefit plans include pension benefit plans and welfare benefit plans. File the applicable return/report for any of the following plans.

(a) Pension benefit plan.—This is an employee pension benefit plan covered by

Page 2

ERISA. The return/report is due whether or not the plan is qualified and even if benefits no longer accrue, contributions were not made this plan year, or contributions are no longer made ("frozen plan" or "wasting trust"). See Section 3 "Final Return/Report" on page 6.

Pension benefit plans required to file include defined benefit plans and defined contribution plans (e.g., profit-sharing, stock bonus, money purchase plans, etc.). The following are among the pension benefit plans for which a return/report must be filed:

(i) Annuity arrangements under Code section 403(b)(1).

(ii) Custodial account established under Code section 403(b)(7) for regulated investment company stock.

(iii) Individual retirement account established by an employer under Code section 408(c).

(iv) Pension benefit plan maintained outside the United States primarily for nonresident aliens if the employer who maintains the plan is:

(A) a domestic employer, or

(B) a foreign employer with income derived from sources within the U.S. (including foreign subsidiaries of domestic employers) and deducts contributions to the plan on its U.S. income tax return. See "Plans Excluded From Filing" below.

(v) Church plans electing coverage under Code section 410(d).

(vi) A plan that covers residents of Puerto Rico, the Virgin Islands, Guam, Wake Island, or American Samoa. This includes a plan that elects to have the provisions of section 1022(i)(2) of ERISA apply.

See "Items To Be Completed on Form 5500" on page 4 for more information about what questions need to be completed by pension plans.

(b) Welfare benefit plan.—This is an employee welfare benefit plan covered by Part 1 of Title I of ERISA. Welfare plans would provide benefits such as medical, dental, life insurance, apprenticeship and training, scholarship funds, severance pay, disability, etc.

See "Items To Be Completed on Form 5500" on page 4 for more information about what questions need to be completed by welfare benefit plans.

(c) Fringe benefit plan.—Group legal services plans described in Code section 120, cafeteria plans described in Code section 125, and educational assistance programs described in Code section 127 are considered fringe benefit plans and generally are required to file the annual information specified by Code section 6039D. However, Code section 127 educational assistance programs which provide only job-related training which is deductible under Code section 162 do not need to file Form 5500.

See "Items To Be Completed on Form 5500" on pages 4 and 5 for more information about how to complete this form for a fringe benefit plan.

B. Plans Excluded From Filing (this does not apply if you are a fringe benefit plan required to file by Code section 6039D).— Do not file a return/report for an employee benefit plan that is any of the following:

(a) A welfare benefit plan which covered fewer than 100 participants as of the beginning of the plan year and is: (i) fully insured, (ii) unfunded, or (iii) a combination of insured and unfunded.

(1) An unfunded welfare benefit plan has its benefits paid as needed directly from the general assets of the employer or the employee organization that sponsors the plan.

(2) A fully insured welfare benefit plan has its benefits provided exclusively through insurance contracts or policies, the premiums of which must be paid directly by the employer or employee organization from its general assets and partly from contributions by its employees or members (which the employer or organization forwards within 3 months of receipt).

(3) A combination unfunded/insured welfare plan has its benefits provided partially as an unfunded plan and partially as a fully insured plan. An example of such a plan is a welfare plan which provides medical benefits as in (1) above and life insurance benefits as in (2) above.

The insurance contracts or policies discussed above must be issued by an insurance company or similar organization (such as Blue Cross, Blue Shield or a health maintenance organization) that can legally do business in any state. A plan meeting (1) above cannot have any assets at any time during the plan year.

"Directly," as used in (1) above, means that the plan cannot use a trust or separately maintained fund (including a Code section 501(c)(9) trust) to hold plan assets or to act as a conduit for the transfer of plan assets.

See 29 CFR 2520.104-20.

Note: *An "employees' beneficiary association as used in Code section 501(c)(9) should not be confused with the employee organization or employer which establishes and maintains (i.e., sponsors) the welfare benefit plan.*

(b) An unfunded pension benefit plan or an unfunded or insured welfare benefit plan: (1) whose benefits go only to a select group of management or highly compensated employees, and (2) which meets the terms of Department of Labor Regulations 29 CFR 2520.104-23 (including the requirement that a notification statement be filed with DOL) or 29 CFR 2520.104-24.

(c) Plans maintained only to comply with workers' compensation, unemployment compensation, or disability insurance laws.

(d) An unfunded excess benefit plan.

(e) A welfare benefit plan maintained outside the United States primarily for persons substantially all of whom are nonresident aliens.

(f) A pension benefit plan maintained outside the United States if it is a qualified foreign plan within the meaning of Code section 404A(e) that does not qualify for the treatment provided in Code section 402(c).

(g) An annuity arrangement described in 29 CFR 2510.3-2(f).

(h) A simplified employee pension (SEP) described in Code section 408(k) which conforms to the alternative method of compliance described in 29 CFR 2520.104-48 or 29 CFR 2520.104-49. A SEP is a pension plan which meets certain minimum

Form 5500—Contd.

qualifications regarding eligibility and employer contributions.

(i) A church plan not electing coverage under Code section 410(d) or a governmental plan.

(j) A welfare benefit plan (other than a fringe benefit plan) that participates in a group insurance arrangement that files a return/report Form 5500 on behalf of the welfare benefit plan. See 29 CFR 2520.104-43.

(k) An apprenticeship or training plan meeting all of the conditions specified in 29 CFR 2520.104-22.

C. Kinds of Filers.—The different types of plan entities that file the forms are described below. (Also see instructions for item 4 on page 7.)

(a) Single-employer plan.—If one employer or one employee organization maintains a plan, file a separate return/report for the plan. If the employer or employee organization maintains more than one plan, file a separate return/report for each plan.

If a member of either a controlled group of corporations, a group of trades or businesses under common control, or an affiliated service group maintains a plan that does not involve other group members, file a separate return/report as a single-employer plan.

If several employers participate in a program of benefits wherein the funds attributable to each employer are available only to pay benefits to that employer's employees, each employer must file a separate return/report.

(b) Plan for controlled group of corporations, group of trades or businesses under common control, or an affiliated service group.—The group is defined in Code sections 414(b), (c), and (m), and are referred to as controlled groups.

If the benefits are payable to participants from the plan's total assets without regard to contributions by each participant's employer, file one return/report for the plan. On the return/report for the plan, complete item 22 only for the controlled group's employees.

Exception: Employers who participate in a pension plan of one of the groups listed above but who are not members of the group must file a separate return/report. The return/report should be filed on Form 5500-C/R regardless of the number of participants. The years you are required to file pages 1 and 3 through 6 as Form 5500-C complete only items 1 through 7a, 9, and 22. The years you file pages 1 and 2 as Form 5500-R complete only items 1 through 7a, 8a, and 8b. These participating employers must enter code F in item 4 of the Form 5500-C/R.

If several employers participate in a program of benefits wherein the funds attributable to each employer are available only to pay benefits to that employer's employees, each employer must file a separate return/report as a single employer plan.

(c) Multiemployer plan.—Multiemployer plans are plans: (1) to which more than one employer is required to contribute, (2) which are maintained pursuant to one or more collective bargaining agreements, and (3) have not made the election under Code section 414(f)(5) and ERISA section 3(37)(E). File one return/report for each of these plans. Contributing e.mployers do not file individually

with respect to such plans. See Code section 414 for more information.

(d) Multiple-employer-collectively-bargained plan.—A multiple-employer-collectively-bargained plan involves more than one employer, is collectively bargained and collectively funded, and, if covered by PBGC termination insurance, had properly elected before 9-27-81 not to be treated as a multiemployer plan under Code section 414(f)(5) or ERISA sections 3(37)(E) and 4001(a)(3). File one return/report for each such plan. Participating employers do not file individually for these plans.

Note: *Filers described in (c) or (d) above complete item 22 only if a plan: (1) benefits employees who are not collective bargaining unit employees, or (2) only covers collective bargaining unit employees and 2% or more of them are professionals.*

(e) Multiple-employer plan (other).— A multiple-employer plan (other) involves more than one employer and is not one of the plans already described. A multiple-employer plan (other) includes only plans whose contributions from individual employers are available to pay benefits to all participants. File one return/report for each such plan.

Exception: Each employer participating in a multiple-employer plan (other) which provides pension benefits must file a Form 5500-C/R regardless of the number of participants. For the years you are required to file pages 1 and 3 through 6 as Form 5500-C, complete only items 1 through 7a, 9, and 22. For the years you file pages 1 and 2 as Form 5500-R, complete only items 1 through 7a, 8a, and 8b. Each participating employer filing the Form 5500-C/R **must** enter code F in item 4.

Note: *If a participating employer is also the sponsor of the multiple-employer plan (other), the plan number on the return/ report filed for the plan should be 333 and if more than one plan they should be consecutively numbered starting with 333.*

The Form 5500-C or Form 5500-R filed by the participating employer should list the appropriate plan number.

If more than one employer participates in the plan and the plan provides that each employer's contributions are available to pay benefits only for that employer's employees who are covered by the plan, one annual return/report must be filed for each participating employer. These filers will be considered single employers and should complete the entire form.

(f) Group insurance arrangement.— A group insurance arrangement is an arrangement which provides benefits to the employees of two or more unaffiliated employers (not in connection with a multiemployer plan or a multiple-employer-collectively-bargained plan), fully insures one or more welfare plans of each participating employer, and uses a trust (or other entity such as a tr.∕e association) as the holder of the insurance contracts and the conduit for payment of premiums to the insurance company.

You do not need to file a separate return/report for a welfare benefit plan that is part of a group insurance arrangement if a consolidated return/report for all the plans in the arrangement was filed by the trust or other entity according to 29 CFR 2520.104-43. Form 5500 is required by 29

CFR 2520.103-2 to be part of the consolidated report.

D. Investment Arrangements Filing Directly With DOL.—Some plans invest in certain trusts, accounts, and other investment arrangements which may file information concerning themselves and their relationship with employee benefit plans directly with DOL (as specified on pages 5 and 6). Plans participating in an investment arrangement as described in paragraphs **a** through **c** below are required to attach certain additional information to the return/report filed with IRS as specified below.

a. Common/Collective Trust and Pooled Separate Account

(i) Definition. For reporting purposes, a "common/collective trust" is a trust maintained by a bank, trust company, or similar institution which is regulated, supervised, and subject to periodic examination by a state or Federal agency for the collective investment and reinvestment of assets contributed thereto from employee benefit plans maintained by more than one employer or controlled group of corporations, as the term is used in Code section 1563. For reporting purposes, a "pooled separate account" is an account maintained by an insurance carrier which is regulated, supervised, and subject to periodic examination by a state agency for the collective investment and reinvestment of assets contributed thereto from employee benefit plans maintained by more than one employer or controlled group of corporations, as the term is used in Code section 1563. See 29 CFR sections 2520.103-3, 2520.103-4, 2520.103-5, and 2520.103-9.

Note: *For reporting purposes, a separate account not considered to be holding plan assets pursuant to 29 CFR 2510.3-101(h)(1)(iii) shall not constitute a pooled separate account.*

(ii) Additional Information Required To Be Attached to the Form 5500 for Plans Participating in Common/Collective Trusts and Pooled Separate Accounts.—A plan participating in a common/collective trust or pooled separate account must complete the annual return/report and attach either: (1) the most recent statement of the assets and liabilities of any common/collective trust or pooled separate account, or (2) a certification that: (A) the statement of the assets and liabilities of the common/ collective trust or pooled separate account has been submitted directly to DOL by the financial institution or insurance carrier; (B) the plan has received a copy of the statement; and (C) includes the EIN and other numbers used by the financial institution or insurance carrier to identify the trusts or accounts in the direct filing made with DOL.

b. Master Trust

(i) Definition. For reporting purposes, a master trust is a trust for which a regulated financial institution (as defined below) serves as trustee or custodian (regardless of whether such institution exercises discretionary authority or control with respect to the management of assets held in the trust), and in which assets of more than one plan sponsored by a single employer or by a group of employers under common control are held.

A "regulated financial institution" means a bank, trust company, or similar financial

Page 3

Form 5500—Contd.

Summary of Filing Requirements for Employers and Plan Administrators (File forms ONLY with IRS)

Type of plan	What to file	When to file
Most pension plans with only one participant or one participant and that participant's spouse	Form 5500EZ	File all required forms and schedules for each plan by the last day of the 7th month after the plan year ends.
Pension plan with fewer than 100 participants	Form 5500-C/R	
Pension plan with 100 or more participants	Form 5500	
Annuity under Code section 403(b)(1) or trust under Code section 408(c)	Form 5500 or 5500-C/R	
Custodial account under Code section 403(b)(7)	Form 5500 or 5500-C/R	
Welfare benefit plan with 100 or more participants*	Form 5500	
Welfare benefit plan with fewer than 100 participants (see exception on page 1 of these instructions)*	Form 5500-C/R	
Pension or welfare plan with 100 or more participants (see instructions for item 29)	Financial statements, schedules, and accountant's opinion	
Pension or welfare plan with benefits provided by an insurance company	Schedule A (Form 5500)	
Pension plan that requires actuarial information	Schedule B (Form 5500)	
Pension or welfare plan with 100 or more participants	Schedule C (Form 5500)	
Pension plan with ESOP benefits	Schedule E (Form 5500)	
Pension plan filing a registration statement identifying separated participants with deferred vested benefits from a pension plan	Schedule SSA (Form 5500)	

*This includes Code section 6039D filers.

institution which is regulated, supervised, and subject to periodic examination by a state or Federal agency. Common control is determined on the basis of all relevant facts and circumstances (whether or not such employers are incorporated). See 29 CFR 2520.103-1(e).

For reporting purposes, the assets of a master trust are considered to be held in one or more "investment accounts." A master trust investment account may consist of a pool of assets or a single asset.

Each pool of assets held in a master trust must be treated as a separate master trust investment account if each plan which has an interest in the pool has the same fractional interest in each asset in the pool as its fractional interest in the pool, and if each such plan may not dispose of its interest in any asset in the pool without disposing of its interest in the pool. A master trust may also contain assets which are not held in such a pool. Each such asset must be treated as a separate master trust investment account.

Financial information must generally be provided with respect to each master trust investment account as specified on pages 5 and 6.

(ii) Additional Information Required To Be Attached to the Form 5500 for Plans Participating in Master Trusts. A plan participating in a master trust must complete the annual return/report and attach a schedule listing each master trust investment account in which the plan has an interest indicating the plan's name, EIN, and plan number and the name of the master trust used in the master trust information filed with DOL (see pages 5 and 6). In tabular format, show the net value of the plan's interest in each investment account at the beginning and end of the plan year, and the net investment gain (or loss) allocated to the plan for the plan year from the investment account (see instructions for items 34c(11) through (15) on page 17).

Note: *If a master trust investment account consists solely of one plan's asset(s) during the reporting period, the plan may report the(se) asset(s) either as an investment account to be reported as part of the master*

trust report filed directly with DOL or as a plan asset(s) which is not part of the master trust (and therefore subject to all instructions pertaining to assets not held in a master trust).

c. 103-12 Investment Entities
Definition. 29 CFR 2520.103-12 provides an alternative method of reporting for plans which invest in an entity (other than an investment arrangement filing with DOL described in **a** or **b** above), the underlying assets of which include "plan assets" (within the meaning of 29 CFR 2510.3-101) of two or more plans which are not members of a "related group" of employee benefit plans. For reporting purposes, a "related group" consists of each group of two or more employee benefit plans (1) each of which receives 10% or more of its aggregate contributions from the same employer or from a member of the same controlled group of corporations (as determined under Code section 1563(a), without regard to Code section 1563(a)(4) thereof); or (2) each of which is either maintained by, or maintained pursuant to a collective bargaining agreement negotiated by, the same employee organization or affiliated employee organizations. For purposes of this paragraph, an "affiliate" of an employee organization means any person controlling, controlled by, or under common control with such organization. See 29 CFR 2520.103-12.

For reporting purposes, the investment entities described above with respect to which the required information is filed directly with DOL constitute "103-12 investment entities" (103-12 IEs).

E. What To File.—This section describes the different categories of the 5500 series of forms and schedules. In addition, this section also lists items to be completed by different types of Form 5500 filers. In addition, this section contains a description of the special filing requirements for plans that invest in certain investment arrangements. For a brief guide illustrating which forms and schedules are required by different types of plans and filers, see the chart above.

Forms

*Form 5500.—*File **Form 5500,** Annual Return/Report of Employee Benefit Plan, annually for each plan with 100 or more participants at the beginning of the plan year.
*Form 5500-C/R.—*File **Form 5500-C/R,** Return/Report of Employee Benefit Plan, for each pension benefit plan, welfare benefit plan, and fringe benefit plan (unless otherwise exempted) with fewer than 100 participants (one-participant plans see "Form 5500EZ" below) at the beginning of the plan year.
Note: *Generally, under the filing requirements explained above, if the number of plan participants increases to 100 or more, or decreases to under 100, from one year to the next, you would have to file a different form from that filed the previous year. However, there is an exception to this rule. You may continue to file the same form you filed last year, provided that at the beginning of this plan year the plan had at least 80 participants, but not more than 120.*
*Form 5500EZ.—*Form **5500EZ,** Annual Return of One-Participant Pension Benefit Plan, should be filed by most one-participant plans.

A one-participant plan is: (1) a pension benefit plan that covers only an individual or an individual and his or her spouse who wholly own a trade or business, whether incorporated or unincorporated; or (2) a pension benefit plan for a partnership that covers only the partners or the partners and the partners' spouses.

See Form 5500EZ and its instructions to see if the plan meets the requirements for filing the form.
*Form 8822.—*Form **8822,** Change of Address, may be used to notify the IRS if the plan's mailing address changes after the return/report has been filed.

Items To Be Completed on Form 5500

Certain kinds of plans and certain kinds of filers that are required to submit an annual Form 5500 are not required to complete the entire form. These are described below, by type of plan. Check the list of headings to see if your plan is affected.

Form 5500—Contd.

1. Welfare Benefit Plans—Welfare benefit plans generally must complete the following items on the Form 5500: 1 through 6a; 6c, 7a(4), b, c, and d; 8a, b, e, and f; 9a, b, c, and f; 10a through d; 11 through 14; 28 through 32; and 34 through 36.

2. Fringe Benefit Plans—For a Form 5500 filed only for fringe benefit plans described in Code sections 120, 125 and 127, complete only items 1 through 6a, 7a(4), 7b, 9a and b, 22h, 22m, and 35g and h. Do NOT file 5500 Schedules A, B, C, E, P or SSA (Form 5500).

If the annual return/report is also for a welfare benefit plan (see "Who Must File" on page 1), complete the above items and those specified for welfare benefit plans in "1" above.

3. Pension Plans—In general, most pension plans (defined benefit and defined contribution) are required to complete all items on the form. However, some items need not be completed by certain types of pension plans, as described below.

a. *Plans exclusively using a tax deferred annuity arrangement under Code section 403(b)(1).* These plans (see "Who Must File" on page 1) need only complete items 1 through 5, 6b (enter code 4), and 9.

b. *Plans exclusively using a custodial account for regulated investment company stock under Code section 403(b)(7).* These plans need only complete items 1 through 5, 6b (enter code 5), and 9.

c. *Individual Retirement Account Plan.*— A pension plan utilizing individual retirement accounts or annuities (as described in Code section 408) as the sole funding vehicle for providing benefits need only complete items 1 through 5, 6b (enter code 6), and 9.

d. *Fully Insured Pension Plan.*—A pension benefit plan providing benefits exclusively through an insurance contract, or contracts that are fully guaranteed and which meet all of the conditions of 29 CFR 2520.104-44 need only. complete items 1 through 29, 32, and 33.

A pension plan which includes both insurance contracts of the type described in 29 CFR 2520.104-44 as well as other assets should limit its reporting in items 34 and 35 to those other assets.

Note: *For purposes of the annual return/report and the alternative method of compliance set forth in 29 CFR 2520.104-44, a contract is considered "allocated" only if the insurance company or organization that issued the contract unconditionally guarantees, upon receipt of the required premium or consideration, to provide a retirement benefit of a specified amount, without adjustment for fluctuations in the market value of the underlying assets of the company or organization, to each participant, and each participant has a legal right to such benefits which is legally enforceable directly against the insurance company or organization.*

e. *Nonqualified pension benefit plans maintained outside the U.S.*—Nonqualified pension benefit plans maintained outside the United States primarily for nonresident aliens required to file a return/report (see "Who Must File" on page 1) need only complete items 1 through 8c, 9 through 12, and 15 through 17.

4. Plans of More Than One Employer— All plans of more than one employer (plans of a controlled group, multiemployer plans, multiple-employer-collectively-bargained plans, and multiple-employer plan (other)) generally should complete all applicable (welfare or pension) items on the form except for item 6d. Only single-employer pension plans must complete this item.

Schedules

The various schedules to be attached to the return/report are listed below.

Note: *All attachments to the Forms 5500, and 5500-C/R must include the name of the plan, the plan sponsor's EIN, and plan number (PN) as found in items 5a, 1b, and 5c, respectively.*

Attach Schedule A (Form 5500), Insurance Information, to Form 5500, or 5500-C/R, if any benefits under the plan are provided by an insurance company, insurance service, or other similar organization (such as Blue Cross, Blue Shield, or a health maintenance organization). (This includes investments with insurance companies such as guaranteed investment contracts (GICs).)

Exceptions: *(1) Schedule A (Form 5500) is not needed if the plan covers only: (a) an individual, or an individual and his or her spouse, who wholly owns a trade or business, whether incorporated or unincorporated; or (b) a partner in a partnership, or a partner and his or her spouse.*

(2) A Schedule A (Form 5500) is not required to be filed with the Form 5500 or Form 5500-C/R if a Schedule A (Form 5500) is filed for the contract as part of the master trust or 103-12 IE information filed directly with DOL.

Do not file a Schedule A (Form 5500) with a Form 5500EZ.

Attach Schedule B (Form 5500), Actuarial Information, to Form 5500, 5500-C/R, or 5500EZ for most defined benefit pension plans. See the instructions for Schedule B.

Attach Schedule C (Form 5500), Service Provider and Trustee Information, to Form 5500. See item 28 and the instructions to Schedule C.

Attach Schedule E (Form 5500), ESOP Annual Information, to Form 5500, 5500-C/R, or 5500EZ for all pension benefit plans with ESOP benefits. See the instructions for Schedule E.

Schedule SSA (Form 5500), Annual Registration Statement Identifying Separated Participants With Deferred Vested Benefits, may be needed for separated participants. See "When To Report Separated Participants" in the instructions for Schedule SSA.

Schedule P (Form 5500), Annual Return of Fiduciary of Employee Benefit Trust.—Any fiduciary (trustee or custodian) of an organization that is qualified under Code section 401(a) and exempt from tax under Code section 501(a) who wants to protect the organization under the statute of limitations provided in Code section 6501(a) must file a Schedule P (Form 5500).

File the Schedule P (Form 5500) as an attachment to Form 5500, 5500-C/R or 5500EZ for the plan year in which the trust year ends.

Other Filings

Reporting Requirements for Investment Arrangements Filing Directly with DOL

Certain investment arrangements for employee benefit plans file financial information directly with DOL. These arrangements include common/collective trusts, pooled separate accounts, master trusts, and 103-12 IEs. Definitions of these investment arrangements may be found on pages 3 and 4. Their DOL filing requirements are described below.

1. Common/Collective Trust and Pooled Separate Account Information To Be Filed Directly With DOL

Financial institutions and insurance carriers filing the statement of the assets and liabilities of a common/collective trust or pooled separate account should identify the trust or account by providing the EIN of the trust or account, or (if more than one trust or account is covered by the same EIN) both the EIN and any additional number assigned by the financial institution or insurance carrier (such as: 99-1234567 Trust No. 1); and a list of all plans participating in the trust or account, identified by the plan number, EIN, and name of the plan sponsor. The direct filing should be addressed to:

Common/Collective Trust (OR)
Pooled Separate Account
Pension and Welfare Benefits
   Administration
U.S. Department of Labor, Room N5644
200 Constitution Avenue, NW
Washington, DC 20210

2. Master Trust Information To Be Filed Directly With DOL

The following information with respect to a master trust must be filed with DOL by the plan administrator or by a designee, such as the administrator of another plan participating in the master trust or the financial institution serving as trustee of the master trust, no later than the date on which the plan's return/report is due. While only one copy of the required information should be filed for all plans participating in the master trust, the information is an integral part of the return/report of each participating plan, and the plan's return/report will not be deemed complete unless all the information is filed within the prescribed time.

Note: *If a master trust investment account consists solely of one plan's asset(s) during the reporting period, the plan may report the(se) asset(s) either as an investment account to be reported as part of the master trust report directly with DOL or as a plan asset(s) which is not part of the master trust (and therefore subject to all instructions pertaining to assets not held in a master trust).*

Each of the following statements and schedules must indicate the name of the master trust and the name of the master trust investment account. The information shall be filed with DOL by mailing it to:

Master Trust
Pension and Welfare Benefits
   Administration
U.S. Department of Labor, Room N5644
200 Constitution Avenue, NW
Washington, DC 20210

Page 5

Form 5500—Contd.

a. The name and fiscal year of the master trust and the name and address of the master trustee.

b. A list of all plans participating in the master trust, showing each plan's name, EIN, PN, and its percentage interest in each master trust investment account as of the beginning and end of the fiscal year of the master trust ending with or within the plan year.

c. A Schedule A (Form 5500) for each insurance or annuity contract held in the master trust.

d. A statement, in the same format as Part I of Schedule C (Form 5500), for each master trust investment account showing amounts of compensation paid during the fiscal year of the master trust ending with or within the plan year to persons providing services with respect to the investment account and subtracted from the gross income of the investment account in determining the net increase (decrease) in net assets of the investment account.

e. A statement for each master trust investment account showing the assets and liabilities of the investment account at the beginning and end of the fiscal year of the master trust ending with or within the plan year, grouped in the same categories as those specified in item 34 of Form 5500.

f. A statement for each master trust investment account showing the income and expenses, changes in net assets, and net increase (decrease) in net assets of each such investment account during the fiscal year of the master trust ending with or within the plan year, in the categories specified in item 35 of Form 5500. In place of item 35a, show the total of all transfers of assets into the investment account by participating plans. In place of item 35j, show the total of all transfers of assets out of the investment account by participating plans.

g. Schedules, in the format set forth in the instructions for item 30 of Form 5500, of the following items with respect to each master trust investment account for the fiscal year of the master trust ending with or within the plan year: assets held for investment, nonexempt party-in-interest transactions, defaulted or uncollectible loans and leases, and 5% transactions involving assets in the investment account. The 5% figure shall be determined by comparing the current value of the transaction at the transaction date with the current value of the investment account assets at the beginning of the applicable fiscal year of the master trust.

3. 103-12 IE Information To Be Filed Directly With DOL

The information described below must be filed with the DOL by the sponsor of the 103-12 IE no later than the date on which the plan's return/report is due before the plan administrator can elect the alternative method of reporting. While only one copy of the required information should be filed for the 103-12 IE, the information is an integral part of the return/report of each plan electing the alternative method of compliance.

The filing address is:

103-12 Investment Entity
Pension and Welfare Benefits
Administration
U. S. Department of Labor, Room N5644

200 Constitution Avenue, NW
Washington, DC 20210

a. The name, fiscal year, and EIN of the 103-12 IE and the name and address of the sponsor of the 103-12 IE. If more than one 103-12 IE is covered by the same EIN, they shall be sequentially numbered as follows: 99-1234567 Entity No. 1.

b. A list of all plans participating in the 103-12 IE, showing each plan's name, EIN, PN, and its percentage interest in the 103-12 IE as of the beginning and end of the fiscal year of the 103-12 IE ending with or within the plan year.

c. A Schedule A (Form 5500) for each insurance or annuity contract held in the 103-12 IE.

d. A statement, in the same format as Part I of Schedule C (Form 5500), for the 103-12 IE showing amounts of compensation paid during the fiscal year of the 103-12 IE ending with or within the plan year to persons providing services to the 103-12 IE.

e. A statement showing the assets and liabilities at the beginning and end of the fiscal year of the 103-12 IE ending with or within the plan year, grouped in the same categories as those specified in item 34 of Form 5500.

f. A statement showing the income and expenses, changes in net assets, and net increase (decrease) in net assets during the fiscal year of the 103-12 IE ending with or within the plan year, grouped in the same categories as those specified in item 35 of Form 5500. In place of item 35a, show the total of all transfers of assets into the 103-12 IE by participating plans. In place of item 35j, show the total of all transfers of assets out of the 103-12 IE by participating plans.

g. Schedules, in the format set forth in the instructions for item 30 of Form 5500 (except item 30d) with respect to the 103-12 IE for the fiscal year of the 103-12 IE ending with or within the plan year. Substitute the term "103-12 IE" in place of the word "plan" when completing the schedules.

h. A report of an independent qualified public accountant regarding the above items and other books and records of the 103-12 IE that meets the requirements of 29 CFR 2520.103-1(b)(5).

Section 3

General Information

Final Return/Report.—If all assets under the plan (including insurance/annuity contracts) have been distributed to the participants and beneficiaries or distributed to another plan (and when all liabilities for which benefits may be paid under a welfare benefit plan have been satisfied), check the "final return/report" box at the top of the form filed for such plan. The year of complete distribution is the last year a return/report must be filed for the plan. For purposes of this paragraph, a complete distribution will occur in the year in which the assets of a terminated plan are brought under the control of PBGC.

For a defined benefit plan covered by PBGC, a PBGC Form 1 must be filed and a premium must be paid until the end of the plan year in which the assets are distributed or brought under the control of PBGC.

Filing the return/report marked "Final return" and indicating that the plan

terminated satisfies the notification requirement of Code section 6057(b)(3).

Signature and Date.—The plan administrator must sign and date all returns/reports filed. The name of the individual who signed as plan administrator must be typed or printed clearly on the line under the signature line. In addition, the employer must sign a return/report filed for a single-employer plan or a plan required to file only because of Code section 6039D (i.e., for a fringe benefit plan).

When a joint employer-union board of trustees or committee is the plan sponsor or plan administrator, at least one employer representative and one union representative must sign and date the return/report.

Participating employers in a multiple-employer plan (other), who are required to file Form 5500-C/R, are required to sign the return/report. The plan administrator need not sign the Form 5500-C/R filed by the participating employer.

Reproductions.—Original forms are preferable, but a clear reproduction of the completed form is acceptable. Sign the return/report after it is reproduced. All signatures must be original.

Change in Plan Year.—Generally only defined benefit pension plans need to get prior approval for a change in plan year. (See Code section 412(c)(5).) Rev. Proc. 87-27, 1987-1 C.B. 769 explains the procedure for automatic approval of a change in plan year. A pension benefit plan that would ordinarily need to obtain approval for a change in plan year under Code section 412(c)(5) is granted an automatic approval for a change in plan year if all the following criteria are met:

1. No plan year exceeds 12 months long.

2. The change will not delay the time when the plan would otherwise have been required to conform to the requirements of any statute, regulation, or published position of the IRS.

3. The trust, if any, retains its exempt status for the short period required to effect the change, as well as for the taxable year immediately preceding the short period.

4. All actions necessary to implement the change in plan year, including plan amendment and a resolution of the board of directors (if applicable), have been taken on or before the last day of the short period.

5. No change in plan year has been made for any of the preceding plan years.

6. In the case of a defined benefit plan, deductions are taken in accordance with section 5 of Rev. Proc. 87-27.

For the first return/report that is filed following the change in plan year, check the box on line C at the top of the form.

Amended Return/Report.—If you file an amended return/report, check box A(2) "an amended return/report" at the top of the form. When filing an amended return, be sure to answer all questions and put a circle around the numbers of the items that have been amended.

How The Annual Return/Report Information May Be Used.—All Form 5500 series return/reports will be subjected to a computerized review. It is, therefore, in the filer's best interest that the responses accurately reflect the circumstances they were designed to report. Annual reports filed

Form 5500—Contd.

under Title I of ERISA must be made available by plan administrators to plan participants and by the Department of Labor to the public pursuant to ERISA section 104.

Section 4

Specific Instructions for Form 5500

Important: Answer all items on the Form 5500 with respect to the plan year, unless otherwise explicitly stated in the item-by-item instructions or on the form itself. Therefore, your responses usually apply to the year entered or printed at the top of the first page of the form. "Yes" and "No" questions are to be marked either "Yes" or "No," but not both. "N/A" cannot be used to respond to a "Yes" or "No" question which is required to be answered by the filer as specified on page 4 or 5 under "Items To Be Completed On Form 5500."

Information To Be Completed at the Top of the Form

First Line at the top of the form— Complete the space for dates when: (1) the 12-month plan year is not a calendar year, or (2) the plan year is less than 12 months (a short plan year).

A. Check box (1) if this is the initial filing for this plan. Do not check this box if you have ever filed for this plan even if it was on a different form (Form 5500 vs. Form 5500-C or Form 5500-R).

Check box (2) if you have already filed for the 1991 plan year and are now submitting an amended return/report to reflect errors and/or omissions on the previously filed return/report.

Check box (3) if the plan no longer exists to provide benefits. See section 3 on page 6 for instructions concerning the requirement to file a final return/report.

Check box (4) if this form is being filed for a period of less than 12 months.

B. Check the box if you made any changes to the preprinted information on page 1.

C. Check the box if the plan year has been changed since the last return/report was filed.

D. Check this box if you filed for an extension of time to file this form. Attach a copy of Form 5558 or a copy of the employer's extension of time to file the income tax return if you are using the exception in "Request for Extension of Time to File" on page 2 of these instructions.

The numbers of the following instructions are the same as the item numbers on the return/report.

Check the information printed in 1 through 6b for accuracy and completeness. Line out any incorrect information and enter the correct information. Complete any incomplete items.

If you did not receive a Form 5500 with the page one information filled in, complete items 1 through 6b as follows:

1a. Enter the name and address of the plan sponsor. If the plan covers only the employees of one employer, enter the employer's name. If the Post Office does not deliver mail to the street address and the sponsor has a P.O. box, show the P.O. box number instead of the street address.

The term "plan sponsor" means—

(i) the employer, for an employee benefit plan that a single employer established or maintains;

(ii) the employee organization in the case of a plan of an employee organization; or

(iii) the association, committee, joint board of trustees, or other similar group of representatives of the parties who establish or maintain the plan, if the plan is established or maintained jointly by one or more employers and one or more employee organizations, or by two or more employers.

Include enough information in item 1(a) to describe the sponsor adequately. For example, "Joint Board of Trustees of Local 187 Machinists" rather than just "Joint Board of Trustees."

For group insurance arrangements, enter the name of the trust or other entity that holds the insurance contracts. In addition, attach a list of all participating employers and their EINs.

A "group insurance arrangement" is an arrangement which provides benefits to the employees of two or more unaffiliated employers (not in connection with a multiemployer plan or a multiple-employer-collectively-bargained plan), fully insures one or more welfare plans of each participating employer, and uses a trust (or other entity such as a trade association) as the holder of the insurance contracts and the conduit for payment of premiums to the insurance company.

1b. Enter the 9-digit employer identification number (EIN) assigned to the plan sponsor/employer. For example, 00-1234567.

Employers and plan administrators who do not have an EIN should apply for one on Form SS-4, available from most IRS or Social Security Administration offices. Send Form SS-4 to the Internal Revenue Service Center to which this form will be sent.

Plan sponsors are reminded that they should use the trust EIN when opening a bank account or conducting other transactions for a plan that requires an employer identification number. The trust may apply for an EIN as explained in the preceding paragraph.

A plan of a controlled group of corporations whose sponsor is more than one of the members of the controlled group should insert only the EIN of one of the sponsoring members. This EIN must be used in all subsequent filings of the annual returns/reports for the controlled group unless there is a change in the sponsor.

If the plan sponsor is a group of individuals, get a single EIN for the group. When you apply for a number, enter on line 1 of Form SS-4 the name of the group, such as "Joint Board of Trustees of the Local 187 Machinists' Retirement Plan."

Note: Although EINs for funds (trusts or custodial accounts) associated with plans are not required to be furnished on the Form 5500 series returns/reports, the IRS will issue EINs for such funds for other reporting purposes. EINs may be obtained by filing Form SS-4 as explained above.

1d. From the list of business codes on pages 19 and 20, enter the one that best describes the nature of the employer's business. If more than one employer is involved, enter the business code for the main business activity.

1e. Plans entering code A or B in item 4 must enter the first six digits of the CUSIP (Committee on Uniform Securities Identification Procedures) number, "issuer number," if one has been assigned to the plan sponsor for purposes of issuing corporate securities. CUSIP issuer numbers are assigned to corporations and other entities which issue public securities listed on stock exchanges or traded over the counter. The CUSIP issuer number is the first six digits of the number assigned to the individual securities which are traded. If the plan sponsor has no CUSIP issuer number, enter "N/A."

2a. If the document constituting the plan appoints or designates a plan administrator other than the sponsor, enter the administrator's name and address. If the plan administrator is also the sponsor, enter "Same." If filing as a group insurance arrangement, enter "Same." If "Same" is entered on 2a, then items 2b and 2c should be left blank.

The term "administrator" means—

(i) the person or group of persons specified as the administrator by the instrument under which the plan is operated;

(ii) the plan sponsor/employer if an administrator is not so designated; or

(iii) any other person prescribed by regulations of the Secretary of Labor if an administrator is not designated and a plan sponsor cannot be identified.

2b. A plan administrator must have an EIN for reporting purposes. Enter the plan administrator's 9-digit EIN here. If the plan administrator has no EIN, apply for one as explained in 1b above.

Employees of an employer are not plan administrators unless so designated in the plan document, even though they engage in administrative functions of the plan. If an employee of the employer is designated as the plan administrator, that employee must get an EIN.

3. If the plan sponsor's/administrator's name, address and EIN are different than what appears on the last return/report filed for this plan, enter the plan sponsor's/administrator's name, address and EIN as it appears on the last return/report filed for this plan.

3c. Indicate if the change in 3a is only a change in sponsorship. "Change in sponsorship" means the plan's sponsor has been changed but no assets or liabilities have been transferred to another plan(s), the plan has not terminated or merged with any other plan, and so forth. Therefore, the plan is now the responsibility of the new sponsor whose name is entered in item 1a of this return/report.

4. From the following list of plan entities choose the one that describes your plan entity and enter the code for it in item 4.

Entity	Code
Single-employer plan	A
Plan of controlled group of corporations or common control employers	B
Multiemployer plan	C
Multiple-employer-collectively-bargained plan	D
Multiple-employer plan (other)	E

Form 5500—Contd.

Group insurance arrangement
(of welfare plans) . . . . F

5a(1). Enter the formal name of the plan, group insurance arrangement, or enough information to identify the plan. This name should be no more than 70 characters long. If the present plan name is larger than this, try to abbreviate it so that it is no more than 70 spaces long.

5b. Enter the date the plan first became effective.

5c. Enter the 3-digit number the employer or plan administrator assigned to the plan. All welfare benefit plan numbers and Code section 6039D plan numbers start at 501. All other plans start at 001.

Once you use a plan number, continue to use it for that plan on all future filings with IRS, DOL and PBGC. Do not use it for any other plan even if you terminated the first plan.

6a. Enter every code from the list below that describes the welfare benefit plan for which this return/report is being filed.

Example: If your plan provides health insurance, life insurance, dental insurance, eye examinations, the four codes A, B, D, and E should be entered. If your plan has a benefit not described by one of the codes, enter "Z" and write in a description of this benefit in the space provided.

A fringe benefit plan (i.e., a Code section 120, 125 or 127 plan) filing because of the reporting requirement under Code section 6039D should enter either code M, N, or O. A plan that is required to file under Title I of ERISA as a welfare plan and under Code section 6039D as a fringe benefit plan should enter the applicable welfare plan and fringe benefit codes.

If you entered code M, N, or O, you must check 6a(2) "No" if the plan is: (1) unfunded, (2) fully insured, or (3) a combination of unfunded/insured as defined on page 2, Section 2B(a).

**Type of Welfare
or Fringe Benefit Plan** | **Code**

Health (other than dental or vision) . . A
Life insurance . . . . B
Supplemental unemployment . . . C
Dental . . . . D
Vision . . . . E
Temporary disability (accident and sickness) . . . . F
Prepaid legal . . . . G
Long-term disability . . . . . . H
Severance pay I
Apprenticeship and training . . . . J
Scholarship (funded) . . . . . . K
Death benefits (other than life ins.) . . L
Code section 120 group legal services plan . . . . M
Code section 125 cafeteria plan . . . N
Code section 127 educational assistance program . . . . . . O
Taft-Hartley Financial Assistance for Employee Housing Expenses . . . P
Other (specify on page 1) . . . . . Z

6b. Pension benefit plans must enter the codes from the list below that describe the type of plan the Form 5500 is being filed for. If none of the codes in the list describe the type of pension plan, enter code "7" and

describe the type of pension plan you are filing for.

Type of Pension Benefit Plan | **Code**

Defined benefit 1

Defined Contribution

Profit-sharing 2A
Stock bonus 2B
Target Benefit 2C
Other money purchase 2D
Other (specify on page 1) 2E
Note: ESOP plans must check 6c(1) or 6c(2).

Other

Defined benefit plan with benefits based partly on balance of separate account of participant (Code section 414(k)) 3
Annuity arrangement of certain exempt organizations (Code section 403(b)(1)) 4
Custodial account for regulated investment company stock (Code section 403(b)(7)) 5
Pension plan utilizing individual retirement accounts or annuities (described in Code section 408) as the sole funding vehicle for providing benefits 6
Other (describe the type of plan) . . . 7

6c(1) and 6c(2). If you check either of these boxes, complete Schedule E (Form 5500) and attach it to the Form 5500-C/R you file for this plan.

6c(2). Check the box for a leveraged ESOP if the plan acquires employer securities with borrowed money or other debt-financing techniques.

6c(3). Check if the plan is a pension plan that provides for individual accounts and permits a participant or beneficiary to exercise independent control over the assets in his or her account (see ERISA section 404(c)).

6c(4). Check this box for pension benefit plans maintained outside the United States primarily for nonresident aliens. See "Kinds of Filers" on page 3 for more information.

6c(5). In the space provided following 6c(8), enter name of the trust and financial institution. Also enter city and state where the trust is maintained. (See page 3 for master trust instructions.)

6c(6). In the space provided following 6c(8), enter name and address of the 103-12 IE. (See page 6 for 103-12 IE instructions.)

6d. For single-employer pension plans enter the date the employer's tax year ends. For example, if the tax year is a calendar year, enter 12-31-91. For all plans with more than one employer, enter "N/A."

6e. Definition of Affiliated Service Group.— In general, Code section 414(m)(2) defines an affiliated service group as a first service organization (FSO) that has:

(1) a service organization (A-ORG) that is a shareholder or partner in the FSO and that regularly performs services for the FSO, or is regularly associated with the FSO in performing services for third persons, and/or

(2) any other organization (B-ORG) if:

(a) a significant portion of the business of that organization consists of performing services for the FSO or A-ORG of a type

historically performed by employees in the service field of the FSO or A-ORG, and

(b) 10% or more of the interest of the B-ORG is held by persons who are highly compensated employees of the FSO or A-ORG.

An affiliated service group also includes a group consisting of an organization whose principal business is performing management functions for another organization (or one organization and other related organizations) on a regular and continuing basis, and the organization for which such functions are so performed by the organization. For a plan maintained by more than one employer, check "Yes" if any such employer is a member of an affiliated service group.

6f. A cash or deferred arrangement described under Code section 401(k) is a part of a qualified defined contribution plan which provides for an election by employees to defer part of their compensation or receive these amounts in cash.

7. The description of "participant" in the instructions below is only for purposes of item 7 of this form.

For welfare benefit plans, dependents are considered to be neither participants nor beneficiaries. For pension benefit plans, "alternate payees" entitled to benefits under a qualified domestic relations order are not to be counted as participants for this item.

"Participant" means any individual who is included in one of the categories below.

7a. Active participants include any individuals who are currently in employment covered by a plan and who are earning or retaining credited service under a plan. This category includes any individuals who are: (i) currently below the integration level in a plan that is integrated with social security, and/or (ii) eligible to elect to have the employer make payments to a Code section 401(k) qualified cash or deferred arrangement. Active participants also include any nonvested individuals who are earning or retaining credited service under a plan. This category **does not** include nonvested former employees who have incurred the break in service period specified in the plan.

For determining if active participants are fully vested, partially vested, or nonvested, consider vesting in employer contributions only.

For purposes of Code section 6039D, (fringe benefit plan) "participant" means any individual who, for a plan year, has had at least one dollar excluded from income by reason of Code section 120, 125, or 127. If you are filing Form 5500 for a welfare plan that is required to file under Title I of ERISA and under Code section 6039D as a fringe benefit plan, the preceding sentence does not apply.

7b. Inactive participants receiving benefits are any individuals who are retired or separated from employment covered by the plan and who are receiving benefits under the plan. This includes former employees who are receiving group health continuation coverage benefits pursuant to Part 6 of ERISA who are covered by the employee welfare benefit plan. This category does not include any individual to whom an insurance company has made an irrevocable commitment to pay all the

Form 5500—Contd.

benefits to which the individual is entitled under the plan.

7c. Inactive participants entitled to future benefits are individuals who are retired or separated from employment covered by the plan and who are entitled to begin receiving benefits under the plan in the future. This category does not include any individual to whom an insurance company has made an irrevocable commitment to pay all the benefits to which the individual is entitled under the plan.

7e. Deceased participants are any deceased individuals who had one or more beneficiaries who are receiving or are entitled to receive benefits under the plan. This category does not include an individual if an insurance company has made an irrevocable commitment to pay all the benefits to which the beneficiaries of that individual are entitled under the plan.

7g. Enter the number of participants included in line 7f who have account balances. For example, for a Code section 401(k) plan, the number entered on line 7g should be the number of participants counted in line 7f who have made a contribution to the plan during this plan year or any prior plan year.

7h(1). If "Yes," file Schedule SSA (Form 5500) as an attachment to Form 5500. **Plan administrators:** Code section 6057(e) provides that the plan administrator must give each participant a statement showing the same information for that participant as is reported on Schedule SSA.

8a. Check "Yes" if an amendment to the plan was adopted regardless of the effective date of the amendment.

8b. Enter the date the most recent amendment was adopted regardless of the date of the amendment or the effective date of the amendment.

8c. Check "Yes" only if the accrued benefits were retroactively reduced. For example, a plan provides a benefit of 2% for each year of service, but the plan is amended to change the benefit to 1½% a year for all years of service under the plan. Do not check "Yes" if accrued benefits were retroactively reduced solely to the extent permitted under a model amendment provided in IRS Notice 88-131, 1988-2 C.B. 546.

8e. Check "Yes" only if an amendment changed the information previously provided to participants by the summary plan description or summary description of modifications.

8f. A revised summary plan description or summary description of modifications must be filed with DOL and distributed to all participants and pension plan beneficiaries no later than 210 days after the close of the plan year in which the amendment(s) was adopted. If the material was distributed and filed since the amendments were adopted (even if after the end of the plan year), check "Yes" to item 8f.

9a. Check "Yes" if the plan was terminated or if the plan was merged or consolidated into another plan. Enter the year of termination if applicable. If you entered a code M, N, or O in 6a(1) and indicated that this is an unfunded plan and you also checked 9a "Yes," you must also check 9b "Yes."

9b. If the plan was terminated and all plan assets were not distributed, file a return/report for each year the plan has assets. In that case, the return/report must be filed by the plan administrator, if designated, or by the person or persons who actually control the plan's property.

If all plan assets were used to buy individual annuity contracts and the contracts were distributed to the participants, check "Yes."

If all the trust assets were legally transferred to the control of another plan or brought under the control of PBGC, check "Yes."

Do not check "Yes" for a welfare benefit plan which is still liable to pay benefits for claims which were incurred prior to the termination date, but not yet paid. See 29 CFR 2520.104b-2(g)(2)(ii).

9h. The Code provides for a nondeductible excise tax on a reversion of assets from a qualified plan.

9i. The employer must report the reversion by filing Form 5330 and pay any applicable tax. The tax will not be imposed upon employers who are tax-exempt entities under Code section 501(a). See instructions for Form 5330.

10a. If this plan was merged or consolidated into another plan(s), or plan assets or liabilities were transferred to another plan(s), indicate which other plan or plans were involved.

10c. Enter the EIN of the sponsor (employer, if for a single-employer plan) of the other plan.

10e. Pension benefit plans must file **Form 5310-A,** Notice of Merger, Consolidation, or Transfer of Plan Assets or Liabilities, at least 30 days before any plan merger or consolidation or any transfer of plan assets or liabilities to another plan.

Caution: *There is a penalty for not filing Form 5310-A on time.*

11. Enter the code for the **funding arrangement** used by the plan for the plan year from the list below.

The "funding arrangement" is the method used during the plan year for the receipt, holding, investment, and transmittal of plan assets prior to the time the plan actually provides the benefits promised under the plan. For purposes of items 11 and 12, the term "trust" includes any fund or account which receives, holds, transmits, or invests plan assets other than an account or policy of an insurance company.

Note: *An employee benefit plan which enters a code 2, 3, or 5 in item 11 and/or 12 must attach a Schedule A (Form 5500), Insurance Information, to provide information pertaining to each contract year ending with or within the plan year. See Schedule A (Form 5500) instructions.*

	Plan Funding Arrangement Codes
Trust	1
Trust and insurance	2
Insurance	3
Exclusively from general assets of sponsor (unfunded)	4
Partially insured and partially from general assets of sponsor	5

Other 6

12. Enter the code for the **benefit arrangement** used by the plan for the plan year from the list below.

The "benefit arrangement" is the method by which benefits were actually provided during the plan year to participants by the plan. For example, if all participants received their benefits from a trust (as defined in 11 above) the plan's benefit arrangement code would be "1." If some benefits come from a trust and some come from an insurance company, the code would be "2." If all benefits were paid from an account or policy of an insurance company, the code would be "3."

	Plan Benefit Arrangement Codes
Trust	1
Trust and insurance	2
Insurance	3
Exclusively from general assets of sponsor (unfunded)	4
Partially insured and partially from general assets of sponsor	5
Other	6

13a. Enter "Yes" if either the contributions to the plan or the benefits paid by the plan are subject to the collective bargaining process, even if the plan is not established and administered by a joint board of trustees. Enter "Yes" even if only some of those covered by the plan are members of a collective bargaining unit which negotiates benefit levels on its own behalf. The benefit schedules need not be identical for all employees under the plan.

13b. All plans entering code C or D on line 4 must enter the 6-digit LM number to identify each sponsoring labor organization which is a party to the collective bargaining agreement. Other plans which are maintained pursuant to collective bargaining agreements should enter the appropriate LM number, if available. The "LM number" is the six-digit Labor-Management file number entered by the sponsoring labor organization in item 1 of the Form LM-2 or LM-3 (Labor Organization Annual Report) filed with the Department of Labor. Accordingly, the LM number(s) should be readily available from the sponsoring labor organization(s). If all sponsoring labor organizations' LM numbers cannot be entered in the spaces provided in item 13b on the form, enter the additional LM numbers on a supplemental sheet to accompany the Form 5500.

14. If either the funding arrangement code (item 11) and/or the benefit arrangement code (item 12) is 2, 3, or 5, at least one Schedule A (Form 5500) must be attached to the Form 5500 filed for pension and welfare plans to provide information concerning the contract year ending with or within the plan year. The insurance company (or similar organization) which provides benefits is required to provide the plan administrator with the information needed to complete the return/report, pursuant to ERISA section 103 (a)(2). If you do not receive this information in a timely manner, contact the insurance company (or similar organization). If information is missing on Schedule A (Form 5500) due to a refusal to provide this information, note this on the Schedule A. If there are no Schedule(s) A attached, enter "0."

Page 9

Form 5500—Contd.

15b. If a waived funding deficiency is being amortized in the current plan year, do not complete (1), (2), and (3), but complete items 1, 2, 3, 7, and 9 of Schedule B (Form 5500). An enrolled actuary need not sign Schedule B under these circumstances.

15b(3). File Form 5330 with IRS to pay the excise tax on any funding deficiency.
Caution: *There is a penalty for not filing Form 5330 on time.*

16. A "top-heavy plan" is a plan which during any plan year is:

(1) any defined benefit plan if, as of the determination date, the present value of the cumulative accrued benefits under the plan for key employees exceeds 60% of the present value of the cumulative accrued benefits under the plan for all employees; and

(2) any defined contribution plan if, as of the determination date, the aggregate of the accounts of key employees under the plan exceeds 60% of the aggregate of the accounts of all employees under the plan.

Each plan of an employer included in a required aggregation group is to be treated as a top-heavy plan if such group is a top-heavy group. See definitions of required aggregation group and top-heavy group, below.

Key Employee—A key employee is any participant in an employer plan who at any time during the plan year, or any of the 4 preceding years, is:

(1) an officer of the employer having an annual compensation greater than 50% of the amount in effect under Code section 415(b)(1)(A),

(2) one of the 10 employees having annual compensation from the employer of more than the limitation in effect under Code section 415(c)(1)(A) and owning (or considered as owning within the meaning of Code section 318) the largest interests in the employer,

(3) a 5% owner of the employer, or

(4) a 1% owner of the employer having an annual compensation from the employer of more than $150,000.

In determining whether an individual is an officer of the employer, no more than 50 employees, or, if less, the greater of 3 employees or 10% of the employees, are to be treated as officers. See Code section 416(i) and T-12 of Regulations section 1.416. A key employee will not include any officer or employee of a governmental plan under Code section 414(d).

Required Aggregation Group—A required aggregation group consists of:

(1) each plan of the employer in which a key employee is or was a participant, and

(2) each other plan of the employer which enables a plan to meet the requirements for nondiscrimination in contributions or benefits under Code section 401(a)(4), or the participation requirements under Code section 410.

Top-Heavy Group—A top-heavy group is an aggregation group if, as of the determination date, the sum of the present value of the cumulative accrued benefits for key employees under all defined benefit plans included in such group and the aggregate of the accounts of key employees under all defined contribution plans in such group exceeds 60% of a similar sum determined for

all employees. To determine if a plan is top-heavy, include distributions made in the 5-year period ending on the determination date. However, do not take into account accrued benefits for an individual who hasn't performed services for the employer during the 5-year period ending on the determination date.

A qualified plan must limit the annual compensation of each employee taken into account for this year to $222,220 adjusted annually for the cost of living. The family members (spouse and lineal descendents under age 19) of 5% owners or one of the 10 most highly compensated employees are treated as a single employee. Qualified plans must comply with this requirement in operation even if the plan has not yet been amended to comply with the Tax Reform Act of 1986.

18a(1). Check "Yes" if the plan distributed any annuity contracts. Check "Yes" even if the plan was terminated.

18a(2). If "Yes" was checked for item 18a(1), the annuity contract must provide that all distributions from it will meet the participant and spousal consent requirements of Code section 417. However, consent is not needed for the distribution of the contract itself. If the contracts contained the Code section 417 requirements check "Yes."

18b. In general, distributions must be made in the form of a qualified joint and survivor annuity for life or a qualified preretirement survivor annuity. An annuity distribution to a single individual (see 18c(1) below), is a qualified joint and survivor annuity. Check "Yes" if distributions in other forms were made, even if those distributions were permissible, e.g., because consent was obtained or was not required.

18c. Generally, within the 90 days prior to the date of any benefit payment or the making of a loan to a participant, you must get the spouse's consent to the payment of the benefit or the use of the accrued benefit for the making of the loan. However, there are some circumstances where obtaining this spousal consent is not required. The following is a partial list of circumstances when spousal consent is not required:

(1) The participant is not married and no former spouse is required to be treated as a current spouse under a qualified domestic relations order issued by a court.

(2) The participant's nonforfeitable accrued benefit in the plan does not have at the time of distribution a present value of more than $3,500.

(3) The benefit is paid in the form of a qualified joint and survivor annuity, i.e., an annuity for the life of the participant with a survivor annuity for the life of the spouse which is not less than 50% of (and is not greater than 100% of) the amount of the annuity which is payable during the joint lives of the participant and the spouse. See Code section 417(b).

(4) The payout is from a profit-sharing or stock bonus plan that pays the spouse the participant's full account balance upon the participant's death, an annuity payment is not elected by the participant, and the profit-sharing or stock bonus plan is not a transferee plan with respect to the participant (i.e., had not received a transfer from a plan

that was subject to the consent requirements with respect to the participant).

(5) The participant had no service under the plan after August 22, 1984.

18d. A plan may not eliminate a subsidized benefit or a retirement option by plan amendment or plan termination.

19. If distributions were not made in accordance with the joint and survivor annuity rules of Code sections 411(a)(11) and 417(e) answer "No." If distributions did comply with Code sections 411(a)(11) and 417(e) or if no distributions were made answer "Yes."

20. The maximum annual benefit that may be provided under a defined benefit plan may not exceed the lesser of $90,000 or 100% of compensation. However, if benefits begin before the social security retirement age, the $90,000 limit must be reduced as described in IRS Notice 87-21, 1987-1 C.B. 458.

In addition, the dollar limitations will be reduced for participants with fewer than 10 years of participation in a defined benefit plan, i.e., a 10% reduction for each year under 10 years of participation.

For defined contribution plans, Code section 415 now provides that the dollar limit on annual additions to a qualified plan may not exceed the greater of $30,000 or 25% of the defined benefit dollar limit for such limitation year. The limitation for defined contributions plans under section 415(c)(1)(A) remains at $30,000 for 1991 since the law provides that it shall not be changed until the section 415(b)(1)(A) limit ($108,963 for 1991) for defined benefit plans exceeds $120,000.

Annual additions to a defined contribution plan will, for years beginning after December 31, 1986, include 100% of all after-tax employee contributions. For participants participating in plans of tax-exempt organizations, the pre-Tax Reform Act limits remain in effect.

The Tax Reform Act of 1986 provides that a participant's previously accrued benefit won't be reduced merely because of the reduction in dollar limits or increases in required periods of participation. The transitional rule applies to an individual who was a participant prior to January 1, 1987 in a plan in existence on May 5, 1986. If this participant's current accrued benefit exceeds the dollar limit under the Tax Reform Act of 1986, but complies with prior law, then the applicable dollar limit for the participant is equal to the current accrued benefit. The term "current accrued benefit" is defined as the participant's accrued benefit as of the close of the last limitation year beginning before January 1, 1987, and expressed as an annual benefit. To compute the defined benefit fraction, the current accrued benefit would replace the dollar limit otherwise used in the denominator of the fraction. The current accrued benefit is also reflected in the numerator of the defined benefit fraction.

21. Employees must begin to receive minimum distributions pursuant to Code section 401(a)(9) by April 1 of the calendar year following the calendar year in which the employee attains age 70½. Once begun, minimum distributions must continue each calendar year.

If your plan was required to make the distributions and did not, check "No." If your plan made the required distributions or if no distributions were made, check "Yes."

Form 5500—Contd.

22. In general, a plan must satisfy one of the coverage tests on each day of the year being tested. However, if the plan satisfies one of the tests on at least one day in each quarter of the year being tested, the plan will be deemed to pass the coverage tests for the entire year provided that the quarterly testing dates reasonably represent the coverage of the plan over the entire plan year. Complete item 22 for the testing date selected by the employer (typically the last day of the plan year). For an alternative testing option see Income Tax Regulations section 1.410(b)-8(a)(4).

If Form 5500 is being filed solely because of Code section 6039D, for item 22, complete only **22h** and **22m**.

Multiemployer plan (code C in item 4) and multiple-employer-collectively-bargained plan (code D in item 4) need to complete line 22 only if a plan: (1) benefits employees who are not collective bargaining unit employees (other than employees required to benefit under the terms of a collective bargaining agreement) or (2) only covers collective bargaining unit employees and 2% or more of them are professionals. Multiple-employer plan (other) filers (Code E in item 4) are not required to complete item **22**. However, the participating employers in multiple-employer plan (other) pension benefit plans are required to complete the applicable questions in item 22 on the Form 5500C/R that they file.

22a. In general, if the employer operated separate lines of business within the meaning of Code section 414(r) for a year, the employer may apply the coverage and discrimination requirements separately to employees in each separate line of business. If **22a** is "Yes," complete **22b** through **22o** for the separate line of business covered by the plan as if the employees of the separate line of business were the sole employees of the employer. If this plan benefits employees in more than one separate line of business, complete item **22** for one of the lines of business and for each additional line of business covered by the plan submit an attachment completed in the same format as item **22**.

22c. Income Tax Regulations section 1.410(b)-7(c) requires the "disaggregation" of certain single plans into two or more separate plans. Each of the disaggregated parts of the plan must then satisfy the coverage requirements under Code section 410(b) as if they were a separate plan. For purposes of item **22c** the following plans must be disaggregated: (i) a plan that has a section 401(k) provision (a qualified cash or deferred arrangement (CODA)) and a provision that is not a 401(k) plan, (ii) a plan that has a section 401(m) provision (employee and matching contributions) and a provision that is not a 401(m) provision, (iii) a plan that has an ESOP provision and a provision that is not an ESOP, and (iv) a plan that benefits both collectively and noncollectively bargained employees (see Income Tax Regulations section 1.410(b)-5(f) for an exception).

If any of the above apply to your plan, complete item 22 for one of the disaggregated plans and for each additional part of the plan that must be disaggregated, submit an attachment completed in the same format as item 22. Also see Income Tax Regulations section 1.410(b)-7(c) for more details on other plans that may have to be disaggregated to satisfy the coverage requirements of code section 410(b).

22d. Under section 1.410(b)-7(d) of the Income Tax Regulations, employers can aggregate any qualified pension or profit sharing plans that are not mandatorily disaggregated under the rules for item **22c** above in order to satisfy the coverage tests. However, the aggregated plan must also satisfy the discrimination rules of section 401(a)(4) on an aggregated basis. Note that a special aggregation rule applies for the purposes of computing the average benefit percentage. See item **22o(1)** below. If the employer aggregates plans for the purposes of the coverage and discrimination tests, check this item "Yes."

22e. Income Tax Regulations section 1.401(a)(4)-9(c) allows an employer to restructure a plan into component plans to satisfy the coverage and discrimination tests. Check "Yes," if the employer is satisfying the coverage and discrimination tests by restructuring the plan, and do not complete the rest of item 22.

22f(1). Check this box if this plan benefited no highly compensated employees (within the meaning of Code section 414(q)). This box should be checked for plans under which no employee receives an allocation or accrues a benefit. See the instructions to item **22m** for the definition of benefiting.

22f(2). Check this box if this plan is a collectively bargained plan that benefits only collectively bargained employees and no more than 2% of the employees who are covered pursuant to such agreement are professional employees. See section 1.410(b)-9 of the Income Tax Regulations.

22g. Check "Yes," if any leased employee, within the meaning of section 414(n), performed services for the employer or any entity aggregated with the employer under Code sections 414(b), (c), or (m).

22h. Enter the total number of employees of the employer. Include all self-employed individuals, common-law employees and leased employees, within the meaning of Code section 414(n), of any of the entities aggregated with the employer under Code section 414(b), (c), or (m).

22i. Enter the total number of excludable employees in the following categories:

(1) Employees who have not attained the minimum age and service requirements of the plan.

(2) Collectively bargained employees. Do not count any employees covered under a collective bargaining agreement if more than 2% of the employees covered pursuant to such agreement are professional employees. See section 1.410 (b)-9 of the Income Tax Regulations.

(3) Nonresident aliens (within the meaning of Income Tax Regulations section 1.410(b)-6(c)).

(4) Employees who fail to accrue a benefit solely because: they fail to satisfy a minimum hour of service or last day requirement under the plan, they do not have more than 500 hours of service, and they are not employed on the last day of the plan year.

22k. See the instructions for item **22m** for the definition of benefiting.

22l. The definition of highly compensated employee is contained in Code section 414(q) and the income tax regulations thereunder.

22m. In general, an employee is benefiting if the employee receives an allocation of contributions or forfeitures, or accrues a benefit under the plan for the plan year. Certain other employees are treated as benefiting even if they fail to receive an allocation of contributions and/or forfeitures, or to accrue a benefit solely because the employee is subject to plan provisions that limit plan benefits, such as a provision for maximum years of service, maximum retirement benefits, or limits designed to satisfy Code section 415. An employee is treated as benefiting under a plan if the employee is eligible to make elective contributions or after-tax employee contributions and matching distributions subject to Code section 401(k) or (m). An eligible employee is treated as benefiting under the plan even if they do not actually make contributions.

22o(1). A plan satisfies the average benefit test if it satisfies both the nondiscriminatory classification test and the average benefit percentage test.

A plan satisfies the nondiscriminatory classification test if benefiting employees are defined by reasonable and objective business criteria set out in the plan and such classification is nondiscriminatory. A classification will be deemed nondiscriminatory if the ratio in item **22o(2)** below is equal to or greater than the safe harbor percentage. The safe harbor percentage is 50%, reduced by ¾ of a percentage point for each percentage point by which the nonhighly compensated employee concentration percentage exceeds 60%. The nonhighly compensated employee concentration percentage is the percentage of all the employees of the employer who are not highly compensated employees. See Income Tax Regulations section 1.410(b)-4.

In general, a plan satisfies the average benefit percentage test if the actual benefit percentage for nonhighly compensated employees is at least 70% of the actual benefit percentage for highly compensated employees. All qualified plans of the employer, including CODAs and plans containing employee or matching contributions (Code section 401(k) or (m)) are aggregated in determining the actual benefit percentages. Do not aggregate plans that may not be aggregated for the purposes of satisfying the ratio percentage test, other than plans subject to Code section 401(k) or (m). In addition, all nonexcludable employees, including those with no benefit under any qualified plan of the employer, are included in determining the actual benefit percentages. See Income Tax Regulation section 1.410(b)-5 for complete details on this computation.

22o(2). In general to compute the ratio, divide the number of nonexcludable employees who benefit under the plan and are not highly compensated by the total number of nonexcludable nonhighly compensated employees; put this result in the numerator (top of the fraction). Divide the number of nonexcludable employees who benefit under the plan and who are highly compensated by the total number of nonexcludable highly compensated employees; put this result in the denominator

Form 5500—Contd.

(bottom of the fraction). Divide the numerator by the denominator and put the result in item 22o(2).

23a. Check "Yes" if it is your intention that this plan qualify under Code section 401(a). Otherwise check "No" and go to item 24a.

23b. If item 23a is "Yes," and you have received a determination letter from IRS, enter the date of the most recent determination letter received.

23c. Check "Yes" if you have applied for a determination letter from IRS but have not received a reply from IRS. Otherwise check "No."

24b. An independent appraiser must be used to ascertain the value of securities, acquired by a plan after December 31, 1986, if the securities aren't readily tradeable on an established securities market.

28a. Check "Yes" if any person (including, when applicable, a corporation or partnership) received, directly or indirectly, $5,000 or more during the plan year for providing services to the plan. For exceptions, see the instructions for Part I of Schedule C (Form 5500). If you checked "Yes," complete Part I of Schedule C (Form 5500), and attach it to Form 5500. Include payments from the plan sponsor which are reimbursable by the plan.

Check "No" if all plan assets are held in a master trust and the master trust report filed with DOL includes a Schedule C that reports all payments to service providers for the master trust.

28b. Include all trustees in office during the plan year. List these trustees on Part II of Schedule C (Form 5500) and attach it to the Form 5500.

28c. Check "Yes" if there has been a termination in the appointment of any person for which a box must be checked in item 28d. In case the service provider is not an individual (i.e., when the service provider is a legal entity such as a corporation, partnership, etc.), check "Yes" when the service provider (not the individual) has been terminated. If item 28c is checked "Yes," complete Part III of Schedule C (Form 5500) and attach the Schedule C to the Form 5500. Otherwise, check "No" and skip to item 28g.

28d. Check all appropriate boxes and complete Part III of Schedule C (Form 5500). At least one box must be checked if item 28c is answered "Yes."

28e. If item 28c is checked "Yes," check 28e "Yes" if, during the two most recent plan years preceding the termination and any subsequent interim period preceding such termination, resignation, or dismissal, there were any disagreements (whether or not the disagreements were a factor in the termination) on any matter of professional judgment which, if not resolved to the satisfaction of the former appointee, would have caused (or did cause) the former appointee to take some action, such as including the subject matter of the disagreement within a written report. For example, check "Yes" if the accountant was terminated as a result of a disagreement over the valuation of plan assets and the accountant would have required that the matter be disclosed in a note to the financial statements. Disagreements not involving a matter of professional judgment, such as the payment or nonpayment of fees, or the

amount of the fee charged should not be included.

28f. If item 28d(1) or 28d(2) has been checked, indicating that an independent qualified public accountant or enrolled actuary has been terminated, the plan administrator must provide the terminated accountant or enrolled actuary with a copy of the explanation for the termination provided in Part III of Schedule C (Form 5500), along with a completed copy of the notice which follows.

Notice To Terminated Accountant or Enrolled Actuary

In accordance with this requirement, I, as plan administrator, verify that the explanation that is either reproduced below or attached to this notice is the explanation concerning your termination as reported on the Schedule C (Form 5500) attached to the 1991 Annual Return/Report Form 5500 for the (enter name of plan).

This return/report is identified in item 1b by the nine-digit

EIN – (enter Employer Identification Number) and in item 5c by the three-digit PN (enter plan number).

Signed

Dated

Any comments concerning this explanation should include the name, EIN, and PN of the plan and be submitted directly to:

Office of Enforcement
Pension and Welfare Benefits
  Administration
U. S. Department of Labor
200 Constitution Avenue, NW
Washington, DC 20210

An explanation of the reasons for the termination of an accountant or enrolled actuary (terminated party) must be provided as part of the annual report (Part III of Schedule C). The plan administrator of the employee benefit plan is also required to provide the terminated party with a copy of this explanation and a notification that the terminated party has the opportunity to comment directly to the Department of Labor concerning any aspect of this explanation.

28g. A Schedule C (Form 5500) must be attached if item 28a, 28b, and/or 28c are checked "Yes." More than one Schedule C may be required if additional space is required to complete any part of the Schedule C. If no Schedule(s) C is required to be attached, enter "0."

29. Employee benefit plans filing the Annual Return/Report Form 5500 are generally required to engage an independent qualified public accountant pursuant to ERISA section 103(a)(3)(A). An independent qualified public accountant's opinion must be attached to Form 5500 unless: (i) the plan is an employee welfare benefit plan which is unfunded, fully insured, or a combination of unfunded and insured, as described in 29 CFR 2520. 104-44(b)(1); (ii) the plan is an employee pension benefit plan whose sole asset(s) consists of insurance contracts which provide that, upon receipt of the premium payment, the insurance carrier fully guarantees the amount of benefit payments attributable to plan participants for that plan year as specified in 29 CFR 2520.104-44(b)(2); or (iii) the plan has elected to defer attaching the accountant's opinion for the first of two plan

years, one of which is a short plan year of 7 months or less as allowed by 29 CFR 2520.104-50. (Also see the instructions for item 29a below.)

Welfare benefit plans sponsored by one employer (or by a controlled group of employers) which use a Code section 501(c)(9) trust are generally not exempt from the requirement of engaging an independent qualified public accountant.

29a. Plans meeting (i) or (ii) above should check "Yes" for item 29a and skip to item 31. Plans meeting (iii) must attach the required explanation and statements in lieu of the opinion and should check "No" to item 29a and "Other" to item 29b, and specify, in the space provided, that "the opinion is to be attached to the next Form 5500 pursuant to 29 CFR 2520.104-50." All other plans should check "No." "N/A" is NOT an acceptable response to this item. If the required accountant's opinion is not attached to the Form 5500, the filing is subject to rejection as incomplete and penalties may be imposed (see page 1).

29b and c. 29CFR 2520.103-1(b) requires that any separate financial statements prepared in order for the independent qualified public accountant to form the opinion and notes to financial statements (or items 34 and 35 if applicable) must be attached to the annual return/report Form 5500. Any separate statements must include the information required to be disclosed in items 34 and 35 of the Form 5500; however, they may be aggregated into categories in a manner other than that used on Form 5500. The separate statements should be either typewritten or printed and consist of reproductions of items 34 and 35 or statements incorporating by reference items 34 and 35. See 29 CFR 2520.103-1(b).

29b(1). Generally, an unqualified opinion is issued when the auditor concludes that the plan's financial statements present fairly, in all material respects, the financial status of the plan as of the end of the period audited, and the changes in its financial status for the period under audit are in conformity with generally accepted accounting principles. Check this box if the plan received an unqualified opinion.

29b(2). Department of Labor Regulations 29 CFR 2520.103-8 and 2520.103-12(d) generally state that the examination and report of an independent qualified public accountant need not extend to: (1) information prepared and certified to by a bank or similar institution or by an insurance carrier which is regulated and supervised and subject to periodic examination by a state or Federal agency, or (2) information concerning a 103-12 IE which is reported directly to the Department of Labor. Check this box if the plan received an accountant's opinion as discussed in 29b(1) above except for the information not audited pursuant to the above regulations.

29b(3). Generally a qualified opinion is issued by an independent qualified public accountant when the plan's financial statements present fairly, in all material respects, the financial position of the plan as of the end of the audit period and the results of its operations for the audit period are in conformity with generally accepted accounting principles except for the effects of one or more matters which are described in

Form 5500—Contd.

the opinion. A disclaimer of opinion is issued when the independent qualified public accountant does not express an opinion on the financial statements because he has not performed an audit sufficient in scope to enable him to form an opinion of the financial statements. Check this box if the plan received a qualified opinion or if a disclaimer of opinion was issued. If the audit was of limited scope pursuant to 29 CFR 2520.103-8 and/or 2520.103-12(d), and no other limitations as to scope or procedures were in effect, then check the box in item 29b(2).

29b(4). Generally an adverse opinion is issued by an independent qualified public accountant when the plan's financial statements do not present fairly, in all material respects, the financial position of the plan as of the end of the audit period and the results of its operations for the audit period in conformity with generally accepted accounting principles. Check this box if the plan received an adverse accountant's opinion.

29b(5). Generally, an independent qualified public accountant's opinion will be described by one of the categories in 29b(1) through (4). Check this box if the accountant's opinion received by the plan is not described by one of the categories in 29b(1) through (4). Explain the nature of the opinion in the space next to this box. If the explanation requires more space, enter "See attached" and on a separate sheet of paper explain in detail the nature of the accountant's opinion. Any attachments should identify the item number and include the plan's name, EIN and PN.

29c and 29d. These items must be answered by all plans required to engage an independent qualified public accountant (item 29a is "No"). The disclosure of the transactions and financial conditions listed in 29c are some of the disclosures required to be made when a plan's financial statements are presented in accordance with generally accepted accounting principles. (Usually these disclosures are contained in the notes

to the financial statements.) If you are unsure as to whether the disclosures presented in or accompanying the plan's financial statements fall within one of the disclosures described in **29c**, you should consult with the plan's independent qualified public accountant.

Check 29c "Yes" and provide the amount involved in 29d if the financial statements or the notes to the statements contain any of the disclosures listed in **29c**. The amount should be determined by adding the amounts of all of the applicable disclosures. For example, if two significant transactions are disclosed between the plan and the sponsor, the amounts, if any, disclosed in the notes should be added together and the total reported.

If you confirm, through consultation with the accountant, if necessary, that the accountant's report, including any applicable financial statements or notes, does not contain any of the disclosures noted in item **29c**, check item **29c** "No" and enter "0" in item **29d**.

30. Plans with assets held in a master trust and/or 103-12 IE (see pages 3 and 4 for the definition of these terms) should complete items **30a, b, c,** and d to report information relating to assets held and transactions occurring outside the master trust and/or 103-12 IE. In determining the 5% figure for item **30d**, subtract the value of plan assets held in the master trust or 103-12 IE from the current value of the plan's total assets at the beginning of the plan year.

"Current value" means fair market value where available. Otherwise, it means the fair value as determined in good faith under the terms of the plan by a trustee or a named fiduciary, assuming an orderly liquidation at time of the determination.

Do not complete sub-items **30a** through **30f** if all plan funds are held in a master trust.

If "Yes" is checked for item(s) **30a, b, c, d, e,** and/or f, schedules must be completed and attached to the Form 5500. If the required schedule is not clearly labeled and

attached to the Form 5500, the filing is subject to rejection as incomplete and penalties may be imposed (see page 1). Any attachments must identify the item number and include the plan's name, EIN, and PN.

30a–30d. If the assets or investment interests of two or more plans are maintained in one trust (except investment arrangements reported in **34c(11)** through **34c(15)** (see page 17)), all entries in the schedules included under items **30a, b,** and **c** which relate to the trust shall be completed by including the plan's allocable portion of the trust. For purposes of item **30d**, the plan's allocable portion of the transactions of the trust shall be combined with the other transactions of the plan, if any, to determine which transactions (or series of transactions) are reportable. Do not include individual transactions of investment arrangements reported in 34c(11) through 34c(15).

For purposes of this form, party-in-interest is deemed to include a disqualified person—see Code section 4975(e)(2). The term "party-in-interest" means, as to an employee benefit plan—

(A) any fiduciary (including, but not limited to, any administrator, officer, trustee or custodian), counsel, or employee of the plan;

(B) a person providing services to the plan;

(C) an employer, any of whose employees are covered by the plan;

(D) an employee organization, any of whose members are covered by the plan;

(E) an owner, direct or indirect, of 50% or more of—(i) the combined voting power of all classes of stock entitled to vote, or the total value of shares of all classes of stock of a corporation, (ii) the capital interest or the profits interest of a partnership, or (iii) the beneficial interest of a trust or unincorporated enterprise that is an employer or an employee organization described in (C) or (D);

(F) a relative of any individual described in (A), (B), (C), or (E);

(Continued on page 15)

30a. Check "Yes" and attach one or both of the following two schedules to the Form 5500 if the plan had any assets held for investment purposes at any time during the plan year. Assets held for investment purposes shall include:

1 Any investment asset held by the plan on the last day of the plan year; and

2 Any investment asset purchased during the plan year and sold before the end of the plan year except:

(i) Debt obligations of the U.S. or any U.S. agency.

(ii) Interests issued by a company registered under the Investment Company Act of 1940 (e. g., a mutual fund).

(iii) Bank certificates of deposit with a maturity of one year or less.

(iv) Commercial paper with a maturity of 9 months, or less, if it is valued in the highest rating category by at least two nationally recognized statistical rating services and is issued by a company required to file reports with the Securities and Exchange Commission under section 13 of the Securities Exchange Act of 1934.

(v) Participations in a bank common or collective trust.

(vi) Participations in an insurance company pooled separate account.

(vii) Securities purchased from a broker-dealer registered under the Securities Exchange Act of 1934 and either:

(A) listed on a national securities exchange and registered under section 6 of the Securities Exchange Act of 1934, or (B) quoted on NASDAQ. Assets held for investment purposes shall not include any investment which was not held by the plan on the last day of the plan year if that investment is reported in the annual report for that plan year in any of the following:

1 The schedule of loans or fixed income obligations in default required by item 30b;

2 The schedule of leases in default or classified as uncollectible required by item 30c;

3 The schedule of reportable transactions required by item 30d; and

4 The schedule of party-in-interest transactions required by items 30e and 30f.

The first schedule required to be attached to the Form 5500 is a schedule of all assets held for investment purposes at the end of the plan year, aggregated and identified by issue, maturity date, rate of interest, collateral, par or maturity value, cost and current value, and, in the case of a loan, the payment schedule. The schedule must use the following or a similar format and the same size paper as the Form 5500.

Note: *In column (a), place an asterisk (*) on the line of each identified person known to be a party-in-interest to the plan. In column (c), include any restriction on transferability of corporate securities. (Include lending of securities permitted under Prohibited Transactions Exemption 81-6.)*

Form 5500—Contd.

The following schedule must be clearly labeled **"Item 30a – Schedule of Assets Held for Investment Purposes."**

(a)	(b) Identity of issue, borrower, lessor, or similar party	(c) Description of investment including maturity date. rate of interest. collateral. par or maturity value	(d) Cost	(e) Current value

The second schedule required to be attached to the Form 5500 is a schedule of investment assets which were both acquired and disposed of within the plan year (see 29 CFR 2520.103-11). The schedule should use the following or a similar format and the same size paper as the Form 5500. The following schedule must be clearly labeled **"Item 30a – Schedule of Assets Held for Investment Purposes."**

(a) Identity of issue, borrower, lessor, or similar party	(b) Description of investment including maturity date. rate of interest, collateral, par or maturity value	(c) Costs of acquisitions	(d) Proceeds of dispositions

Note: Participant loans under an individual account plan with investment experience segregated for each account, that are made in accordance with 29 CFR 2550.408b-1 and that are secured solely by a portion of the participant's vested accrued benefit, may be aggregated for reporting purposes in item 30a. Under identity of borrower enter "Participant loans," under rate of interest enter the lowest rate and the highest rate charged during the plan year (e.g., 8%-10%), under the cost and proceeds columns enter "-0-", and under current value enter the total amount of these loans.

    30b. Check "Yes" and attach the following schedule to the Form 5500 if the plan had any loans or fixed income obligations in default or determined to be uncollectible as of the end of the plan year. Include obligations where the required payments have not been made by the due date. With respect to notes and loans, the due date, payment amount and conditions for default are usually contained in the note or loan documents. Defaults can occur at any time for those obligations which require periodic repayment. Generally loans and fixed income obligations are considered uncollectible when payment has not been made and there is little probability that payment will be made. A loan by the plan is in default when the borrower is unable to pay the obligation upon maturity. A fixed income obligation has a fixed maturity date at a specified interest rate. List any loans by the plan which are in default and any fixed income obligations which have matured, but have not been paid, for which it has been determined that payment will not be made. The schedule should use the following or similar format and the same size paper as the Form 5500. The following schedule must be clearly labeled **"Item 30b – Schedule of Loans or Fixed Income Obligations."**

    Note: *In column (a), place an asterisk (*) on the line of each identified person known to be a party-in-interest to the plan. Include all loans that were renegotiated during the plan year. Also, explain what steps have been taken or will be taken to collect overdue amounts for each loan listed.*

(a)	(b) Identity and address of obligor	(c) Original amount of loan	Amount received during reporting year		(f) Unpaid balance at end of year	(g) Detailed description of loan including dates of making and maturity, interest rate, the type and value of collateral, any renegotiation of the loan and the terms of the renegotiation and other material items	Amount overdue	
			(d) Principal	(e) Interest			(h) Principal	(i) Interest

    30c. Check "Yes," and attach to Form 5500 the following schedule if the plan had any leases in default or classified as uncollectible. The schedule should use the following or a similar format and the same size paper as Form 5500. The following schedule must be clearly labeled **"Item 30c – Schedule of Leases in Default or Classified as Uncollectible."**

    A lease is an agreement conveying the right to use property, plant or equipment for a stated period. A lease is in default when the required payment(s) has not been made. An uncollectible lease is one where the required payments have not been made and for which there is little probability that payment will be made. *Also, explain what steps have been taken or will be taken to collect overdue amounts for each lease listed.*

(a)	(b) Identity of lessor/lessee	(c) Relationship to plan, employer, employee organization or other party-in-interest	(d) Terms and description (type of property, location and date it was purchased, terms regarding rent, taxes, insurance, repairs, expenses, renewal options, date property was leased)	(e) Original cost	(f) Current value at time of lease	(g) Gross rental receipts during the plan year	(h) Expenses paid during the plan year	(i) Net receipts	(j) Amount in arrears

    30d. Check "Yes" and attach to the Form 5500 the following schedule if the plan had any reportable transactions (see 29 CFR 2520.103-6). The schedule should use the following or a similar format and the same size paper as the Form 5500.

    A reportable transaction includes:

    1. A single transaction within the plan year in excess of 5% of the current value of the plan assets;

    2. Any series of transactions with, or in conjunction with, the same person, involving property other than securities, which amount in the aggregate within the plan year (regardless of the category of asset and the gain or loss on any transaction) to more than 5% of the current value of plan assets;

    3. Any transaction within the plan year involving securities of the same issue if within the plan year any series of transactions with respect to such securities amount in the aggregate to more than 5% of the current value of the plan assets; and

    4. Any transaction within the plan year with respect to securities with, or in conjunction with, a person if any prior or subsequent single transaction within the plan year with such person, with respect to securities, exceeds 5% of the current value of plan assets.

    The 5% figure is determined by comparing the current value of the transaction at the transaction date with the current value of the plan assets at the beginning of the plan year.

Page 14

Form 5500—Contd.

If the assets of two or more plans are maintained in one trust, the plan's allocable portion of the transactions of the trust shall be combined with the other transactions of the plan, if any, to determine which transactions (or series of transactions) are reportable (5%) transactions. This does not apply to investment arrangements whose current value is reported in items 34c(11) through 34c(15). Instead, for investments in common/collective trusts, pooled separate accounts, 103-12 IEs and registered investment companies, determine the 5% figure by comparing the transaction date value of the acquisition and/or disposition of units of participation or shares in the entity with the current value of the plan assets at the beginning of the plan year. Do not complete item 30d if all plan funds are held in a master trust. Plans with assets in a master trust which have other transactions should determine the 5% figure by subtracting the current value of plan assets held in the master trust from the current value of all plan assets at the beginning of the plan year. Do not include individual transactions of investment arrangements reported in items 34c(11) through 34c(15).

In the case of a purchase or sale of a security on the market, do not identify the person from whom purchased or to whom sold.

The following schedule must be clearly labeled **"Item 30d – Schedule of Reportable Transactions."**

(a) Identity of party involved	(b) Description of asset (include interest rate and maturity in case of a loan)	(c) Purchase price	(d) Selling price	(e) Lease rental	(f) Expense incurred with transaction	(g) Cost of asset	(h) Current value of asset on transaction date	(i) Net gain or (loss)

30e and f. Check "Yes" and attach the following schedule to the Form 5500 if the plan had any nonexempt transactions with a party-in-interest.

For purposes of this form, party-in-interest is deemed to include a disqualified person (see Code section 4975(e)(2)). The term "party-in-interest" is defined on page 13. Nonexempt transactions with a party-in-interest include any direct or indirect:

1. Sale or exchange, or lease, of any property between the plan and a party-in-interest.
2. Lending of money or other extension of credit between the plan and party-in-interest.
3. Furnishing of goods, services, or facilities between the plan and a party-in-interest.
4. Transfer to, or use by or for the benefit of, a party-in-interest, of any income or assets of the plan.
5. Acquisition, on behalf of the plan, of any employer security or employer real property in violation of ERISA section 407(a).
6. Dealing with the assets of the plan for a fiduciary's own interest or own account.
7. Acting in a fiduciary's individual or any other capacity in any transaction involving the plan on behalf of a party (or represent a party) whose interests are adverse to the interests of the plan or the interests of its participants or beneficiaries.
8. Receipt of any consideration for his or her own personal account by a party-in-interest who is a fiduciary for any party dealing with the plan in connection with a transaction involving the income or assets of the plan.

Do not check "Yes" for item 30e or 30f, or list transactions that are statutorily exempt under Part 4 of Title I of ERISA, or administratively exempt under ERISA section 408(a), or exempt under Code sections 4975(c) and 4975(d), or include transactions of a 103-12 IE with parties other than the plan. You may indicate that an application for an administrative exemption is pending.

If you are unsure as to whether a transaction is exempt or not, you should consult with either the plan's independent qualified public accountant or legal counsel or both.

Set out each transaction with the information set forth below in the following or similar format using the same size paper as the Form 5500. The following schedules must be clearly labeled as appropriate **"Item 30e — Schedule of Nonexempt Transactions"** and/or **"Item 30f — Schedule of Nonexempt Transactions."**

If a nonexempt prohibited transaction occurred with respect to a disqualified person, file Form 5330 with IRS to pay the excise tax on the transaction.

(a) Identity of party involved	(b) Relationship to plan, employer or other party-in-interest	(c) Description of transactions including maturity date, rate of interest, collateral, par or maturity value	(d) Purchase price	(e) Selling price	(f) Lease rental	(g) Expenses incurred in connection with transaction	(h) Cost of asset	(i) Current value of asset	(j) Net gain or (loss) on each transaction

(Continued from page 13)

(G) a corporation, partnership, or trust or estate of which (or in which) 50% or more of: (i) the combined voting power of all classes of stock entitled to vote or the total value of shares of all classes of stock of such corporation, (ii) the capital interest or profits interest of such partnership, or (iii) the beneficial interest of such trust or estate is owned directly or indirectly, or held by, persons described in (A), (B), (C), (D) or (E);

(H) an employee, officer, director (or an individual having powers or responsibilities similar to those of officers or directors), or a 10% or more shareholder, directly or indirectly, of a person described in (B), (C), (D), (E), or (G), or of the employee benefit plan; or

(I) a 10% or more (directly or indirectly in capital or profits) partner or joint venturer of a person described in (B), (C), (D), (E), or (G).

30g. Employer Security.—An employer security is any security issued by an employer (including affiliates) of employees covered by the plan. These may include common stocks, preferred stocks, bonds, zero coupon bonds, debentures, convertible debentures, notes, and commercial paper. Generally, a publicly traded security is a security which is bought and sold on a recognized market (e.g., NYSE, AMEX, over the counter, etc.) for which there is a pool of willing buyers and sellers. Securities which are listed on a market but for which there does not exist a pool of willing buyers and sellers are not publicly traded.

Qualifying Employer Security.—An employer security which is a stock or a "marketable obligation" is considered a qualifying

employer security. For purposes of this definition, the term "marketable obligation" means a bond, debenture, note, certificate, or other evidence of indebtedness (obligation) if: *(i)* such obligation is acquired—

   (A) on the market, either: (1) at the price of the obligation prevailing on a national securities exchange which is registered with the Securities and Exchange Commission, or (2) if the obligation is not traded on such a national securities exchange, at a price not less favorable to the plan than the offering price for the obligation as established by current bid and asked prices quoted by persons independent of the issuer;

   (B) from an underwriter, at a price: (1) not in excess of the public offering price for the obligation as set forth in a prospectus or offering circular filed with the Securities and Exchange Commission, and (2) at which a substantial portion of the same issue is

Page 15

Form 5500—Contd.

acquired by persons independent of the issuer; or

(C) directly from the issuer, at a price not less favorable to the plan than the price paid currently for a substantial portion of the same issue by persons independent of the issuer;

(ii) immediately following the acquisition of such obligation—

(A) not more than 25% of the aggregate amount of obligations issued in such issue and outstanding at the time of acquisition is held by the plan, and

(B) at least 50% of the aggregate amount referred to in subparagraph (A) is held by persons independent of the issuer; and

(iii) immediately following the acquisition of the obligation, not more than 25% of the assets of the plan is invested in obligations of the employer or an affiliate of the employer.

For purposes of the qualifying employer security definition, the term "stock" must meet the following conditions:

1. No more than 25% of the aggregate amount of stock of the same class issued and outstanding at the time of acquisition is held by the plan, and

2. At least 50% of the aggregate amount of stock described in the preceding paragraph is held by persons independent of the issuer.

For exceptions to the above, see ERISA section 407(f).

30h. Generally, as it relates to this question, an appraisal by an unrelated third party is an evaluation of the value of a security prepared by an individual or firm who knows how to judge the value of securities and does not have an ongoing relationship with the plan or plan fiduciaries except for preparing the appraisal. Non-publicly traded securities are generally held by few people and not traded on a stock exchange.

32a(1). Generally, every plan official of an employee benefit plan who "handles" funds or other property of such plan must be bonded. Generally a person shall be deemed to be handling funds or other property of a plan, so as to require bonding, whenever his or her duties or activities with respect to given funds are such that there is a risk that such funds could be lost in the event of fraud or dishonesty on the part of such person, acting either alone or in collusion with others. Section 412 of ERISA and Regulations 29 CFR 2580 provide the bonding requirements, including the definition of "handling" (29 CFR 2580.412-6), the permissible forms of bonds (29 CFR 2580.412-10), the amount of the bond (29 CFR 2580, subpart C), and certain exemptions such as the exemption for unfunded plans, certain banks and insurance companies (ERISA section 412), and the exemption allowing plan officials to purchase bonds from surety companies authorized by the Secretary of the Treasury as acceptable reinsurers on Federal bonds (29 CFR 2580.412-23).

Check "Yes" only if the plan itself (as opposed to the plan sponsor or administrator) is a named insured under a fidelity bond covering plan officials and if the plan is protected as described in 29 CFR 2580.412-18.

Plans are permitted under certain conditions to purchase fiduciary liability insurance. These policies do not protect the plan from dishonest acts and are not bonds which should be reported in question 32.

32a(2). Indicate the aggregate amount of coverage available for all claims.

32b(1). Check "Yes" if the plan has suffered or discovered any loss as the result of a dishonest or fraudulent act(s).

32b(2). If item 32b(1) has been answered "Yes," enter the full amount of the loss. If the full amount of the loss has not yet been determined, provide and disclose that the figure is an estimate, such as "Approximately $1,000."

Note: *Willful failure to report is a criminal offense. See ERISA section 501.*

33a. If you are uncertain as to whether the plan is covered under the PBGC termination insurance program, check the box "Not determined" and contact the PBGC and request a coverage determination. Welfare and fringe benefit plans do not complete this item.

34 and 35. You can use either the cash, modified accrual, or accrual basis for recognition of transactions in items 34 and 35, as long as you use one method consistently.

Round off all amounts in items 34 and 35 to the nearest dollar. Any other amounts are subject to rejection. Check all subtotals and totals carefully.

Caution: *Do not mark through the printed line descriptions and insert your own description as this may cause additional correspondence due to a new computerized review of the Form 5500.*

"Current value" means fair market value, where available. Otherwise, it means the fair value as determined in good faith under the terms of the plan by a trustee or a named fiduciary, assuming an orderly liquidation at the time of the determination.

If the assets of two or more plans are maintained in one trust, such as when an employer has two plans which are funded through a single trust (except investment arrangements reported in items 34c(11) through 34c(15)), complete items 34 and 35 by entering the plan's allocable part of each line item.

If assets of one plan are maintained in two or more trust funds, report the combined financial information in items 34 and 35.

Fully insured, unfunded, and unfunded/ insured welfare plans, and fully insured pension plans meeting the conditions of 29 CFR 2520.104-44, need not complete items 34 and 35. To determine if your welfare benefit plan is fully insured, unfunded, or unfunded/insured, see page 2.

To determine if your pension plan is fully insured, see page 5.

Exception: *Plans which are both welfare and fringe benefit plans must complete items 35g and 35h.*

34. Column (a) should be used to enter the current value of plan assets and liabilities as of the beginning of the plan year. Column (b) should be used to enter the current value of plan assets and liabilities as of the end of the plan year.

Amounts reported in column (a) must be the same as reported for corresponding line items in column (b) of the return/report for the preceding plan year.

34a. Total noninterest-bearing cash includes, among other things, cash on hand or cash in a noninterest-bearing checking account.

34b(1). Noncash basis filers should include contributions due the plan by the employer but not yet paid. Do not include other amounts due from the employer such as the reimbursement of an expense or the repayment of a loan.

34b(2). Noncash basis filers should include contributions withheld by the employer from participants and amounts due directly from participants which have not yet been received by the plan. Do not include the repayment of participant loans.

34b(3). Noncash basis filers should include income from investment income earned but not yet received by the plan.

34b(4). Noncash basis filers should include amounts due to the plan which are not includable in items 34b(1)–(3) above. These may include amounts due from the employer or another plan for expense reimbursement or from a participant for the repayment of an overpayment of benefits.

34c(1). Include all assets which earn interest in a financial institution account including interest bearing checking accounts, passbook savings accounts, et al., or in a money market fund.

34c(3). Include securities issued or guaranteed by the U.S. Government or its designated agencies such as U.S. Savings Bonds, Treasury bonds, Treasury bills, FNMA, and GNMA.

34c(4). Include investment securities issued by a corporate entity at a stated interest rate repayable on a particular future date such as most bonds, debentures, convertible debentures, commercial paper and zero coupon bonds. Do not include debt securities of Governmental units or municipalities reported under 34c(3) or 34c(17).

"Preferred" means any of the above securities that are publicly traded on a recognized securities exchange and the securities have a rating of "A" or above. If the securities are not "preferred" they are listed as "Other".

34c(5)(A). Include stock issued by corporations which is accompanied by preferential rights such as the right to share in distributions of earnings at a higher rate or has general priority over the common stock of the same entity. Include the value of warrants convertible into preferred stock.

34c(5)(B). Include any stock which represents regular ownership of the corporation and is not accompanied by preferential rights plus the value of warrants convertible into common stock.

34c(6). Include the value of the plan's participation in a partnership or joint venture if the underlying assets of the partnership or joint venture are not considered to be plan assets under 29 CFR 2510.3-101. Do not include the value of a plan's interest in a partnership or joint venture which is a 103-12 IE (see the instructions for 34c(11) through 34c(15), below).

34c(7)(A). Include the current value of real property owned by the plan which produces income from rentals, etc. This property is not to be included in item 34e, buildings and other property used in plan operations.

Form 5500—Contd.

34c(7)(B). Include the current value of real property owned by the plan which is not producing income or used in plan operations.

34c(8)(A). Include the current value of all loans made by the plan to provide mortgage financing to purchasers (other than plan participants) of residential dwelling units, either by making or participating in loans directly or by purchasing mortgage loans originated by a third party. (For participant loans, see 34c(9)(A) and (B), below.)

34c(8)(B). Include the current value of all loans made by the plan to provide mortgage financing to purchasers (other than participants) of commercial real estate, either by making or participating in the loans directly or by purchasing mortgage loans originated by a third party. (For participant loans, see 34c(9)(A) and (B), below).

34c(9)(A). Include the current value of all loans to participants which are made by the plan to provide mortgage financing to participants who were purchasers of real property, irrespective of whether the mortgage was for residential, commercial or farm property.

34c(9)(B). Include the balance of any loans made to participants which were not reported in item 34c(9)(A).

34c(10). Include all loans made by the plan which are not to be reported elsewhere in item 34 such as loans for construction, securities loans, and other miscellaneous loans.

34c(11) through 34c(15). In items **34c(11)** through **34c(15),** enter the current value of the plan's interest at the beginning and end of the plan year. If some plan funds are held in these investment arrangements, and other plan funds are held in other funding media, complete all applicable sub-items of item 34 with regard to assets held in other funding media.

A plan investing in common/collective trusts or pooled separate accounts should attach to the return/report either the statement of assets and liabilities of the common/collective trust or pooled separate account or the certification discussed on page 3 of these instructions.

The value of the plan's interest in a master trust is the sum of the net values of the plan's interest in master trust investment accounts. The net values of such interests are obtained by multiplying the plan's percentage interest in each master trust investment account by the net assets of the investment account (total assets minus total liabilities) at the beginning and end of the plan year.

34c(16). You can use the same method for determining the value of the insurance contracts reported in 34c(16) that you used for line 6e of Schedule A (Form 5500) as long as the contract values are stated as of the beginning and end of the plan year.

34c(17). Other investments include options, index futures, repurchase agreements, and state and municipal securities among other things.

34d. See 30g on page 16 for the definition of employer security.

34e. Include the current (not book) value of the buildings and other property used in the operation of the plan. Buildings or other property held as plan investments should be reported in item 34c(7)(A) or (B), or 34d(2).

Do not include the value of future pension payments in items 34g, 34h, 34i, 34j or 34k.

34g. Noncash basis plans should include the total amount of benefit claims which have been processed and approved for payment by the plan.

34h. Noncash basis plans should include the total amount of obligations owed by the plan which were incurred in the normal operations of the plan and have been approved for payment by the plan but have not been paid.

34i. Acquisition Indebtedness.— "Acquisition indebtedness," for debt-financed property other than real property, means the outstanding amount of the principal debt incurred:

(1) by the organization in acquiring or improving the property;

(2) before the acquisition or improvement of the property if the debt was incurred only to acquire or improve the property; or

(3) after the acquisition or improvement of the property if the debt was incurred only to acquire or improve the property and was reasonably foreseeable at the time of such acquisition or improvement.

For further explanation, see Code section 514(c).

34j. Noncash basis plans should include amounts owed for any liabilities which would not be classified as benefit claims payable, operating payables, or acquisition indebtedness.

34l. Column (b) must equal the sum of column (a) plus items 35i and 35j.

35a(1). Include the cash contributions received and/or (for accrual basis plans) due to be received.

35a(2). Use the current value, at date contributed, of securities or other noncash property.

35b(1)(A). Include the interest earned on interest-bearing cash. This is derived from investments which are includable in 34c(1), including earnings from sweep accounts, STIF accounts, etc.

35b(1)(B). Include the interest earned on certificates of deposit. This is the interest earned on the investments which are reported on line 34c(2).

35b(1)(C). Include the interest earned on U.S. Government securities. This is the interest earned on the investments which are reported on line 34c(3).

35b(1)(D). Generally, this is the interest earned on securities which are reported on lines 34c(4)(A) and (B) and 34d(1).

35b(1)(E). Include the interest earned on the investments which are reported on lines 34c(8)(A) and (B) and 34c(9)(A).

35b(1)(F). Include the interest earned on the investments which are reported on lines 34c(9)(B) and 34c(10).

35b(1)(G). Include any interest not reported in 35b(1)(A)–(F).

35b(2) (A) and (B). Generally, these dividends are from the investments which are reported in items 34c(5)(A) and (B) and 34d(1).

For accrual basis plans, include any dividends declared for stock held on the date of record, but not yet received as of the end of the plan year.

35b(3). Generally, rents represent the income earned on the real property which is

reported in items 34c(7)(A) and 34d(2). Rents should be entered as a "Net" figure. Net rents are determined by taking the total rent received and subtracting all expenses directly associated with the property. If the real property is jointly used as income producing property and for the operation of the plan, that portion of the expenses attributable to the income producing portion of the property should be netted against the total rents received.

35b(4). Column (b), total of net gain (loss) on sale of assets, should reflect the sum of the net realized gain (or loss) on each asset held at the beginning of the plan year which was sold or exchanged during the plan year and each asset which was both acquired and disposed of within the plan year.

Note: *As current value reporting is required for the Form 5500, assets are revalued to current value at the end of the plan year. For purposes of this form, the increase or decrease in the value of assets since the beginning of the plan year (if held on the first day of the plan year) or their acquisition date (if purchased during the plan year) is reported in item 35b(5) below, with two exceptions: (1) the realized gain (or loss) on each asset which was disposed of during the plan year is reported in 35b(4) (NOT in 35b(5)), and (2) the net investment gain (or loss) from certain investment arrangements is reported in items 35b(6) through 35b(10).*

The sum of the realized gain (or loss) of all assets sold or exchanged during the plan year is to be calculated by—

(1) entering the sum of the amount received for these former assets in 35b(4), column (a), line (A),

(2) entering in 35b(4), column (a), line (B), the sum of the current value of these former assets as of the beginning of the plan year, for those assets on hand at the beginning of the plan year, or the purchase price for those assets acquired during the plan year, and

(3) subtracting (B) from (A) and entering this result on line c in column (b).

A negative figure should be placed in parentheses.

35b(5). Subtract the current value of assets at the beginning of the year plus the cost of any assets acquired during the plan year from the current value of assets at the end of the year to obtain this figure. A negative figure should be placed in parentheses. Do not include the value of assets reportable in items 35b(4) and 35b(6) through 35b(10).

35b(6) through (10). Report all earnings, expenses, gains or losses, and unrealized appreciation or depreciation which were included in computing the net investment gain (or loss) from these investment arrangements here. If some plan funds are held in any of these investment arrangements and other plan funds are held in other funding media, complete all applicable sub-items of item 35 to report plan earnings, and expenses, relating to the other funding media.

The net investment gain (or loss) allocated to the plan for the plan year from the plan's investment in these investment arrangements is equal to:

(A) the sum of the current value of the plan's interest in each investment arrangement at the end of the plan year,

Form 5500—Contd.

(B) minus the current value of the plan's interest in each investment arrangement at the beginning of the plan year,

(C) plus any amounts transferred out of each investment arrangement by the plan during the plan year, and

(D) minus any amounts transferred into each investment arrangement by the plan during the plan year.

Enter the net gain as a positive number or the net loss in parentheses.

35c. Include any other plan income earned that is not included in 35a or 35b. Do not include transfers from other plans which should be reported in item 35j.

35d. Add all amounts in column (b) and enter the total income.

35e. If distributions include securities or other property, use the current value at date distributed for this item. See page 16 for the definition of current value. If this return/report is being filed only for a fringe benefit plan (or for both a fringe benefit plan and a welfare benefit plan which is exempt from completing item 35), you must complete items 35g and 35h (reasonable estimates will be acceptable for these figures).

35e(1). Include the current value of all cash, securities or other property at the date of distribution.

35e(2). Include payments to insurance companies and similar organizations such as Blue Cross, Blue Shield, and health maintenance organizations for the provision of plan benefits, e.g., paid-up annuities, accident insurance, health insurance, vision care, dental coverage, etc.

35e(3). Include payments made to other organizations or individuals providing benefits. Generally, these are individual providers of welfare benefits such as legal services, day care services, training and apprenticeship services.

35f. Interest expense is a monetary charge for the use of money borrowed by the plan. This amount should include the total of interest paid or to be paid (for accrual basis plans) during the plan year.

35g. Expenses incurred in the general operations of the plan are classified as administrative expenses. Report all administrative expenses (by specified category) paid by or charged to the plan, including those which were not subtracted from the gross income of common/collective trusts, pooled separate accounts, master trust investment accounts, and 103-12 IEs in determining their net investment gain(s) or loss(es). If this return/report is filed only for a fringe benefit plan and NOT for a welfare benefit plan, do not include overhead expenses such as utilities and photocopying expenses. Also, if you are filing for an educational assistance program described in Code section 127, do not include expenses for job-related training which are deductible under Code section 162.

35g(1). Include all of the plan's expenditures such as salaries and payment of premiums to provide benefits to plan employees (e.g., health insurance, life insurance, etc.).

35g(2). Include the total fees paid (or in the case of accrual basis plans, costs incurred during the plan year but not paid as of the end of the plan year) by the plan for outside accounting services. These may include the fee(s) for the annual audit of the plan by an independent qualified public accountant, for payroll audits, and for accounting/bookkeeping services. These do not include amounts paid to plan employees to perform accounting functions.

35g(3). Include the total fees paid (or in the case of accrual basis plans, costs incurred during the plan year but not paid as of the end of the plan year) to an actuary for services rendered to the plan.

35g(4). Include the total fees paid (or in the case of accrual basis plans, costs incurred during the plan year but not paid as of the end of the plan year) to a contract administrator for performing administrative services for the plan. For purposes of the return/report, a contract administrator is any individual, partnership, or corporation, responsible for managing the clerical operations (e.g., handling membership rosters, claims payments, maintaining books and records) of the plan on a contractual basis. Do not include salaried staff or employees of the plan or banks, or insurance carriers.

35g(5). Include the total fees paid (or in the case of accrual basis plans, costs incurred during the plan year but not paid as of the end of the plan year) to an individual, partnership or corporation (or other person) for advice to the plan relating to its investment portfolio. These may include fees paid to manage the plan's investments, fees for specific advice on a particular investment, and fees for the evaluation of the plan's investment performance.

35g(6). Include total fees paid (or in the case of accrual basis plans, costs incurred during the plan year but not paid as of the end of the plan year) to a lawyer for services rendered to the plan. Include fees paid for rendering legal opinions, litigation, and advice but not for providing legal services as a benefit to plan participants.

35g(7). Include the total fees paid (or in the case of accrual basis plans, costs incurred during the plan year but not paid as of the end of the plan year) for valuations or appraisals to determine the cost, quality, or value of an item. These may include the fee(s) paid for appraisals of real property (real estate, gemstones, coins, etc.), and a valuation of closely held securities for which there is no ready market.

35g(8). Include the total fees and expenses paid to or on behalf of plan trustees (or in the case of accrual basis plans, costs incurred during the plan year but not paid as of the end of the plan year). These may include reimbursement of expenses associated with trustees such as lost time, seminars, travel, meetings, etc.

35g(9). Other expenses are those that cannot be associated definitely with items 35g(1) through 35g(8). All miscellaneous expenses are also included in this figure. These may include expenses for office supplies and equipment, cars, telephone, postage, rent, and expenses associated with the ownership of a building used in the operation of the plan.

35h. Add column (b) of items 35e(4), 35f, and 35g(10).

35i. Subtract item 35h from item 35d.

35j. Include in this reconciliation figure any transfers of assets into or out of the plan resulting from mergers and consolidations of plans or associated with benefit liabilities which are also being transferred. A transfer is not a shifting of assets or liabilities from one investment medium to another used for a single plan (e.g., between a trust and an annuity contract). Transfers out should be shown in parentheses.

35k. Include the amount of net assets at the beginning of the year. This amount must equal item 34l, column (a).

35l. Include the amount of net assets at the end of the year. This amount must equal item 34l, column (b).

Form 5500—Contd.

Codes for Principal Business Activity and Principal Product or Service

These industry titles and definitions are based, in general, on the Enterprise Standard Industrial Classification System authorized by the Regulatory and Statistical Analysis Division, Office of Information and Regulatory Affairs, Office of Management and Budget, to classify enterprises by type of activity in which they are engaged.

AGRICULTURE, FORESTRY, AND FISHING
Code
0120 Field crop.
0150 Fruit, tree nut, and vegetable.
0180 Horticultural specialty.
0230 Livestock.
0270 Animal specialty.

Agricultural services and forestry:
0740 Veterinary services.
0750 Animal services, except veterinary.
0780 Landscape and horticultural services.
0790 Other agricultural services.
0800 Forestry.

Farms:

Fishing, hunting, and trapping:
0930 Commercial fishing, hatcheries, and preserves.
0970 Hunting, trapping, and game propagation.

MINING
Metal mining:
1010 Iron ores.
1070 Copper, lead and zinc, gold and silver ores.
1098 Other metal mining.
1150 Coal mining.

Oil and gas extraction:
1330 Crude petroleum, natural gas, and natural gas liquids.
1380 Oil and gas field services.

Nonmetallic minerals (except fuels) mining:
1430 Dimension, crushed and broken stone; sand and gravel.
1498 Other nonmetallic minerals, except fuels.

CONSTRUCTION
General building contractors and operative builders:
1510 General building contractors.
1531 Operative builders.

Heavy construction contractors:
1611 Highway and street construction.
1620 Heavy construction, except highway.

Special trade contractors:
1711 Plumbing, heating, and air conditioning.
1721 Painting, paperhanging, and decorating.
1731 Electrical work.
1740 Masonry, stonework, and plastering.
1750 Carpentering and flooring.
1761 Roofing and sheet metal work.
1771 Concrete work.
1781 Water well drilling.
1790 Miscellaneous special trade contractors.

MANUFACTURING
Food and kindred products:
2010 Meat products.
2020 Dairy products.
2030 Preserved fruits and vegetables.
2040 Grain mill products.
2050 Bakery products.
2060 Sugar and confectionery products.
2081 Malt liquors and malt.
2088 Alcoholic beverages, except malt liquors and malt.
2089 Bottled soft drinks and flavorings.
2096 Other food and kindred products.
2100 Tobacco manufacturers.

Textile mill products:
2228 Weaving and textile finishing.
2250 Knitting mills.
2298 Other textile mill products.

Apparel and other textile products:
2315 Men's and boys' clothing.

Code
2345 Women's and children's clothing.
2388 Hats, caps, millinery, fur goods, and other apparel and accessories.
2390 Misc. fabricated textile products.

Lumber and wood products:
2415 Logging camps and logging contractors, sawmills, and planing mills.
2430 Millwork, plywood, and related products.
2498 Other wood products, including wood buildings and mobile homes.
2500 Furniture and fixtures.

Paper and allied products:
2625 Pulp, paper, and board mills.
2699 Other paper products.

Printing, publishing, and allied industries:
2710 Newspapers.
2720 Periodicals.
2735 Books, greeting cards, and miscellaneous publishing.
2799 Commercial and other printing, and printing trade services.

Chemical and allied products:
2815 Industrial chemicals, plastics materials, and synthetics.
2830 Drugs.
2840 Soap, cleaners, and toilet goods.
2850 Paints and allied products.
2898 Agricultural and other chemical products.

Petroleum refining and related industries (including those integrated with extraction):
2910 Petroleum refining (including those integrated with extraction).
2998 Other petroleum and coal products.

Rubber and miscellaneous plastics products:
3050 Rubber products, plastics footwear, hose, and belting.
3070 Misc. plastics products.

Leather and leather products:
3140 Footwear, except rubber.
3198 Other leather and leather products.

Stone, clay, glass, and concrete products:
3225 Glass products.
3240 Cement, hydraulic.
3270 Concrete, gypsum, and plaster products.
3298 Other nonmetallic mineral products.

Primary metal industries:
3370 Ferrous metal industries; miscellaneous primary metal products.
3380 Nonferrous metal industries.

Fabricated metal products, except machinery and transportation equipment:
3410 Metal cans and shipping containers.
3428 Cutlery, hand tools, and hardware; screw machine products, bolts, and similar products.
3430 Plumbing and heating, except electric and warm air.
3440 Fabricated structural metal products.
3460 Metal forgings and stampings.
3470 Coating, engraving, and allied services.
3480 Ordnance and accessories, except vehicles and guided missiles.
3490 Miscellaneous fabricated metal products.

Machinery, except electrical:
3520 Farm machinery.
3530 Construction, mining and materials handling machinery, and equipment.
3540 Metalworking machinery.
3550 Special industry machinery, except metalworking machinery.
3560 General industrial machinery.
3570 Office, computing, and accounting machines.

Code
3598 Engines and turbines, service industry machinery, and other machinery, except electrical.

Electrical and electronic machinery, equipment, and supplies:
3630 Household appliances.
3665 Radio, television, and communication equipment.
3670 Electronic components and accessories.
3698 Other electric equipment.

Transportation equipment:
3710 Motor vehicles and equipment.
3725 Aircraft, guided missiles, and parts.
3730 Ship and boat building and repairing.
3798 Other transportation equipment.

Measuring and controlling instruments; photographic and medical goods, watches and clocks:
3815 Scientific instruments and measuring devices; watches, and clocks.
3845 Optical, medical, and ophthalmic goods.
3860 Photographic equipment and supplies.
3998 Other manufacturing products.

TRANSPORTATION, COMMUNICATION, ELECTRIC, GAS, SANITARY SERVICES
Transportation:
4000 Railroad transportation.

Local and interurban passenger transit:
4121 Taxicabs.
4189 Other passenger transportation.

Trucking and warehousing:
4210 Trucking, local and long distance.
4289 Public warehousing and trucking terminals.

Other transportation including transportation services:
4400 Water transportation.
4500 Transportation by air.
4600 Pipelines, except natural gas.
4722 Passenger transportation arrangement.
4723 Freight transportation arrangement.
4799 Other transportation services.

Communication:
4825 Telephone, telegraph, and other communication services.
4830 Radio and television broadcasting.

Electric, gas, and sanitary services:
4910 Electric services.
4920 Gas production and distribution.
4930 Combination utility services.
4990 Water supply and other sanitary services.

WHOLESALE TRADE
Durable:
5010 Motor vehicles and automotive equipment.
5020 Furniture and home furnishings.
5030 Lumber and construction materials.
5040 Sporting, recreational, photographic, and hobby goods, toys, and supplies.
5050 Metals and minerals, except petroleum and scrap.
5060 Electrical goods.
5070 Hardware, plumbing, and heating equipment.
5083 Farm machinery and equipment.
5089 Other machinery, equipment, and supplies.
5098 Other durable goods.

Nondurable:
5110 Paper and paper products.
5129 Drugs, drug proprietaries, and druggists' sundries.
5130 Apparel, piece goods, and notions.
5140 Groceries and related products, except meats and meat products.
5147 Meats and meat products.
5150 Farm product raw materials.
5160 Chemicals and allied products.
5170 Petroleum and petroleum products.
5180 Alcoholic beverages.
5190 Miscellaneous nondurable goods.

Form 5500—Contd.

RETAIL TRADE

Code

Building materials hardware, garden supply, and mobile home dealers:

5211 Lumber and other building materials dealers.
5231 Paint, glass and wallpaper stores.
5251 Hardware stores.
5261 Retail nurseries and garden stores.
5271 Mobile home dealers.

General merchandise:

5331 Variety stores.
5398 Other general merchandise stores.

Food stores:

5411 Grocery stores.
5420 Meat and fish markets and freezer provisioners.
5431 Fruit stores and vegetable markets.
5441 Candy, nut, and confectionary stores.
5451 Dairy products stores.
5460 Retail bakeries.
5490 Other food stores.

Automotive dealers and service stations:

5511 New car dealers (franchised).
5521 Used car dealers.
5531 Auto and home supply stores.
5541 Gasoline service stations.
5551 Boat dealers.
5561 Recreational vehicle dealers.
5571 Motorcycle dealers.
5599 Aircraft and other automotive dealers.

Apparel and accessory stores:

5611 Men's and boys' clothing and furnishings.
5621 Women's ready-to-wear stores.
5631 Women's accessory and specialty stores.
5641 Children's and infants' wear stores.
5651 Family clothing stores.
5661 Shoe stores.
5681 Furriers and fur shops.
5699 Other apparel and accessory stores.

Furniture, home furnishings, and equipment stores:

5712 Furniture stores.
5713 Floor covering stores.
5714 Drapery, curtain, and upholstery stores.
5719 Home furnishings, except appliances.
5722 Household appliance stores.
5732 Radio and television stores.
5733 Music stores.

Eating and drinking places:

5812 Eating places.
5813 Drinking places.

Miscellaneous retail stores:

5912 Drug stores and proprietary stores.
5921 Liquor stores.
5931 Used merchandise stores.
5941 Sporting goods stores and bicycle shops.
5942 Book stores.
5943 Stationery stores.
5944 Jewelry stores.
5945 Hobby, toy, and game shops.
5946 Camera and photographic supply stores.
5947 Gift, novelty, and souvenir shops.
5948 Luggage and leather goods stores.
5949 Sewing, needlework, and piece goods stores.
5961 Mail order houses.

Code

5962 Merchandising machine operators.
5963 Direct selling organizations.
5982 Fuel and ice dealers (except fuel oil and bottle gas dealers).
5983 Fuel oil dealers.
5984 Liquefied petroleum gas (bottled gas).
5992 Florists.
5993 Cigar stores and stands.
5994 News dealers and newsstands.
5996 Other miscellaneous retail stores.

FINANCE, INSURANCE, AND REAL ESTATE

Banking:

6030 Mutual savings banks.
6060 Banking holding companies.
6090 Banks, except mutual savings banks and bank holding companies.

Credit agencies other than banks:

6120 Savings and loan associations.
6140 Personal credit institutions.
6150 Business credit institutions.
6199 Other credit agencies.

Security, commodity brokers, dealers, exchanges, and services:

6212 Security underwriting syndicates.
6218 Security brokers and dealers, except underwriting syndicates.
6299 Commodity contract brokers and dealers; security and commodity exchanges; and allied services.

Insurance:

6355 Life insurance.
6356 Mutual insurance, except life or marine and certain fire or flood insurance companies.
6359 Other insurance companies.
6411 Insurance agents, brokers, and services.

Real estate:

6511 Real estate operators (except developers) and lessors of buildings.
6516 Lessors of mining, oil, and similar property.
6518 Lessors of railroad property and other real property.
6531 Real estate agents, brokers and managers.
6541 Title abstract offices.
6552 Subdividers and developers, except cemeteries.
6553 Cemetery subdividers and developers.
6599 Other real estate.
6611 Combined real estate, insurance, loans and law offices.

Holding and other investment companies:

6742 Regulated investment companies.
6743 Real estate investment trusts.
6744 Small business investment companies.
6749 Holding and other investment companies, except bank holding companies.

SERVICES

Hotels and other lodging places:

7012 Hotels.
7013 Motels, motor hotels, and tourist courts.
7021 Rooming and boarding houses.
7032 Sporting and recreational camps.
7033 Trailer parks and camp sites.
7041 Organizational hotels and lodging houses on a membership basis.

Code

Personal services:

7215 Coin-operated laundries and dry cleaning.
7219 Other laundry, cleaning and garment services.
7221 Photographic studios, portrait.
7231 Beauty shops.
7241 Barber shops.
7251 Shoe repair and hat cleaning shops.
7261 Funeral services and crematories.
7299 Miscellaneous personal services.

Business services:

7310 Advertising.
7340 Services to buildings.
7370 Computer and data processing services.
7392 Management, consulting, and public relations services.
7394 Equipment rental and leasing.
7398 Other business services.

Automotive repair and services:

7510 Automotive rentals and leasing, without drivers.
7520 Automobile parking.
7531 Automobile top and body repair shops.
7538 General automobile repair shops.
7539 Other automobile repair shops.
7540 Automobile services, except repair.

Miscellaneous repair services:

7622 Radio and TV repair shops.
7628 Electrical repair shops, except radio and TV.
7641 Reupholstery and furniture repair.
7680 Other miscellaneous repair shops. Motion pictures:
7812 Motion picture production, distribution, and services.
7830 Motion picture theaters.

Amusement and recreation services:

7920 Producers, orchestras, and entertainers.
7932 Billiard and pool establishments.
7933 Bowling alleys.
7980 Other amusement and recreation services.

Medical and health services:

8011 Offices of physicians.
8021 Offices of dentists.
8031 Offices of osteopathic physicians.
8041 Offices of chiropractors.
8042 Offices of optometrists.
8048 Registered and practical nurses.
8050 Nursing and personal care facilities.
8060 Hospitals.
8071 Medical laboratories.
8072 Dental laboratories.
8098 Other medical and health services.

Other services:

8111 Legal services.
8200 Educational services.
8911 Engineering and architectural services.
8932 Certified public accountants.
8933 Other accounting, auditing, and bookkeeping services.
8999 Other services not classified elsewhere.

TAX-EXEMPT ORGANIZATIONS

9002 Church plans making an election under section 410(d) of the Internal Revenue Code.
9319 Other tax-exempt organizations.
9904 Governmental instrumentality or agency.

Form 5500—Contd.

SCHEDULE A (Form 5500)	**Insurance Information**	OMB No. 1210-0016

SCHEDULE A
(Form 5500)
Department of the Treasury
Internal Revenue Service

Department of Labor
Pension and Welfare Benefits Administration

Pension Benefit Guaranty Corporation

Insurance Information

This schedule is required to be filed under section 104 of the Employee Retirement Income Security Act of 1974.

▶ **File as an Attachment to Form 5500 or 5500-C/R.**

▶ Insurance companies are required to provide this information as per ERISA section 103(a)(2).

OMB No. 1210-0016

1991

This Form Is Open to Public Inspection

For calendar year 1991 or fiscal plan year beginning _____ , 1991 and ending _____ , 19 ____ .

▶ **Part I must be completed for all plans required to file this schedule.**
▶ **Part II must be completed for all insured pension plans.**
▶ **Part III must be completed for all insured welfare plans.**

▶ Enter master trust or 103-12 IE name in place of "sponsor" and specify investment account or 103-12 IE in place of "plan" if filing with DOL for a master trust or 103-12 IE.

Name of plan sponsor as shown on line 1a of Form 5500 or 5500-C/R

Employer identification number

Name of plan

Enter three-digit plan number ▶

Part I	**Summary of All Insurance Contracts Included in Parts II and III**

Group all contracts in the same manner as in Parts II and III.

1 Check appropriate box: **a** ☐ Welfare plan   **b** ☐ Pension plan   **c** ☐ Combination pension and welfare plan

2 Coverage:

(a) Name of insurance carrier	(b) Contract or identification number	(c) Approximate number of persons covered at end of policy or contract year	Policy or contract year	
			(d) From	(e) To

3 Insurance fees and commissions paid to agents and brokers:

(a) Contract or identification number	(b) Name and address of the agents or brokers to whom commissions or fees were paid	(c) Amount of commissions paid	(d) Fees paid	
			Amount	Purpose

Total

4 Premiums due and unpaid at end of the plan year ▶ $ _____ : Contract or identification number ▶ _____

Part II	**Insured Pension Plans** Provide information for each contract on a separate Part II. Where individual contracts are provided, the entire group of such individual contracts with each carrier may be treated as a unit for purposes of this report.

▶ Contract or identification number ▶

5 Contracts with allocated funds, for example, individual policies or group deferred annuity contracts:
  a State the basis of premium rates ▶ ....
  b Total premiums paid to carrier . . . .
  c If the carrier, service, or other organization incurred any specific costs in connection with the acquisition or retention of the contract or policy, other than reported in 3 above, enter amount . . . .
     Specify nature of costs ▶

6 Contracts with unallocated funds, for example, deposit administration or immediate participation guarantee contracts. Do not include portions of these contracts maintained in separate accounts:
  a Balance at the end of the previous policy year . . . .
  b Additions: (i) Contributions deposited during year . . . .
     (ii) Dividends and credits . . . .
     (iii) Interest credited during the year . . . .
     (iv) Transferred from separate account . . . .
     (v) Other (specify) ▶ ....
     (vi) Total additions . . . .
  c Total of balance and additions (add **a** and **b**(vi)) . . . .
  d Deductions:
     (i) Disbursed from fund to pay benefits or purchase annuities during year . . .
     (ii) Administration charge made by carrier . . . .
     (iii) Transferred to separate account . . . .
     (iv) Other (specify) ▶ ....
     (v) Total deductions . . . .
  e Balance at end of current policy year (subtract **d**(v) from **c**) . . . .
7 Separate accounts: Current value of plan's interest in separate accounts at year end . . . .

For Paperwork Reduction Act Notice, see page 1 of the Instructions for Form 5500 or 5500-C/R.   Cat. No. 13505I   **Schedule A (Form 5500) 1991**

Form 5500—Contd.

Part III   Insured Welfare Plans

Provide information for each contract on a separate Part III. If more than one contract covers the same group of employees of the same employer(s) or members of the same employee organization(s), the information may be combined for reporting purposes if such contracts are experience-rated as a unit. Where individual contracts are provided, the entire group of such individual contracts with each carrier may be treated as a unit for purposes of this report.

8	(a) Contract or identification number	(b) Type of benefit	(c) List gross premium for each contract	(d) Premium rate or subscription charge

9   Experience-rated contracts: **a** Premiums: *(i)* Amount received . . . .

     (ii)   Increase (decrease) in amount due but unpaid . . . .

     (iii)   Increase (decrease) in unearned premium reserve . . . .

     (iv)   Premiums earned, add *(i)* and *(ii)*, and subtract *(iii)* . . . .

   b   Benefit charges: *(i)* Claims paid . . . .

     (ii)   Increase (decrease) in claim reserves . . . .

     (iii)   Incurred claims (add *(i)* and *(ii)*) . . . .

     (iv)   Claims charged . . . .

   c   Remainder of premium: *(i)* Retention charges (on an accrual basis)—

     (A)   Commissions . . . .

     (B)   Administrative service or other fees . . . .

     (C)   Other specific acquisition costs . . . .

     (D)   Other expenses . . . .

     (E)   Taxes. . . . .

     (F)   Charges for risks or contingencies . . . .

     (G)   Other retention charges . . . .

     (H)   Total retention . . . .

     (ii)   Dividends or retroactive rate refunds. (These amounts were ☐ paid in cash, or ☐ credited.) .

   d   Status of policyholder reserves at end of year: *(i)* Amount held to provide benefits after retirement . .

     (ii)   Claim reserves . . . .

     (iii)   Other reserves . . . .

   e   Dividends or retroactive rate refunds due. (Do not include amount entered in **c***(ii)*.) . . . .

10   Nonexperience-rated contracts: **a** Total premiums or subscription charges paid to carrier. . . . . .

   b   If the carrier, service, or other organization incurred any specific costs in connection with the acquisition or retention of the contract or policy, other than reported in 3 above, report amount . . . .

     Specify nature of costs ▶ ....

....

....

If additional space is required for any item, attach additional sheets the same size as this form.

General Instructions

This schedule must be attached to Form 5500 or 5500-C/R for every defined benefit, defined contribution, and welfare benefit plan where any benefits under the plan are provided by an insurance company, insurance service, or other similar organization.

Specific Instructions

(References are to the line items on the form.)

Information entered on Schedule A (Form 5500) should pertain to contracts with policy or contract years ending with or within the plan year (for reporting purposes, a year cannot exceed 12 months). **Exception:** If the insurance company maintains records on the basis of a plan year rather than a policy or contract year, the information entered on Schedule A (Form 5500) may pertain to the plan year instead of the policy or contract year.

Include only the contracts issued to the plan for which this return/report is being filed.

Plans Participating in Master Trust(s) and 103-12 IEs—See the Form 5500 or Form 5500-C/R instructions for "Reporting Requirements for Investment Arrangements Filing With DOL."

Line 2(c).—Since the plan coverage may fluctuate during the year, the administrator should estimate the number of persons that were covered by the plan at the end of the policy or contract year.

Where contracts covering individual employees are grouped, entries should be determined as of the end of the plan year.

Lines 2(d) and (e).—Enter the beginning and ending dates of the policy year for each contract listed under column (b). Enter "N/A" in column (d) if separate contracts covering individual employees are grouped.

Line 3.—Report all sales commissions in column (c) regardless of the identity of the recipient. Do not report override commissions, salaries, bonuses, etc., paid to a general agent or manager for managing an agency, or for performing other administrative functions.

Fees to be reported in column (d) represent payments by insurance carriers to agents and brokers for items other than commissions (e.g., service fees, consulting fees, and finders fees).

Note: *For purposes of this item, commissions and fees include amounts paid by an insurance company on the basis of the aggregate value (e.g., policy amounts, premiums) of contracts or*

policies (or classes thereof) placed or retained. The amount (or pro rata share of the total) of such commissions or fees attributable to the contract or policy placed with or retained by the plan must be reported in column (c) or (d), as appropriate.

Fees paid by insurance carriers to persons other than agents and brokers should be reported in Parts II and III on Schedule A (Form 5500) as acquisition costs, administrative charges, etc., as appropriate. For plans with 100 or more participants, fees paid by employee benefit plans to agents, brokers, and other persons are to be reported on Schedule C (Form 5500).

Line 5a.—The rate information called for here may be furnished by attachment of appropriate schedules of current rates filed with appropriate state insurance departments or by a statement as to the basis of the rates.

Line 6.—Show deposit fund amounts rather than experience credit records when both are maintained.

Line 8(d).—The rate information called for here may be furnished by attachment of the appropriate schedules of current rates or by a statement as to the basis of the rates.

Form 5500—Contd.

SCHEDULE B (Form 5500) Department of the Treasury Internal Revenue Service Department of Labor Pension and Welfare Benefits Administration Pension Benefit Guaranty Corporation	**Actuarial Information** This schedule is required to be filed under section 104 of the Employee Retirement Income Security Act of 1974, referred to as ERISA, and section 6059(a) of the Internal Revenue Code, referred to as the Code. ▶ **Attach to Form 5500, 5500-C/R, or 5500EZ if applicable.** ▶ **See separate instructions.**	OMB No. 1210-0016 19**91** **This Form Is Open to Public Inspection**

For calendar plan year 1991 or fiscal plan year beginning   , 1991, and ending   , 19

▶ **Read the specific instructions** before attempting to complete this form.

▶ **Please complete every item on this form.** If an item does not apply, enter **"N/A."** ▶ **Round off amounts to nearest dollar.**

▶ **Caution:** *A penalty of $1,000 will be assessed for late filing of this report unless reasonable cause is established.*

Name of plan sponsor as shown on line 1a of Form 5500, 5500-C/R, or 5500EZ	**Employer identification number**

Name of plan	Enter three-digit plan number ▶			**Yes**	**No**

1   Has a waiver of a funding deficiency for this plan year been approved by the IRS? . . . .
     If "Yes," attach a copy of the IRS approval letter.

2   Is a waived funding deficiency of a prior plan year being amortized in this plan year? . . . .

3   Have any of the periods of amortization for charges described in Code section 412(b)(2)(B) been extended by IRS?
     If "Yes," attach a copy of the IRS approval letter.

4a   Was the shortfall funding method the basis for this plan year's funding standard account computations?. . .

  b   Is this plan a multiemployer plan which is, for this plan year, in reorganization as described in Code section 418 or ERISA section 4241? . . . .
     If "Yes," you are required to attach the information described in the instructions.

5   Has a change been made in funding method for this plan year? . . . .
     If "Yes," attach either a copy of the letter showing IRS approval or state the applicable Revenue Procedure authorizing approval if used.

6   Operational information:

  a   Enter the most recent actuarial valuation date ▶ ....

  b   Enter the date of the last independent appraisal of property such as real estate, collectibles and closely held stock, etc.
     Date ▶ ....

  c   Current value of the assets accumulated in the plan as of the beginning of this plan year . . . . .

  d   Current liability as of beginning of plan year:

	(1) No. of Persons	**(2) Vested Benefits**	**(3) Total Benefits**
(i) For retired participants and beneficiaries receiving payments .			
(ii) For terminated vested participants			
(iii) For active participants			
(iv) Total			

  e   Expected current liability increase as of mo. .... day ..... yr. ...... attributable to benefits accruing during the plan year . . . .

  f   Expected benefit payments . . . .

7   Contributions made to the plan for the plan year by employer(s) and employees:

(a) Month Day Year	**(b)** Amount paid by employer	**(c)** Amount paid by employees	**(a)** Month Day Year	**(b)** Amount paid by employer	**(c)** Amount paid by employees
			Total		

Statement by Enrolled Actuary (see instructions before signing):

To the best of my knowledge, the information supplied in this schedule and on the accompanying statements, if any, is complete and accurate, and in my opinion each assumption used in combination, represents my best estimate of anticipated experience under the plan. Furthermore, in the case of a plan other than a multiemployer plan, each assumption used (a) is reasonable (taking into account the experience of the plan and reasonable expectations) or (b) would, in the aggregate, result in a total contribution equivalent to that which would be determined if each such assumption were reasonable. In the case of a multiemployer plan, the assumptions used, in the aggregate, are reasonable (taking into account the experience of the plan and reasonable expectations).

....	....
Signature of actuary	Date
....	....
Print or type name of actuary	Most recent enrollment number
....	....
Firm name and address	Telephone number (including area code)

For Paperwork Reduction Act Notice, see the instructions for Form 5500   Cat. No. 13507E   **Schedule B (Form 5500) 1991**

Form 5500—Contd.

8 Funding standard account and other information:
  a Accrued liability as determined for funding standard account as of (enter date) ▶ ....
  b Value of assets as determined for funding standard account as of (enter date) ▶ ....
  c Unfunded liability for spread-gain methods with bases as of (enter date) ▶ ....
  d *(i)* Actuarial gains or (losses) for period ending ▶ ....
     (ii) Shortfall gains or (losses) for period ending ▶ ....
  e Amount of contribution certified by the actuary as necessary to reduce the funding deficiency to zero, from **9o** or **10h** (or the attachment for **4b** if required). . . . .

9 Funding standard account statement for this plan year ending ▶ ....
  Charges to funding standard account:
  a Prior year funding deficiency, if any . . . .
  b Employer's normal cost for plan year as of mo. .... day .... yr. ....
  c Amortization charges: Balance
     (i) Funding waivers (outstanding balance as of mo. ..... day ..... yr. ..... ▶ $..................)
     (ii) Other than waivers (outstanding balance as of mo. ..... day .... yr. .... ▶ $..................)
  d Interest as applicable on **a**, **b**, and **c** . . . .
  e Additional funding charge, if applicable (see line 13, page 3) . . . .
  f Additional interest charge due to late quarterly contributions . . . .
  g Total charges (add **a** through **f**) . . . .
  Credits to funding standard account:
  h Prior year credit balance, if any . . . .
  i Employer contributions (total from column (b) of item 7). . . . .
  j Amortization credits (outstanding balance as of mo. ..... day ..... yr. ..... ▶ $..................)
  k Interest as applicable to end of plan year on **h**, **i**, and **j**. . . . .
  l Miscellaneous credits:
     (i) FFL credit before reflecting 150% of current liability component. . . . .
     (ii) Additional credit due to 150% of current liability component . . . . . .
     (iii) Waived funding deficiency . . . .
     (iv) Total. . . . .
  m Total credits (add **h** through **l**) . . . .
  Balance:
  n Credit balance: if **m** is greater than **g**, enter the difference . . . .
  o Funding deficiency: if **g** is greater than **m**, enter the difference . . . .
  Reconciliation:
  p Current year's accumulated reconciliation account:
     (i) Due to additional funding charge as of the beginning of the plan year. . .
     (ii) Due to additional interest charges as of the beginning of the plan year . .
     (iii) Due to waived funding deficiency:
        (a) Reconciliation outstanding balance as of mo. ...... day ...... yr. ......
        (b) Reconciliation amount (**9c(i)** balance minus **9p(iii)(a)**) . . . .
     (iv) Total as of mo. .... day .... yr. . . . .

10 Alternative minimum funding standard account (omit if not used):
  a Was the entry age normal cost method used to determine entries in line 9, above. . . . . ☐ Yes   ☐ No
     If "No," do not complete **b** through **h**.
  b Prior year alternate funding deficiency, if any . . . .
  c Normal cost . . . .
  d Excess, if any, of value of accrued benefits over market value of assets . . . .
  e Interest on **b**, **c**, and **d**. . . . .
  f Employer contributions (total from columns (b) of item 7) . . . .
  g Interest on **f** . . . .
  h Funding deficiency: if the sum of **b** through **e** is greater than the sum of **f** and **g**, enter difference

Form 5500—Contd.

Schedule B (Form 5500) 1991   Page **3**

11 Actuarial cost method used as the basis for this plan year's funding standard account computation:

   a ☐ Attained age normal   **b** ☐ Entry age normal   **c** ☐ Accrued benefit (unit credit)
   d ☐ Aggregate   **e** ☐ Frozen initial liability   **f** ☐ Individual level premium
   g ☐ Other (specify) ▶

12 Checklist of certain actuarial assumptions:

	Pre-retirement		Post-retirement	
a Rates specified in insurance or annuity contracts	☐ Yes	☐ No	☐ Yes	☐ No
b Mortality table code:	/////	/////	/////	/////
(i) Males				
(ii) Females				
c Interest rate:	/////	/////	/////	/////
(i) Current liability		%		%
(ii) All other calculated values		%		%
d Retirement age			/////	/////
e Expense loading		%		%
f Annual withdrawal rate:	Male	Female	/////	/////
(i) Age 25	%	%		
(ii) Age 40	%	%		
(iii) Age 55	%	%		
g Ratio of salary at normal retirement to salary at:	/////	/////	/////	/////
(i) Age 25		%	%	
(ii) Age 40		%	%	
(iii) Age 55		%	%	

h Estimated investment return on actuarial value of plan assets for the year ending on the valuation date   %

13 Additional Required Funding Charge—Multiemployer plans or plans with NO unfunded current liability or plans with 100 or fewer participants check the box at the right and do not complete **a** through **r** below ☐

   a Current liability as of valuation date
   b Adjusted value of assets as of valuation date (subtract line **9h** from line **8b**)
   c Funded current liability percentage (**b** divided by **a**)   %
   d Unfunded current liability as of valuation date (subtract **b** from **a**)
   e Outstanding balance of unfunded old liability as of valuation date
   f Liability attributable to any unpredictable contingent event benefit
   g Unfunded new liability (subtract **e** and **f** from **d**)
   h Unfunded new liability amount (_____ % of **g**)
   i Unfunded old liability amount
   j Deficit reduction contribution (add **h** and **i**)
   k Net amortization charge for certain bases
   l Unpredictable contingent event amount:
      (i) Benefits paid during year attributable to unpredictable contingent event
      (ii) Unfunded current liability percentage (subtract the percentage on **13c** from 100%)   %
      (iii) Transition percentage   %
      (iv) Enter the product of lines *(i)*, *(ii)*, and *(iii)*.
      (v) Amortization of all unpredictable contingent event liabilities
      (vi) Enter the greater of line *iv* or line *v*
   m Additional funding charge as of valuation date (excess of **j** over **k** (if any) plus **l***(vi)*)
   n Assets needed to increase current liability percentage to 100% (line **d**)
   o Lesser of **m** or **n**
   p Interest adjustment
   q Additional funding charge (add **o** and **p**)
   r Adjustment for plans with more than 100 but less than 150 participants (_____ % of **q**)

14 Has this form been prepared and signed subject to the qualification under Income Tax Regulations section 301.6059-1(d)(5)? (See instructions.)   ☐ Yes ☐ No

Form 5500—Contd.

Department of the Treasury Internal Revenue Service	Department of Labor Pension and Welfare Benefits Administration	Pension Benefit Guaranty Corporation

1991 Instructions
for Schedule B (Form 5500)

Actuarial Information

(Code references are to the Internal Revenue Code. ERISA refers to the Employee Retirement Income Security Act of 1974.)

General Instructions

Who Must File.—The employer or plan administrator of a defined benefit plan that is subject to the minimum funding standards (see Code section 412 and Part 3 of Title I of ERISA) must file this schedule as an attachment to the return/report filed for this plan year.

Note: *(1) For split-funded plans, the costs and contributions reported on Schedule B should include those relating to both trust funds and insurance carriers.*

(2) For plans with funding standard account amortization charges and credits see the instructions for lines 9c and 9j regarding attachment.

Statement by Enrolled Actuary.—An enrolled actuary must sign Schedule B. The signature of the enrolled actuary may be qualified to state that it is subject to attached qualifications. See Income Tax Regulations section 301.6059-1(d) for permitted qualifications. A stamped or machine produced signature is not acceptable. In addition, the actuary may offer any other comments related to the information contained in Schedule B.

Specific Instructions

(References are to line items on the form.)

4a. Only certain collectively bargained plans may elect the shortfall funding method (see regulations under Code section 412). Advance approval from the IRS of the election of the shortfall method of funding is NOT required if it is first adopted for the first plan year to which Code section 412 applies. However, advance approval from IRS is required if the shortfall funding method is adopted at a later time, if a specific computation method is changed, or if the shortfall method is discontinued.

4b. Attach an explanation of the basis for the determination that the plan is in reorganization for this plan year. Also attach a worksheet showing for this plan year **(i)** the amounts considered contributed by employers, **(ii)** any

amount waived by IRS, **(iii)** the development of the minimum contribution requirement (taking into account the applicable overburden credit, cash-flow amount, contribution bases and limitation on required increases on the rate of employer contributions), and **(iv)** the resulting accumulated funding deficiency, if any, which is to be reported on line 8e in lieu of an amount from line 9o.

5. Changes in funding methods include changes in actuarial cost method, changes in asset valuation method, and changes in the valuation date of plan costs and liabilities or of plan assets. Generally, these changes require IRS approval. If approval was granted by an individual ruling letter for this plan, attach a copy of the letter. If approval was granted pursuant to a regulation, class ruling, or revenue procedure, attach a copy of the items required by the applicable regulation, ruling, or revenue procedure.

6a. The valuation for a plan year may be as of any date in the year, including the first and last. Valuations must be performed within the period specified by ERISA section 103(d) and Code section 412(c)(9).

6c. Enter the current value of total assets as of the beginning of the plan year, as shown on Form 5500 or Form 5500-C/R.

6d, 6e, and 6f. All plans regardless of the number of participants must provide the information indicated in accordance with these instructions.

With the exception of the interest rate, each actuarial assumption used in calculating the current liability reported in line 12 should reflect the best estimate of the plan's future experience solely with respect to that assumption applicable to the plan on an ongoing (rather than a terminating) basis. The actuary must take into account rates of early retirement and the plan's early retirement provisions as they relate to benefits, where these would significantly affect the results. With the exception of line 6e, no salary scale projections should be used in computing the present values.

The interest rate used to compute the current liability must be in accordance with guidelines issued by the Internal Revenue Service.

The current liability must be computed in accordance with guidelines issued by the Internal Revenue Service.

Omit from lines **6d, 6e,** and **6f** liabilities fully funded by annuity and insurance contracts other than any contract funds not allocated to individuals.

6d. Enter the current liability as of the beginning of the plan year. Do not include the liability attributable to benefits accruing during the plan year.

Column (1)—If the valuation date is not the beginning of the plan year, enter the number of participants as of the most recent valuation date.

Column (2)—Include only the portion of the current liability attributable to vested benefits.

Column (3)—Include the current liability attributable to all benefits, both vested and nonvested.

6e. Enter the amount by which the current liability is expected to increase due to benefits accruing during the plan year. One year's salary scale may be reflected. This amount is included in the full funding limitation calculation.

6f. Enter the amount of benefit payments expected to be paid during the plan year.

7. Show all employer and employee contributions for the plan year, and employer contributions made not later than 2½ months (or the later date allowed under Code section 412(c)(10) and ERISA section 302(c)(10)) after the end of the plan year. Show only contributions actually made to the plan by the date Schedule B is signed. Certain employer contributions must be made in quarterly installments, see Code section 412(m).

Add the amounts in both columns (b) and (c) and enter the result on the total line.

8a. If the attained age normal, aggregate, frozen initial liability, or other

Form 5500—Contd.

method that does not develop an accrued liability is used, enter "N/A."

8b. Enter the value of assets determined in accordance with Code section 412(c)(2) or ERISA section 302(c)(2).

8d(ii). For the methods to be used to determine the shortfall gain (loss) see the regulations under Code section 412.

8e. Enter amount from line 9o. However, if the alternative method is elected and line 10h is smaller than line 9o, enter the amount from line 10h. Multiemployer plans in reorganization, see instruction 4b. File Form 5330 with the IRS to pay 10% excise tax (5% in the case of a multiemployer plan) on the funding deficiency.

9. Under the shortfall method of funding, the *normal cost* in the funding standard account is the charge per unit of production (or per unit of service) multiplied by the actual number of units of production (or units of service) which occurred during the plan year. Each amortization installment in the funding standard account is similarly calculated.

9c and 9j. If there are any amortization charges or credits, attach the maintenance schedule of funding standard account base. The attachment should clearly indicate the type of base (i.e., original unfunded liability, amendments, actuarial losses, etc.), the outstanding balance of each base, the number of years remaining in the amortization period, and the amortization amount.

The outstanding balance may be as of any day in this plan year.

9c(i). Amortization for waivers must be based on the mandated interest rate.

9c(ii). If a credit described in line 9l(ii) was entered on the prior year's Schedule B, establish a new base equal to the amount of the credit and amortize the base over a 10-year period .at the valuation rate.

9e. Enter the required additional funding charge from line 13r (or 13q if 13r does not apply). Enter "N/A" if line 13 is not applicable.

For corporations described in section 806(b) of the Steel Import Stabilization Act, enter the lesser of line 13r and the transition charge provided under Act section 9303(e) of OBRA 1987. Include an attachment outlining the calculation of the transition charge.

9f. Interest is charged for the entire period of underpayment. Refer to IRS Notice 89-52, 1989-1, C.B. 692, for a description of how this amount is calculated.

Note: *Notice 89-52 was issued prior to the amendment of section 412(m)(1) by the Revenue Reconciliation Act of 1989. Rather than using the rate in the Notice, the applicable interest rate for this purpose is the greater of (1) 175% of the*

Federal mid-term rate at the beginning of the plan year or **(2)** the rate used to determine the current liability. All other descriptions of the additional interest charge contained in Notice 89-52 still apply.

9l(i). Enter the excess, if any, of the accumulated funding deficiency, disregarding the credit balance, if any, over the full funding limitation (FFL) before reflecting the 150% current liability component.

9l(ii). If the full funding limitation after reflecting the 150% current liability component is less than the full funding limitation before reflecting the 150% current liability component, enter the amount which absent the 150% current liability component would have been required.

Note: *The sum of lines 9l(i) and 9l(ii) is the excess of the accumulated funding deficiency over the full funding limitation (i.e., the full funding credit under Code section 412(c)(6)).*

9l(iii). Enter a credit for a waived funding deficiency for the current plan year (Code section 412(b)(3)(C)). If a waiver of a funding deficiency is pending, it is not to be reported as a credit but as a funding deficiency. If the waiver is granted, an amended Schedule B (Form 5500) should be filed to report it.

9p. The reconciliation account is comprised of those components which upset the balance equation of Income Tax Regulations section 1.412(c)(3)-1(b).

9p(i). The accumulation of additional funding charges for prior plan years must be included. Enter the sum of line 9p(i) (increased by one year's interest at the valuation rate) and line 9e, both from the prior year's Schedule B (Form 5500).

Example: *Enter the 1989 additional charge with one year's interest plus the 1990 additional funding charge.*

9p(ii). The accumulation of additional interest charges due to late or unpaid quarterly installments for prior plan years must be included. Enter the sum of line 9p(ii) (increased with one year's interest at the valuation rate) and line 9f, both from the prior year's Schedule B (Form 5500).

Example: For 1991, enter the 1989 additional interest charges with one year's interest at the valuation rate, plus the 1990 additional interest charges.

9p(iii)(a). If a waived funding deficiency is being amortized at an interest rate that differs from the valuation rate, enter the prior year's "reconciliation waiver outstanding balance" increased with one year's interest at the valuation rate and decreased with the year end amortization amount based on the mandated interest rate.

This amount must be as of the same date entered in line 9(c)(i).

9p(iv). Enter the sum of lines (i), (ii), and (iii)(b) (each adjusted with interest at the valuation rate, if necessary).

Note: *The net outstanding balance of amortization charges and credits minus the prior year's credit balance minus the amount on line 9p(iv) (each adjusted with interest at the valuation rate, if necessary) must equal the unfunded liability.*

10a. If the entry age normal cost method was not used to determine the entries on line 9, the alternative minimum funding standard account may not be used.

10d. The value of accrued benefits should exclude benefits accrued for the current plan year. The market value of assets should be reduced by the amount of any contributions for the current plan year.

11. Enter only the primary method used. If the plan uses one actuarial cost method in one year as the basis of establishing an accrued liability for use under the frozen initial liability method in subsequent years, answer as if the frozen initial liability method were used in all years.

For a modified individual level premium method for which actuarial gains and losses are spread as a part of future normal cost, check the box for 11g and describe the cost method. For the shortfall funding method, check the appropriate box for the underlying actuarial cost method used to determine the annual computation charge.

12. If gender-based statistics are used in developing plan costs, enter those rates where appropriate in line 12. Note that requests for gender-based cost information do not suggest that gender-based benefits are legal. Complete all blanks. Enter "N/A" if not applicable.

If unisex tables are used, enter the values in both the male and female columns.

Attach a statement of actuarial assumptions (if not fully described by line 12), and actuarial methods used to calculate: (i) the figures shown in lines 8, 9, and 10 (if not fully described by line 11), and (ii) the value of assets shown on line 8b. The statement is to include a summary of the principal eligibility and benefit provisions upon which the valuation was based, an identification of benefits not included in the calculation, and other facts, such as any change in actuarial assumptions or cost methods and justifications for any such change. Also, include any other information needed to fully and fairly disclose the actuarial position of the plan.

12a. Check "Yes," if the rates in the contract were used (e.g., purchase rates at retirement).

Page 2

Form 5500—Contd.

12b. Enter the mortality table code as follows:

Table	Code
1937 Standard Annuity	1
a-1949 Table	2
Progressive Annuity Table	3
1951 Group Annuity	4
1971 Group Annuity Mortality	5
1971 Individual Annuity Mortality	6
UP-1984	7
1983 I.A.M	8
1983 G.A.M.	9
Other	10
None	11

Where an indicated table consists of separate tables for males and females, add F to the female table (e.g., 4F). When a projection is used with a table, follow the code with "P" and the year of projection (omit the year if the projection is unrelated to a single calendar year); the identity of the projection scale should be omitted. When an age setback or setforward is used, indicate with "−" or "+" and the years. For example, if for females the 1951 Group Annuity Table with Projection C to 1971 is used with a 5-year setback, enter "4P71-5." If the table is not one of those listed, enter "10" with no further notation. If the valuation assumes a maturity value to provide the post-retirement income without separately identifying the mortality, interest and expense elements, under "post-retirement," enter on line 12b the value of $1.00 of monthly pension beginning at the age shown on line 12d, assuming the normal form of annuity for an unmarried person; in this case enter "N/A" on lines 12c and 12e.

12c(i). Enter the interest rate used to determine the current liability on line 6. The rate used must be in accordance with the guidelines issued by the IRS. See Notice 90-11, 1990-1 C.B. 319.

12c(ii). Enter the assumption as to the expected interest rate (investment return) used to determine all other calculated values with the exception of current liability and liabilities determined under the alternative minimum funding standard (line 10). If the assumed rate varies with the year, enter the weighted average of the assumed rate for 20 years following the valuation date.

12d. If each participant is assumed to retire at his/her normal retirement age, enter the age specified in the plan as normal retirement age; do not enter "NRA." Otherwise, enter the assumed retirement age. If the valuation uses rates of retirement at various ages, enter the estimated average whole age at which participants are assumed to retire.

12e. If there is no expense loading, enter "-0-". If there is a single expense loading not separately identified as pre-retirement or post-retirement, enter it

under pre-retirement and enter "N/A" under post-retirement. Where expenses are assumed other than as a percent of plan costs or liabilities, enter the assumed expense as a percent of calculated normal cost.

12f. Enter rates to the nearest 0.1%. If select and ultimate rates which vary with both age and years of service are used, enter the rates for a new participant at the age shown and enter "S" before the rate.

12g. Enter the salary ratio for the age indicated to the nearest 1%.

12h. Enter the estimated rate of return on the actuarial value of plan assets for the one year period ending on the valuation date. For this purpose, the rate of return is determined by using the formula $2I/(A + B − I)$, where I is the dollar amount of investment return under the asset valuation method used for the plan, A is the actuarial value of the assets one year ago, and B is the actuarial value of the assets on the current valuation date.

Note: *If the actuary feels that the result of using the formula above does not represent the true estimated rate of return on the actuarial value of plan assets for the one year period ending on the valuation date, line 12h should still be completed according to the instructions above, and the actuary may attach a statement to Schedule B showing both the actuary's estimate of the rate of return and the actuary's calculations of that rate.*

13. Multiemployer plans or plans with NO unfunded current liability or plans with 100 or fewer participants should check this box and skip lines 13a through 13r.

A plan has 100 or fewer participants only if there were 100 or fewer participants (both active participants and non active participants) on each day of the preceding plan year taking into account participants in all defined benefit plans maintained by the same employer who are also employees of such employer.

13a. Enter the current liability as of the valuation date. If the valuation date is the beginning of the plan year, this amount is the same as line 6d(iv) column (3) "total benefits." Otherwise, adjust the current liability by interest (at the rate used to determine current liability).

13b. Enter the actuarial value of assets (reduced by the prior year's credit balance) as of the valuation date. If the prior year's credit balance (line 9h) was determined at a date other than the valuation date, adjust the balance with the appropriate interest adjustment before subtracting. Do not make any adjustment to reflect a prior year's funding deficiency.

13c. Enter the adjusted actuarial value of assets expressed as a percentage of

current liability. Round off to two decimal places (e.g., 28.72%).

13e. Enter the outstanding balance of the unfunded old liability as of the valuation date.

Note: *In the case of a collectively bargained plan, this amount must be increased by the unamortized portion of any "unfunded benefit increase liability" in accordance with Code section 412(l)(3)(C).*

13f. Enter the liability with respect to any unpredictable contingent event benefit that was included on line 13a, whether or not such event had occurred.

13g. This amount is the unfunded new liability. It will be recalculated each year. If the result is negative, enter -0-.

13h. If the unfunded new liability is -0-, enter $0 for unfunded new liability amount. If the unfunded new liability amount is greater than -0-, calculate the amortization percentage as follows:

(1) If the funded current liability percentage (line 13c) is less than or equal to 35%, enter 30%.

(2) If the funded current liability percentage exceeds 35%, reduce 30% by the product of 25% and the amount of such excess; round off to two decimal places, and enter the resulting percentage.

The unfunded new liability amount is equal to the above calculated percentage of the unfunded new liability.

13i. Enter the amortization of the outstanding balance of the unfunded old liability as of the valuation date (line 13e). In the case of a collectively bargained plan, the unfunded old liability amount to be entered on line 13i must include the amortization of any unfunded existing benefit increase liability calculated in accordance with Code section 412(l)(3)(C)(ii). On a separate attachment show the breakdown of the various liabilities being amortized, the outstanding balance of each liability, the number of years remaining in the amortization period, and the amortization amount.

Any such amortization amount must be determined based on: (1) the current liability interest rate in effect at the beginning of the plan year, and (2) use the valuation date as the due date of the amortization payment. The amortization period must be the remainder of the originial 18-year period that applies when the amortization began.

Any such amortization amount must be redetermined each year based on the outstanding balance (line 13e). If the plan becomes fully funded as a current liability basis, the unfunded old liability (including any arising from collectively bargained plans) will be considered fully amortized.

13j. Enter the sum of lines 13h and 13i. This amount is the deficit reduction contribution at the valuation date.

13k. When entering the net amortization amounts for certain bases include only charges (included on line 9c) and credits (included on line 9j) attributable to original unfunded liability, amendments, funding waivers, charges resulting from a "switchback" arising from the utilization of the alternative minimum, and "offsetable bases" as described in Announcement 90-87, I.R.B. 1990-30 23 which were shown as an attachment to your 1989 Schedule B.

If a base resulted from combining and/or offsetting pre-existing bases among which were bases not designated in the preceding paragraph, then such resulting base may not be included in this line 13k.

Regardless of how the attachment (schedule of bases described in the instructions for lines 9c and 9j) is prepared, enter the amount assuming the payment was on the valuation date.

13l. Item I does not apply to the unpredictable contingent event benefits (and liabilities attributable thereto) for which the event occurred before the first plan year beginning after December 31, 1988.

13l(i). Enter the total of all benefits paid during the previous plan year that would not have been paid had the unpredictable contingent event not occurred.

13l(ii). Enter 100% minus the funded current liability percentage (line 13c).

13l(iii). Enter 10% for plan years beginning in 1991. (See Code section 412(l)(5)(B))

13l(v). Amortization should be based on the current liability interest rate and assume beginning of year payments for a seven-year period.

Note: *Alternative calculation of unpredictable contingent event amount is available for the first year of amortization. Refer to Code section 412(l)(5)(D) for a description. If alternative is used, include an attachment describing the calculation.*

13p. Enter the applicable amount of interest, based on the current liability interest rate, to bring the additional funding charge (line 13o) to the end of the plan year.

13r. If the plan had 150 or more participants on each day of the preceding plan year, enter N/A. If the plan had less than 150 participants but more than 100 participants on each day of the preceding plan year, only an applicable percentage of line 13q is charged to the funding standard account. The same aggregation rule described in the instructions for line 13 applies.

The applicable percentage is calculated as follows:

(i) Determine the excess of the greatest number of participants during the preceding plan year over 100.

(ii) The applicable percentage is 2% of such excess.

This amount (or line 13q, if line 13r is N/A) will also be entered on line 9e.

14. Generally, if the actuary signs the required certification statement on the actuarial report, but "materially qualifies" that statement, the certification is invalid. However, Income Tax Regulations section 301.6059-1(d) lists certain qualifying statements that the actuary is allowed to make. Among them is a statement that in his or her opinion, the report fully reflects the requirements of the statute, but does not conform to the requirements of a regulation or ruling that the actuary believes is contrary to that statute (Income Tax Regulations section 301.6059-1(d)(5)).

Check the "Yes" box on line 14 if the report is being signed subject to this qualification. If a funding deficiency or a disallowed contribution would have resulted for this plan year had the report conformed to the requirements of a regulation or ruling under the subject statute, the actuary must state that on an attachment to Schedule B.

Form 5500—Contd.

SCHEDULE P	**Annual Return of Fiduciary**	OMB No. 1210-0016
(Form 5500)	**of Employee Benefit Trust**	**1991**
Department of the Treasury Internal Revenue Service	▶ File as an attachment to Form 5500, 5500-C/R, or 5500EZ. ▶ For the Paperwork Reduction Notice, see page 1 of the Form 5500 instructions.	

For trust calendar year 1991 or fiscal year beginning _____, 1991, and ending _____ 19_____

1a Name of trustee or custodian

b Number, street, and room or suite no. (If a P.O. box, see the instructions for Form 5500, 5500-C/R, or 5500EZ.)

c City or town, state, and ZIP code

Please type or print

2 Name of trust

3 Name of plan if different from name of trust

4 Have you furnished the participating employee benefit plan(s) with the trust financial information required to be reported by the plan(s)? . . . . ☐ Yes ☐ No

5 Enter the plan sponsor's employer identification number as shown on Form 5500, 5500-C/R, or 5500EZ . . . . ▶

Under penalties of perjury, I declare that I have examined this schedule, and to the best of my knowledge and belief it is true, correct, and complete.

Signature of fiduciary ▶ _____ Date ▶ _____

Instructions

(Section references are to the Internal Revenue Code.)

A. Purpose of Form

You may use this schedule to satisfy the requirements under section 6033(a) for an annual information return from every section 401(a) organization exempt from tax under section 501(a).

Filing this form will start the running of the statute of limitations under section 6501(a) for any trust described in section 401(a), which is exempt from tax under section 501(a).

B. Who May File

(1) Every trustee of a trust created as part of an employee benefit plan as described in section 401(a).

(2) Every custodian of a custodial account described in section 401(f).

C. How To File

File Schedule P (Form 5500) for the trust year ending with or within any participating plan's plan year. Attach it to the Form 5500, 5500-C/R, or 5500EZ filed by the plan for that plan year.

Schedule P (Form 5500) must be filed only as an attachment to a Form 5500, 5500-C/R, or 5500EZ. A separately filed Schedule P (Form 5500) will not be accepted.

If the trust or custodial account is used by more than one plan, file one Schedule P (Form 5500). File it as an attachment to one of the participating plan's returns/reports. If a plan uses more than one trust or custodial account for its funds, file one Schedule P (Form 5500) for each trust or custodial account.

D. Signature

The fiduciary (trustee or custodian) must sign this schedule. If there is more than one fiduciary, one of them, authorized by the others, may sign.

E. Other Returns and Forms That May Be Required

(1) Form 990-T.—For trusts described in section 401(a), a tax is imposed on income derived from business that is unrelated to the purpose for which the trust received a tax exemption. Report such income and tax on **Form 990-T,** Exempt Organization Business Income Tax Return. (See sections 511 through 514 and the related regulations.)

(2) Form 1099-R.—If you made payments or distributions to individual beneficiaries of a plan, report these payments on Form 1099-R. (See sections 6041 and 6047 and the related regulations.)

(3) Forms 941 or 941E.—If you made payments or distributions to individual beneficiaries of a plan, you are required to withhold income tax from those payments unless the payee elects not to have the tax withheld. Report any withholding tax on Form 941 or 941E. (See Form 941 or 941E, and Circular E, Pub. 15.)

Form 5500—Contd.

SCHEDULE SSA (Form 5500)	**Annual Registration Statement Identifying Separated** **Participants With Deferred Vested Benefits** Under Section 6057(a) of the Internal Revenue Code	OMB No. 1210-0016 19**91**
Department of the Treasury Internal Revenue Service	► File as an attachment to Form 5500 or 5500-C/R. ► For Paperwork Reduction Act Notice, see page 1 of the instructions for Form 5500 or 5500-C/R.	This Form Is NOT Open to Public Inspection

For the calendar year 1991 or fiscal plan year beginning , 1991, and ending , 19

► **This schedule must be filed for each plan year in which one or more participants with deferred vested benefit rights separated from the service covered by the plan. See instructions on when to report a separated employee.**

► **Type or print in ink all entries on this schedule. File the originals.**

► **All attachments to this schedule should have entries only on the front of the page.**

1a Name of sponsor (employer if for a single employer plan)

    Number, street, and room or suite no. (If a P.O. box, see the instructions for 1a.)

    City or town, state, and ZIP code

1b Sponsor's employer identification number

1c Is this a plan to which more than one employer contributes? . . ☐ Yes ☐ No

2a Name of plan administrator (if other than sponsor)

    Number, street, and room or suite no. (If a P.O. box, see the instructions for 1a.)

    City or town, state, and ZIP code

2b Administrator's employer identification no.

3a Name of plan

3b Plan number. ►

4 Have you notified each separated participant of his or her deferred benefit? . . . . ► ☐ Yes ☐ No

5 Separated participants with deferred vested benefits (if additional space is required, see instruction, "What To File"):

(a) Social security number	(b) Name of participant	Enter code for nature and form of benefit		(e) Defined benefit plan—periodic payment	Amount of vested benefit		(h) Plan year in which participant separated
		(c) Type of annuity	(d) Payment frequency		(f) Units or shares	(g) Total value of account	

The Following Information Is Optional (See Specific Instruction 6.)

6 Use this item to report: (i) separated participants with deferred vested benefits who were previously reported on Schedule SSA (Form 5500) and who have received part or all of their vested benefits or who have forfeited their benefits during the plan year for which this schedule is being filed, and (ii) to delete participants erroneously reported on a prior Schedule SSA (Form 5500).

Note: Participants listed in this item, because they have received part of their vested benefits, must also be reported in item 5 above listing their remaining vested benefits.

(a) Social security number	(b) Name of participant	Enter code for nature and form of benefit		(e) Defined benefit plan—periodic payment	Amount of vested benefit		(h) Plan year in which participant separated
		(c) Type of annuity	(d) Payment frequency		(f) Units or shares	(g) Total value of account	

Under penalties of perjury, I declare that I have examined this report, and to the best of my knowledge and belief, it is true, correct, and complete.

Signature of plan administrator ►   Date ►

Cat. No. 13506T   Schedule SSA (Form 5500)

Form 5500—Contd.

General Instructions

Note: *Please type or print all information and submit original copy only.*

Who Must File.—The plan administrator must file this schedule for any plan year for which a separated plan participant is reported under "When To Report a Separated Participant," below.

What To File.—File this schedule and complete all items. If you need more space, use either: (1) additional copies of Schedule SSA, completing only items 1, 3, 5, and 6 of the additional copies, or (2) additional sheets the same size as the schedule containing the information asked for in items 1, 3, 5, and 6. The information required in items 5 and 6 should be listed in the same format as items 5 and 6 on Schedule SSA. Enter information on the front of the attachment only.

You may submit machine-generated computer listing showing the information required in items 5 and 6 in lieu of completing items 5 and 6 on the schedule. Complete items 1 through 4 on Schedule SSA and enter in items 5 and 6 a statement that a list is attached. On each page of the computer list, enter the name of the sponsor, the EIN, the plan name, and the plan number. The list must be in the same format as items 5 and 6.

How To File.—File as an attachment to Form 5500 or 5500-C/R.

When To Report a Separated Participant.—In general, *for a plan to which only one employer contributes,* a participant must be reported on Schedule SSA if:

1. The participant separates from service covered by the plan in a plan year, and

2. The participant is entitled to a deferred vested benefit under the plan.

The separated participant must be reported no later than on the Schedule SSA filed for the plan year following the plan year in which separation occurred. The participant may be reported earlier (i.e., on the Schedule SSA filed for the plan year in which separation occurred). Once separated participants have been reported on a Schedule SSA, they should not be reported on a subsequent year's Schedule SSA.

However, a participant is not required to be reported on Schedule SSA if, before the date the Schedule SSA is required to be filed (including any extension of time for filing), the participant:

1. Is paid some or all of the deferred vested retirement benefit,

2. Returns to service covered by the plan, or

3. Forfeits all of the deferred vested retirement benefit.

In general, *for a plan to which more than one employer contributes,* a participant must be reported on Schedule SSA if:

1. The participant incurs two successive one-year breaks in service (as defined in the plan for vesting purposes) in service computation periods, and

2. The participant is (or may be) entitled to a deferred vested benefit under the plan.

The participant must be reported no later than on the Schedule SSA filed for the plan year in which the participant completed the second of the two consecutive one-year breaks in service. The participant may be reported earlier (i.e., on the Schedule SSA filed for the plan year in which he or she separated from service or completed the first one-year break in service).

However, a participant is not required to be reported on Schedule SSA if, before the date the Schedule SSA is required to be filed (including any extension of time for filing), the participant:

1. Is paid some or all of the deferred vested retirement benefit,

2. Accrues additional retirement benefits under the plan, or

3. Forfeits all of the deferred vested retirement benefit.

Cessation of Payment of Benefits.—As described above in "When To Report a Separated Participant," a participant is not required to be reported on Schedule SSA if, before the date the Schedule SSA is required to be filed (including any extension of time for filing), some of the deferred vested benefit to which the participant is entitled is paid to the participant. If payment of the deferred vested benefit ceases before all of the benefit is paid to the participant, the benefit to which the participant remains entitled must be reported on the Schedule SSA filed for the plan year following the last plan year within which any of the benefit was paid to the participant. However, a participant is not required to be reported on Schedule SSA on account of a cessation of payment of benefits if, before the date the schedule is required to be filed (including any extension of time for filing), the participant:

1. Returns to service covered by the plan,

2. Accrues additional retirement benefits under the plan, or

3. Forfeits the remaining benefit.

Separation of a Re-employed Employee.—The deferred vested benefit reported on the current Schedule SSA for a re-employed employee who is again separated from service must include only the benefit not previously reported in or for prior years. Generally, the benefit to be shown on the current filing will be the benefit earned during the re-employment period.

Caution: *A penalty may be assessed if Schedule SSA (Form 5500) is not timely filed.*

Specific Instructions

1a.—If your post office does not deliver mail to your street address and you have a P.O. box, enter your P.O. box number instead of the street address.

4.—Check "Yes" if you have complied with the requirements of Code section 6057(e). The notification to each participant must include the information set forth on this schedule and the information about any contributions made by the participant and not withdrawn by the end of the plan year. Any benefits that are forfeitable if the participant dies before a certain date must be shown on the statement.

5(a).—Enter the exact social security number of each participant listed.

If the participant is a foreign national employed outside of the United States who does not have a social security number, enter the participant's nationality.

5(b).—Enter each participant's name exactly as it appears on the participant's social security card or the employer's payroll records for purposes of reporting to the Social Security Administration.

5(c).—From the following list, select the code that describes the type of annuity that will be provided for the participant. Enter the type of annuity that normally accrues under the plan at the time of the participant's separation from service covered by the plan (or for a plan to which more than one employer contributes at the time the participant incurs the second consecutive one-year break in service under the plan).

  a. A single sum

  b. Annuity payable over fixed number of years

  c. Life annuity

  d. Life annuity with period certain

  e. Cash refund life annuity

  f. Modified cash refund life annuity

  g. Joint and last survivor life annuity

  m. Other

5(d).—From the following list, select the code that describes the benefit payment frequency during a 12-month period.

  a. Lump sum

  b. Annually

  c. Semiannually

  d. Quarterly

  e. Monthly

  m. Other

5(e).—For a defined benefit plan, enter the amount of the periodic payment that a participant would normally be entitled to receive under 5(c), commencing at normal retirement age. However, if it is more expedient to show the amount of periodic payment the participant would be entitled to receive at early retirement date, enter that amount.

For a plan to which more than one employer contributes, if the amount of the periodic payment cannot be accurately determined because the plan administrator does not maintain complete records of covered service, enter an estimated amount and add the letter "X" in column 5(c) in addition to the annuity code to indicate that it is an estimate. If, from records maintained by the plan administrator, it cannot be determined whether the participant is entitled to any deferred vested benefit, but there is reason to believe he or she may be entitled, leave column 5(e) blank and enter "Y" in column 5(c) in addition to the annuity code.

5(f).—For a defined contribution plan, if the plan states that a participant's share of the fund will be determined on the basis of units, enter the number of units credited to the participant.

If, under the plan, participation is determined on the basis of shares of stock of the employer, enter the number of shares and add the letter "S" to indicate shares. A number without the "S" will be interpreted to mean units.

5(g).—For defined contribution plans, enter the value of the participant's account at the time of separation.

6.—If, after a participant has been reported on Schedule SSA, the participant:

  (i) is paid some or all of the deferred vested retirement benefit, or

  (ii) forfeits all of the deferred vested retirement benefit,

the plan administrator may, at its option, request that the participant's deferred vested benefit be deleted from Social Security Administration's records. Information reported in item 6, columns (a) through (g), is to be the exact information previously reported on Schedule SSA for the participant.

If this option is chosen because the participant is paid some of the deferred vested benefit, the reporting requirements described in "Cessation of Payment of Benefits" above apply if payment of the benefit ceases before all of the benefit is paid to the participant.

Also, if a person was erroneously reported on a prior Schedule SSA, use item 6 to delete this information from Social Security Administration's records.

Signature.—This form must be signed by the plan administrator. If more than one Schedule SSA is filed for one plan, only page one should be signed.

GLOSSARY

For further explanation of these terms, with annotations, see *Employee Benefits Dictionary*, published by BNA Books.

Accrued Benefit   Pension credits earned for years of service under a defined benefit pension plan expressed in terms of an annual benefit beginning at normal retirement age; the balance in each employee's account under a defined contribution pension plan.

Accumulated Funding Deficiency   A deficit balance in a pension plan's funding standard account, which means that the required minimum contributions have not been made by the plan.

Actuarial Assumptions   Estimates made by actuaries on which pension costs are based, using factors such as rate of interest on plan investments and rate of deaths, terminations, disabilities, and early retirements.

Actuarial Cost Methods   Different methods used for accounting and tax purposes to allocate the expected cost of a pension plan for the service of the employees covered by that plan. The general purpose of an actuarial cost method is to assign to each year the cost assumed to have accrued in that year.

Actuary   A professional technician or mathematician who computes premium rates, dividends, and risks according to probabilities based on statistical records for insurance and pensions.

Administrator   A person or firm designated by a pension or welfare plan or employer to handle day-to-day details of record keeping, claims handling, and filing of reports.

Amortization   Periodic payments to gradually reduce liabilities or obligations of pension plans and prorating of fund surpluses over a period of years.

Annuity   A contract that provides income for a specified period of time, often for life.

Assignment of Benefits   Assigning to an alternate payee the right to receive all or a portion of a benefit payable to a participant under a pension plan. This generally occurs in divorce or separation settlements.

Back Loading   Providing a higher or faster rate of benefit accrual for later years of service in a pension plan than for earlier years.

Basic Benefits   Retirement benefits that are nonforfeitable because the employee has met all the pension plan's requirements. These are insured by the Pension Benefit Guaranty Corporation up to statutorily set limits.

Beneficiary   The person designated to receive benefits under an employee benefit plan in the event of the death of the person covered by the plan.

Break in Service   A calendar or plan year or other consecutive 12-month period during which an employee has 500 or fewer hours of service.

Buy-Back Provision   An arrangement whereby, if a terminating employee withdraws his or her own contributions when he or she is 50 percent vested or less, a pension plan that cancels the rest of his or her benefits must allow the employee to buy back the forfeited benefits by repaying the withdrawn amounts.

Cafeteria Plan   Also called a "flexible benefit plan," this program permits employees to select from employer-provided taxable and nontaxable benefits. Nontaxable benefits include group term life insurance (up to certain amounts) and health, disability, and accident benefits.

Cash or Deferred Arrangements   Plans under which employees are permitted to have a percentage of pre-taxed salary transferred to a retirement plan. Also known as 401(k) plans.

Cliff Vesting   A vesting schedule under which an employee must be 100 percent vested after 10 years of service, with no vesting prior to the 10th year. Beginning in 1989, employees must be 100 percent vested after 5 years, except for collectively bargained plans, which may continue to use 10 years.

Contributory Plan   A pension plan to which employees contribute as well as employers, either voluntarily or as a condition for participation in the pension plan.

Current Liability   A standard used to measure whether a pension plan is underfunded by calculating the plan's liability on the basis of the value of all accrued benefits, both vested and nonvested, as if the plan were terminating.

Deficit Reduction Contribution   For a pension plan that is less than 100 percent funded, an additional amount that an employer must contribute to the pension plan over and above the required minimum annual contribution. This additional payment consists of a portion of old liabilities (such as benefit increases granted before 1988), which must be amortized over 18 years, and a portion of new liabilities (such as benefit increases or other plan amendments).

Defined Benefit Plan   A pension plan providing a definite formula for calculating the benefit to be paid to employees at retirement, such as a flat monthly amount, a percentage of salary, or a percentage of salary times years of service.

Defined Contribution Plan   A pension plan in which fixed contributions are made to an individual account for each employee. The retirement benefit is dependent on amounts contributed to the account and any income, expenses, gains, losses, and forfeitures of accounts of other employees.

Disqualified Person   A term used in the tax section of ERISA to describe individuals responsible for managing or providing services to employee benefit plans; comparable to the term "party-in-interest."

Distress Termination   The termination of a pension plan of a financially troubled company with an underfunded plan.

Early Retirement Age   An age earlier than normal retirement age at which a pension plan provides that an employee may begin to receive benefits, although the benefit may be lower than the amount would be at normal retirement age.

Elapsed-Time Method   A method for measuring hours of service of an employee from the date of employment to the date of severance.

Eligibility Requirements   Conditions an employee must satisfy to become a participant in a pension plan, such as completing one year of service and reaching age 21.

Employee Benefit Plan   A welfare or pension plan established or maintained by an employer engaged in commerce or in any industry or activity affecting commerce or by an employee organization representing employees in these activities.

Employee Pension Plan   A pension plan established to provide retirement income to employees or that results in the deferral of income by employees.

Employee Stock Ownership Plan (ESOP)   A stock bonus pension plan in which benefits are distributed in the stock of the employer with contributions not dependent on profits.

Employee Welfare Plan   A plan providing medical, surgical, or hospital care or benefits, as well as benefits in the event of sickness, accident, disability, death, or unemployment or other benefits, including apprenticeship or other training programs or day care, scholarship funds, or prepaid legal services.

Enrolled Actuary   An actuary who prepares reports for government agencies who must satisfy requirements (be approved for enrollment) set by the Joint Board for the Enrollment of Actuaries.

Equivalencies   Methods for measuring hours of service of an employee that credit employees with 1,000 hours of service when they have worked an equivalent amount of time. An equivalency system may use time periods such as days, weeks, shifts, or payroll periods.

Fiduciary   A person who exercises authority or control over the management or disposition of an employee benefit plan or its assets.

Flexible Compensation Plan   See "Cafeteria Plan."

Forfeiture   Loss of the right to a pension benefit by an employee who terminates employment before becoming vested. Also, a contribution by an employer for nonvested, terminated employees that can be applied to reducing future employer contributions.

Funding   The process of accumulating assets on a regular, systematic basis to meet benefit obligations of a pension plan.

Funding Standard Account   An account that every pension plan under ERISA must maintain to determine whether the plan is meeting the minimum funding standards imposed by the law.

Graded Vesting   A vesting schedule under which an employee is 20 percent vested after three years of service and gains 20 percent each year thereafter, with full vesting after seven years.

Guaranteed Benefits   Vested accrued pension benefits insured by the Pension Benefit Guaranty Corporation in the event of the termination of a pension plan.

Highly Compensated Employees   Employees who are either 5-percent owners, officers, employees who earned more than $75,000 annually, or employees who earned more than $50,000 annually and were among the top 20 percent of employees by pay.

Hour of Service   An hour for which an employee is paid, or is entitled to payment, for the performance of duties for the employer. This concept is used to determine employee rights and benefits under a pension plan.

Individual Retirement Account   A retirement account to which a person not covered by an employer-provided pension plan can make annual tax-deductible contributions for up to $2,000 or 100 percent of compensation, whichever is less, and up to $2,250 for worker and nonworking spouse.

Insured Event   The event that requires the Pension Benefit Guaranty Corporation to assume responsibility for the payment of pension benefits—plan termination in the case of a single-employer plan and insolvency for multiemployer plans.

Integration   The practice of taking into account Social Security benefits when calculating private pension plan benefits by excluding employees whose earnings are less than the Social Security taxable wage base, providing a higher level of benefits for earnings above the base than is provided for earnings below, or subtracting a percentage of the Social Security benefit from the pension.

Joint and Survivor Annuity   An automatic form of pension payment for a married employee (unless waived) by which an annuity is paid for the life of the employee and, upon the employee's death, half of the benefit is paid to the surviving spouse.

Keogh Plan   A type of pension plan that self-employed individuals can establish and to which they can make annual tax-deductible contributions of up to $30,000 or 25 percent of income, whichever is less.

Money Purchase Plan   Another name for a defined contribution pension plan under which contribution rates are fixed, usually as a percentage of salary, and an employee's benefit depends on the amount of the contributions, investment earnings, and expenses.

Multiemployer Plan   A collectively bargained pension plan to which more than one employer contributes.

Normal Costs   Annual cost to a pension plan for the benefits accrued that year by employees and administrative expenses.

Normal Retirement Age   The age established by a pension plan when retirement normally occurs, usually age 65.

Participant   An employee eligible to receive benefits from an employee pension or welfare plan or whose beneficiaries may be eligible to receive such benefits.

Participation   The term used to describe the status of an employee who is covered by an employee benefit plan after having satisfied eligibility requirements such as one year of service and attainment of the minimum age.

Party-in-Interest   Any individual with an interest in an employee benefit plan, such as an administrator, officer, fiduciary, trustee, custodian, counsel, or employee. Also, a person providing services to a plan or an employee organization whose members are covered by the plan.

Past-Service Liability   The liability of a pension plan for the benefits credited for service before the establishment of the plan or for retroactive benefit increases.

Pension Benefit Guaranty Corporation   The nonprofit independent government corporation established to insure pension benefits in the event of plan terminations.

Plan Termination   The final phase of a pension plan when benefit accruals cease and all participants become 100 percent vested.

Plan Year   The 12-month period used in administration of pension plans, which may be the calendar year, fiscal year, or 12-month period from the anniversary date of the plan to one year later.

Portability   The right of an employee at termination of employment to take vested benefits in cash and transfer the funds to an Individual Retirement Account or another pension plan.

Preemption   The procedure whereby portions of ERISA covering reporting, disclosure, fiduciary responsibility, participation and vesting, funding, and plan termination insurance supersede state law that would otherwise be applicable.

Profit-Sharing Plan   A pension plan established and maintained by an employer to provide for the participation in its profits by its employees or their beneficiaries.

Prohibited Group   Shareholders, officers, and highly paid employees on behalf of whom pension plans seeking tax-favored status must not discriminate.

Prohibited Transaction   Certain activities that are prohibited by ERISA from taking place between an employee benefit plan and a party-in-interest such as the sale, exchange, or leasing of property.

Prudence Rule   A requirement that fiduciaries carry out their duties with the care, skill, prudence, and diligence that a prudent person acting in a like capacity and familiar with such matters would use under conditions prevailing at the time.

Qualified Plans   Employee benefit plans that meet Internal Revenue Service requirements for tax deductibility of employer contributions up to specified amounts.

Reportable Events   Certain events that may indicate possible termination of a pension plan that must be reported by a plan administrator to the Pension Benefit Guaranty Corporation, such as a failure to meet minimum funding standards.

Simplified Employee Pension (SEP)   A pension plan under which the employer makes contributions to Individual Retirement Accounts for employees in amounts up to a maximum of $30,000 per year or 15 percent of compensation, whichever is less.

Standard Termination   The termination of a pension plan when there are sufficient assets in the plan to pay all vested and nonvested benefits owed to employees.

Summary Plan Description   A description of the major features of an employee benefit plan written in language that can be easily understood by all employees covered by the plan.

Target Benefit Plan   A pension plan that uses a formula to determine a target benefit for each employee with the employer's contribution then geared toward meeting that benefit obligation.

Tax-Qualified Plans.   See "Qualified Plans."

Termination Liability   The liability of an employer for both vested and nonvested benefits of participants if the pension plan is terminated. Used synonymously with the term "current liabilities."

Thrift or Savings Plan   A pension plan that requires employee contributions as a condition for participation in the plan. Employer contributions match or equal some fraction of the employee contribution.

Top-Heavy Plan   A pension plan under which the value of benefits for key employees (officers and owners) exceeds 60 percent of the value of benefits for ordinary employees.

Unfunded Liabilities   The benefit obligations of an employee benefit plan that are not covered by assets of the plan.

Unpredictable Contingent Events   Plant shutdowns or reductions in the work force that could not be predicted but that might cause a pension plan to become underfunded. If such an event takes place, the employer is responsible for additional contributions to the plan beyond the minimum funding requirement for that year.

Vesting   The process by which an employee, after satisfying service requirements, acquires a nonforfeitable right to pension benefits even if he or she leaves the job before retirement. An accrued benefit attributable to the employee's own contribution is always 100 percent vested.

Withdrawal Liability   The responsibility of an employer pulling out of a multiemployer pension plan for its share of the plan's unfunded vested liabilities.

Year of Service   A 12-month period during which an employee works at least 1,000 hours. Used to determine eligibility for participation in a pension plan and the satisfaction of requirements for vesting as well as the determination of accrued benefits.

INDEX

215

T

V

W

Y